NO EXCUSES

NO EXCUSES

The Making of a Head Coach

Bob Stoops
and
Gene Wojciechowski

LITTLE, BROWN AND COMPANY

New York   Boston   London

Little, Brown and Company
Hachette Book Group
1290 Avenue of the Americas, New York, NY 10104
littlebrown.com

First Edition: September 2019

Little, Brown and Company is a division of Hachette Book Group, Inc. The Little, Brown name and logo are trademarks of Hachette Book Group, Inc.

The publisher is not responsible for websites (or their content) that are not owned by the publisher.

The Hachette Speakers Bureau provides a wide range of authors for speaking events. To find out more, go to hachettespeakersbureau.com or call (866) 376-6591.

ISBN 978-0-316-45592-3
LCCN 2019944218

10 9 8 7 6 5 4 3 2 1

LSC-C

Printed in the United States of America

To my family from Youngstown — my parents, Ron Sr. and Dee; my brothers, Ron Jr., Mike, and Mark; my sisters, Kathy and Maureen...to my own family — Carol, Mackie, Isaac, and Drake...and to my OU family. Boomer.

Contents

Contents

NO EXCUSES

Introduction

Legacy

Friday, April 13, 2018

I'm standing on a small stage in the middle of the Bennett Event Center at the State Fair Park in Oklahoma City, my wife, Carol, and our three children alongside me. And the truth is, I don't know what to do with my hands.

I'm not an event center type of guy. The football field has always been my stage. From childhood through adulthood, I've lived large parts of my life within the confines of that field: 53 and 1/3 yards wide and 120 yards long from end zone to end zone. Its dimensions have never changed, but I have. And so has the college game—and all that surrounds it.

I'm fifty-seven years old, and I'm 99 percent sure I will never coach football again. That realization hadn't hit me like a helmet to the underside of the chinstrap until recently. I love football, and football has loved me back. But it was now time to quit. It was time to do what so few people in my profession—or any profession—ever get to do: write my own ending, control my own coaching time clock.

Right now, I wouldn't care if the ghost of Vince Lombardi knocked on my door and asked if I'd coach the Green Bay Packers. I wouldn't care if an athletic director tried to money-whip me into a return. At this exact moment—except for that 1 percent of uncertainty—I'm done. Finished. Content. But I'm also a little unsettled, a tiny bit scared, and, at times, a complete mess on football Saturdays. Mostly confident and comfortable with my decision, but still unsure of the future.

How did I get to this place in my life? What caused me to walk away from the game I still love, from the players I adored coaching, from the assistants and staff that had become my second family, from the three-plus-hour jolt of electricity I got from being in the middle of the mayhem, from the competition I craved, from the kind of money that makes knees buckle—from the wins, and even the losses?

The college football media experts say I could have coached another five or ten years, easy. My boss wanted me to stay, and my family wouldn't have minded if I had kept coaching. The fans didn't want me out. My accountant was for it. So why? Why leave when nobody was showing me the door?

That's the reason I'm writing this book—to explain how I got from point A to point R—as in "resignation." And, along the way, how I somehow got from the steel town of Youngstown, Ohio, to the University of Oklahoma, a place that values what I value: consistency, integrity, loyalty, and winning.

The record book says I'm the seventeenth winningest coach by percentage and the nineteenth winningest by total victories in the history of major college football. It says I'm OU's winningest head coach ever. But I know that my success was all due to the work of our players, our coaches, and our staff. I was just part of the equation.

I was lucky enough to be a link in an OU football chain that began in the late nineteenth century and resulted in 896 victories (number seven on the all-time list), forty-eight conference titles, seven national championships, and seven Heisman Trophy winners. Say "OU" to college football fans from coast to coast, and they'll know what you mean. It is the university of Bs: Brian Bosworth, Barry Switzer, Sam Bradford, Billy Vessels, Baker Mayfield, Bud Wilkinson, and Billy Sims.

The easy decision would have been to stay at OU. But there was an intersection between the evolution of college football and the evolution of my own life. And when I got to that intersection, I saw the sign—a metaphorical stop sign—and I knew I had fulfilled my purpose at OU.

The recruiting. The travel. The late-night phone calls you hope never come. The early-morning wake-up calls. The cheaters. The agents. The renegade boosters and alums. The mind-numbing and mind-boggling

NCAA rules that often defy logic. The hours. The toll it takes on your family. The media. The social media. The social issues — racism, #MeToo, academics, player rights — that rightfully deserve and demand your attention. The uninformed expectations. It all became a Molotov cocktail of reasons that it was time to leave.

I wasn't beaten down by the job; I loved it. That's why I was so lucky. I got to choose the when, the where, and the how. So many coaches have those decisions made for them. They get fired — or sometimes they just stay too long, which is almost worse. I've never been fired, and I was determined never to stay too long.

So I'm standing on a stage in the same building where they have trade shows and car auctions — and I decide this isn't the time or place to explain to the more than twelve hundred people seated at 120 tables across a six-acre facility why I'm no longer OU's football coach.

Instead, this is supposed to be a night of celebration, an evening of thank-yous. Me to them. Them to me. But I can't shake the idea that it also feels a little bit like a wake — except that I'm not dead. I'm just moving from this stage...from point R to another part of my life. And I'm good with that.

I recognize nearly every face in the crowd. There are University of Oklahoma dignitaries, hundreds of former OU players, dozens of former and current assistant coaches, big-money boosters and influential alumni, national and local media representatives, bowl game officials, athletic directors, cheerleaders and band members, a contingent of family and friends from my hometown of Youngstown, Heisman Trophy winners, and athletic department staff members.

Even the event center waitstaff has quit clearing dessert plates in anticipation of the big moment. Police and security details poke their heads into the vast room as the band begins to play the OU anthem: "Boomer Sooner." On some sort of invisible cue, the entire audience rises and applauds.

Across the way — maybe a thirty-five-yard pass from my small stage to his large stage — is my longtime friend Toby Keith, the megastar country singer from nearby Moore, Oklahoma. He has his right cowboy boot planted atop a black speaker box, his guitar resting on his knee. Like everyone else, he is waiting for me to say something... *anything*.

During my eighteen seasons as head coach at Oklahoma, I gave hundreds of speeches, did thousands of interviews, made countless public appearances. I call it "Being Bob Stoops." There's Bob Stoops the husband, the father, the brother, the son, the friend, the guy who loves nothing better than sitting on a beach drinking a cold beer pulled out of a $3.99 Styrofoam cooler, or grilling steaks in the backyard, or trading stories with buddies on the golf course, or sitting in the bleachers watching his kids play sports, or going to church, or stopping by the OU Children's Hospital, or playing with the dogs, or simply sharing a laugh with Carol while watching TV in the family room.

And then there is *the* Bob Stoops, who happily and proudly represents all things Oklahoma. I love the state, love its people, love its work ethic and sense of community, love its competitiveness, love its devotion to the University of Oklahoma. But that version of me has to get outside my comfort zone. I'm not an introvert, but I'm not an extrovert, either. I'd rather eat green flies than do a media interview. I'm not a schmoozer. Small talk isn't my strength. In a perfect world, I'd rather not be the center of attention.

But you can't live life in a vacuum, which is why I've tried to embrace "Being Bob Stoops." After all, it isn't difficult to be nice to people, especially when they've been so nice to you. So you shake every hand extended, you pose for every photo, you look each person in the eyes and listen, really listen, as they tell you why OU football matters to them. And on occasion, you grit your teeth as a well-meaning OU fan tells you how and why you screwed up a game.

But now, as I squint into the lights hanging from the metal stage piping overhead, as I feel Carol's hand against mine, as my children—Mackie, Isaac, and Drake—stand nearby, as I catch glimpses of my former players looking up at me from stage's edge, I suddenly can't speak. A thousand thoughts, but not a single word. I'm not an emotional person by nature, but this is different. Everything is different.

When you're a high school senior growing up in blue-collar Youngstown and you see a Rust Belt city fall to its knees on Black Monday in 1977— when the steel plants started to close and tens of thousands of people lost their jobs, and then you hear the worry in the voices of your own parents…you never think that forty-one years later, you're going to be here on this stage, the centerpiece of a "Salute to Stoops" gala.

When your fifty-four-year-old dad suffers a fatal heart attack on the sideline while coaching a high school football game in 1988 and your life is turned upside down by the loss of your hero, of the toughest, most honorable and honest man you've ever known…you never think that thirty years later, you'll have an out-of-body experience and watch people stand in line to get their photos taken with a life-size cardboard cutout of you. You never imagine looking into the gala crowd and seeing your mom trying to make sense of the Bob Stoops "Bob"blehead to the right of her water glass.

I'm holding a microphone, but there is only the hiss of feedback as I stand there, overwhelmed by a moment I never saw coming eighteen-plus years earlier—or, for that matter, ever. I'm fidgeting. It all seems so surreal. Behind me is the just-unveiled, nearly forty-five-hundred-pound, more than thirteen-foot-high statue of the winningest coach in Oklahoma's 124-year football history. More wins than the man sitting at table 44: Switzer, whose badass swagger and fearlessness had earned my attention and admiration as far back as high school. More wins than the incomparable Wilkinson, who once registered forty-seven victories in a row. More wins than Bennie Owen, whose OU teams had few peers in the early 1900s.

I glance back at the bronze statue…a statue of me. This can't be possible. Stoops bobbleheads and signature white visors for each person at the gala…a Bob Stoops statue towering behind me. My former players in front of me. My family to the side of me.

"I got to tell you," I say to the crowd, "I love my players."

I start to say something else, but it's no use; I have to compose myself. I have to get this *right*. I hand the microphone to Carol, the rock of our family. She'll know what to say. She always knows what to say.

"There is no statue if not for you," she says, glancing down at the former players. "It happens to look like Bobby, but it's you."

Yes. Exactly! There is no statue, no 190 career victories, no national championship, no conference championships, no coach-of-the-year awards, no number-one rankings, no bowl game wins, no losing seasons in eighteen years…no nothing without those players, who left bits and pieces of themselves on football fields across the country for OU and me—who trusted me.

After Carol finishes her lovely tribute to all those who helped us during our journey, she looks at me as if to say, "OK, I've done my part." She hands me the microphone. It's time.

I take a deep breath.

"Yeah, where do I begin—this huge journey," I say. "It starts back in Youngstown, Ohio."

I tell everyone about my parents, Ron Sr. and Dee. Our family didn't have any money—football coaches and teachers at Catholic high schools don't make much—but we had everything else. We had love. We had discipline. We had loyalty. We had pride.

I talk about the old neighborhood: working-class families, sons and daughters of immigrants, people trying to survive after the city lost nearly 60 percent of its population and more than half of its tax revenue in the decades after the steel plants went belly-up. We were closer to Pittsburgh than Cleveland, but the Browns were our team. Football was our sport. Fighting—our street in the neighborhood versus another street three blocks away—was our pastime. And, just so you know, in Iowa and Youngstown, they still call me Bobby.

I talk about Iowa offering me a scholarship when no other major program in the country was interested.

I talk about my accidental coaching career and the men I worked for and learned from: Iowa's Hayden Fry (who gave me my coaching start)... Hall of Famer; Kansas State's Bill Snyder...Hall of Famer; Florida's Steve Spurrier, who is one of my closest friends and has had a huge influence on my life...Hall of Famer. And then there is my OU consigliere, Switzer... Hall of Famer. Do you know how intimidating, how daunting it was to walk into a building named the Barry Switzer Center and see his coaching records on the wall (157–29–4, three national championships)?

I talk about taking the Oklahoma job in late 1998, when OU was a shadow of its former dynastic self. I stood on the steps of Evans Hall and promised no excuses and hard work. I even remember what I told the OU faithful on that day twenty years ago: "If it happens where we're back where we're supposed to be, it won't be because of me."

And it wasn't. It was because of us: the administration, the coaches, the support staff, the fans, and the players. It's always about the players.

I got paid $650,000 that first year. I might have done it for free, or close to it.

I look down and see Tommie Harris, one of thirty-seven first-team All-Americas I coached at OU. Harris, a defensive tackle from Killeen, Texas, played for me from 2001 to 2003, and he was impossible to block. I almost felt sorry for opposing offensive linemen. *Almost.*

I pause. I have to compose myself again.

"Funny," I say, "nothing gets me emotional, except looking at them."

I'm in awe of what Tommie did on football fields, but I cherish what he did away from them, too. So I tell a story to the crowd about the day Tommie's dad visited one of our practices and later left a note with my administrative assistant. The note read, "I love you, and I'm praying for you."

The next day, I had walked up to Tommie during the team stretching exercises and tapped him on the cleats with my foot. "Hey, your dad left me a nice note yesterday. Tell him I said thanks."

Tommie smiled. "Coach, that wasn't my dad. That was me."

Those are the moments that mean more than any win, any award, any paycheck.

I see former OU All-America defensive tackle Gerald McCoy, now a six-time Pro Bowl player for the Carolina Panthers. He first came to my OU football camp when he was thirteen or fourteen years old. He was from the south side of Oklahoma City, which can be a tough place to live.

Gerald says kids like him didn't usually make it out of south Oklahoma City to OU. Gerald not only made it, but he made an impact. He was just nineteen and a true freshman when his mother, Patricia, died of a heart attack only a few weeks before his first game. She was in her fifties when she died—just like my dad. Our entire team attended her funeral. We were part of their family; they were part of ours.

I talk about my athletic director Joe Castiglione, the man who hired me; outgoing OU president David Boren; my staff and assistant coaches, who worked with me, not for me. It was Castiglione who addressed the crowd during my introduction on December 1, 1998, saying, "This is an incredibly important day in OU history."

Well, it was important to me and my family. And, in retrospect, I hope it was important to the OU community.

I talk about Carol, my college sweetheart and the love of my life. Whatever we are as a family, it's because of Carol. During the tough times in my personal and coaching life—and there have been plenty—it was Carol who helped get me through the rough spots.

"With my kids," I say, "did the best I could. Carol, she's the best. Tough. Has courage. Encouraging. A great leader."

Many a morning, before the sun had even thought about coming up, I'd quietly slip out of the bedroom and head to work. But before I left, there'd almost always be an encouraging Stick'Ems note on the bathroom mirror. And whenever I'd question myself, or feel sorry for myself, or simply be down after a tough loss, Carol would ask a simple question: "Why do you do this?"

And the answer would always be the same: "Because I love the competition, I love coaching, I love my players and staff."

"Well, then?" Carol would ask.

And she was right. You can't embrace competition without embracing the risks of losing. You can't love coaching without learning to love its challenges and sacrifices.

For fifty years of my life, I either played football or coached it. I played the game in front of our house at 865 Detroit Avenue, in the streets and backyards of my neighborhood, and at Pemberton Park in Youngstown. I played it for my dad at Cardinal Mooney High School, played it at Iowa with no ligament in one of my knees, coached it at Iowa, at Kent State, Kansas State, Florida, and Oklahoma. And the truth is, it's like I never worked a day in my life. I feel like I should have paid those schools for letting me coach.

There's a statue of me now. Talk about surreal. And it's right across from Coach Switzer's statue.

I've met US presidents. I've played in the Pebble Beach Pro-Am. I've traveled around the world. I've hung out backstage with the greatest country singers in the world. I've met movie stars, television stars, World Wrestling Entertainment stars, and rock stars.

More important, I've been able to spend time with kids at the Children's

Hospital at OU Medicine, kids that will melt your heart with their smiles and humble you with their courage.

I've met tornado victims. Special Olympians. Doctors. Nurses. Soldiers. Police officers. Fire fighters. Heroes.

Me? I'm just a former football coach.

Anyway, can you believe it? Can you believe any of it?

Years ago, I made a promise to myself. I wasn't going to coach into my seventies. I wasn't going to ignore reality or heredity. After all, my dad died of a heart attack, and I've had my own heart issues during my adult life. Maybe Coach Spurrier had it right when he said I didn't want to go "from the sidelines to the graveyard." And I wasn't going to contort that promise, even if it looked like I might have a great team, a Heisman Trophy candidate, or that I could win a national championship.

But now I'm done. Visor and whistle retired for good. I became part of Oklahoma football history on June 7, 2017. That's when I resigned. That's when I took a leap of faith into the next part of my life, whatever that might look like.

I'm where I want to be. With my family. With my friends. With my former players. With the people who matter most to me. And not that it was ever a hardship—in fact, it was an honor—but I don't have to "be" Bob Stoops anymore.

Now I'm just a dad and a husband, which are damn good things to be. One of my sons is on the OU football roster. I'm a guy lucky enough to see Jason White, the first player I ever signed at OU—and the first Heisman winner I ever coached—around town here in Norman.

All I ever wanted to do was help the OU program. I'd like to be remembered as someone who was a good steward, who stood up for what was right.

Earlier in the night, I had chatted with about fifteen local media members, many of whom I'd known for years. As we wrapped up the session, one of them asked if I was going to write a book.

While I still was coaching, the answer would always have been no. A minute spent working on another project would have been a minute less spent making OU better. Call it Catholic guilt—or Youngstown work ethic—but that's how I always felt.

But all that changed in June 2017.

I may no longer be coaching, but I still have something to say, something to pass along. Resigning didn't change that. In fact, it makes the next phase of my life possible.

Yes, I'm out of coaching and out of the confines of that 53-and-1/3-yard by 120-yard field, but I'm not out of football. Football is, and always will be, a part of my life.

So I stand on a stage and say thank you, but not goodbye. I remind everyone that I'm not dead; I'm just not coaching again. I'm ready for the future, but I understand the value of the past.

How did I get on this stage? Why is there a statue of me? Why do I owe so much to so many?

In my case, the past holds the answer. Always the past.

Chapter One

Family

Two parents. Six kids. One dog. One three-bedroom, thirteen-hundred-square-foot Cape Cod house. Working-class blue around all of our collars.

Four brothers stuffed into one bedroom upstairs. No bathroom up there, so we made the basement bathroom ours. Gaping holes in the bedroom wall from our wrestling battles, the occasional bloodstain on the blue shag carpeting. Two sisters in a downstairs room. Mom and Dad in theirs, also downstairs. Wally, our jet-black shepherd/Labrador mix, adding to the chaos.

Neighborhood kids walking in and out of our front and back doors like they were family—which they were. The Bearaduces on one side of us. The Browns and then the Braydiches on the other side. The Mastrans, of course, had the best backyard for a playing field.

A detached garage just big enough to squeeze a car into. A side driveway. A small front porch with a brick wraparound exterior. A modest front yard.

Mass and grade school at St. Dominic's. Little League. Pop Warner. Baseball. Basketball. Boxing. Wiffle ball. Soccer. Swimming.

We had very little, but we didn't know it. And we didn't care. Life was simple and good if you were a son or daughter of Ron and Evelyn Stoops of 865 Detroit Avenue, Youngstown, Ohio.

I am the third of those six children. Born September 9, 1960, Robert Anthony Stoops—or Bobby to family, friends, and, later, Iowans. My middle name honors my maternal grandfather, Tony. My first name honors my dad's youngest brother. In fact, my uncle Bob likes to tell people that he's the *real* Bob Stoops. I'll give him this much: he's the original. We always called him Super Bob, or Sup for short.

So if you're keeping track, it goes like this: Ron Sr. and Evelyn (Dee to family and friends), and then Ron Jr. (born in 1957), Kathy (1958), me (1960), Mike (1961), Maureen (we call her Reenie—1963), and Mark (1967). Six kids in ten years.

My dad was a history teacher and coach at Cardinal Mooney High School, which is on the south side of the city. He taught American history as well as physical education classes. In the fall, he was the defensive coordinator, and in the spring, he was the head baseball coach. In between, he officiated intramural basketball games and was the official scorekeeper for the varsity basketball team. To help make ends meet, he also painted houses during the summer. It became the family business.

My mom was a housewife, and later, when we were all old enough for school, she worked at an optometrist's office and eventually in the front office at Mooney.

For years, even decades, there was some kind of Stoops presence at Cardinal Mooney. All six of us kids got our diplomas there. The school was named after Cardinal Edward Mooney, who had been raised in Youngstown and later became the archbishop of Detroit. In 1957, he gave the benediction at the second inauguration of President Dwight Eisenhower.

Former San Francisco 49ers owner Edward DeBartolo Jr. is a Mooney alum. So is current 49ers co-owner Denise DeBartolo York. Then there are the boxing champion Ray "Boom Boom" Mancini (he lived behind us, on Cambridge Street), the Pelini football brothers Bo and Carl, former NFL team executive Carmen Policy, former Michigan Wolverine and Los Angeles Raider Ed Muransky (he lived five houses away on Zedaker Street), Texas offensive coordinator Tim Beck and former teammate Myke Clarett, who died in 2012 and whose son is former Ohio State running back Maurice Clarett.

The school's motto left no room for confusion: "Sanctity, Scholarship, Discipline." Those words fit my dad's sensibilities. He adhered to his core beliefs, and he made damn sure we adhered to them, too.

He had sayings like, "If you're going to do it half-ass, then don't do it." Or, "If you're going to do it, do it right." It was boilerplate Greatest Generation stuff, but it was true and authentic—and the sentiment applies as much today as it did back then.

Dad didn't have a lot of rules for us. He didn't care if we grew our hair over our ears or if we cranked up the volume on our Bruce Springsteen (*Born to Run*), Bob Seger (*Beautiful Loser* or *Stranger in Town*), or Stevie Wonder (*Songs in the Key of Life*) albums and eight-track tapes. He taught by example, not with a series of lectures out of a parenting handbook. He was the kind of guy who would stay up late to shine our school shoes.

Almost by osmosis, we embraced his values of honesty, compassion, integrity, commitment, devotion, and perspective. He was our family's North Star.

We learned hard work from Dad. He was very detailed in anything that he did. He was a perfectionist. Even the way he kept his baseball scorecard or basketball scorebook—it was done in different colors and everything printed just so. It was the same when he painted houses, so much attention to detail. You could see the amount of pride he took in a job well done.

—Mike Stoops

The guy would mop locker rooms, pick up dirty towels, make sure it was perfectly clean. Mr. Stoops had an incredible way. He was nice to the All-Americans, the All-City, the All-State kids he coached, but he would gravitate to the kid who didn't play, who was trying hard but might not have the necessary talent.

—Jerry Williams, Cardinal Mooney teammate

I played Pop Warner with Bobby and Michael, and high school football, of course… Going into my junior year, I was slated as the starting tailback. We were doing summer sessions, and I weighed a buck thirty-two. But I wanted to be a fighter from day one. I finally told Mr. [Don] Bucci, "I'm not going to play football no more. I want to be a fighter."

Second period in school was my free period, so I'd go to the gym and work out. Mr. Stoops saw me and said, "Hey, Ray, you going to give up football?"

I told him I was.

He said, "Then, Ray, you go out and be the best fighter you can be, and you make us proud."

You don't know how that makes a kid in high school feel. It meant the world to me. I loved that man. He never spoke down to me. He gave me the affirmation I needed.

—Ray Mancini

Dad was quick to laugh and had a joyful, easygoing quality to him. He loved to tell a joke. Even though he wasn't an extrovert, he had a way of connecting with players. He accepted each player's personality for what it was, and they all could sense his openness and trust. That was another father's lesson to his sons.

He didn't swear ("horseshit" was his exception), but just below the surface was an intensity and temper that could bubble up in a moment's time. It was best to be in another area code when that happened. I inherited that same trait from him.

Imagine all eight of us at Sunday Mass, crammed into a pew for an hour, expected to behave. No chance, especially with us four boys. I'd nudge Ron Jr. or elbow Mike. They'd elbow me back. Maybe we'd start giggling. My dad would say nothing. Instead, you'd feel the hard pinch of his fingers on your ear. Or his viselike grip on your arm. He was a man of few words, but he didn't need many to convey his displeasure.

My parents loved us unconditionally, but our relationship wasn't based on us being equals. They were our parents, not our friends—and we were their children. We obeyed. We respected. That was the way of the world—or, at least, the way of our world.

Every team, every family has its glue person, the one who holds it all together. That was my mom. Caring, generous, supportive, a constant. Like a lot of moms, she was the counterbalance to my dad's intensity. She was competitive, but in a different, more subtle way. But, like my dad, she was a worker bee. Dad and Mom were the perfect pair. As parents, they bad-copped/good-copped us. You can guess who played which part.

During the summers, we'd leave the house at 8:00 a.m. and not come home until 8:00 p.m. We'd maybe pop in for a lunch sandwich and then disappear. We did what kids did back then: we just played…all day, all night—and only returned when we heard our parents call for us to come in. Played touch football in the streets, tackle football in the park. Our street against your street in pickup basketball. Shorthanded baseball games where if you hit it to right field, it was an automatic out. Wiffle ball rules that dictated a single if you reached the house sidewalk, a double if you cleared the tree in the front yard.

The Browns' house got the worst of this, as it was in the direct line of fire during our baseball games. I quit counting the number of times we broke one of their windows or dented their aluminum siding. My dad would wearily retrieve his repair kit from the house and do his best to fix the damage.

Within eight houses of ours were a baseball field, a football field, tennis courts, a pool, and acres of woods. On some summer nights, Mom would give us a package of hot dogs and we'd go into the woods, make a little fire, and cook them on a stick over the open flame.

St. Dominic was the Catholic church of choice on our street. But depending on your last name, you might go to St. Matthias or Saints Cyril and Methodius, or St. Pat's down on the south side.

If we wanted to go swimming at the Southside pool, we'd find a pole, stick a nail in the end of it, and then stab at any nearby garbage. Collect enough trash, and they'd waive the ten-cent entrance fee. And if that didn't work, we'd jump the pool fence at night and have the place to ourselves. It was only a block from our house.

We were a little rough around the edges in Youngstown. We played a game called "hide the strap." I don't know who invented it, but I know this: you couldn't get away with playing it these days. Someone would call the cops.

Summer evenings were the preferred time for this neighborhood game. The humidity didn't matter, and the heat might still be pushing ninety degrees—but we'd all show up, including the girls, wearing pants, long-sleeve shirts, socks, and shoes. You had to gear up to play "hide the strap."

We'd take our crew and head over to Roxbury three streets away, or to Cambridge just one street over, and challenge those kids. The rules of the game were simple: someone would hide a thick leather belt in one of the backyards. Whoever found it first could take it and start flailing away at anyone within swing radius.

The kid with the belt would chase the other kids until they reached a designated home base, which was usually someone's front porch. Until then, they were fair game. If you were being chased, you had better be able to zig and zag—and God forbid you should trip and fall! If you did, you were going to leave with a few belt welts on your arms and legs.

We had our own homes and parents, of course, but the truth was, we were all one.

My best friend growing up was Jimmy "Snake" Braydich. We called him that because his favorite team was the Oakland Raiders, and his favorite player was Kenny "The Snake" Stabler. Snake's dad died in 1966, leaving behind a widow with five boys to raise. Snake had a pragmatism about him. He didn't suffer fools. He was my fourth "brother," and in time, his own siblings became extensions of our family—especially the youngest, Mark...or "Moke," as we called him. We'd bring them all on vacations with us, to football and basketball games. That's just what you did back then.

In our neighborhood, especially when it came to the Braydiches and the Bearaduces, we didn't ring doorbells or knock on doors. We just walked in as if their houses were ours. That's what everyone did. And there was no refuge from discipline in a neighbor's house. It was like there was a NATO treaty between all the neighborhood parents. They kept all of us in line. If they told you to do something, it was as if your own parents had told you to do it.

We were regulars at the Pemberton Park ballfields, where my dad still played softball. He was drafted out of high school as a shortstop by the Washington Senators and then drafted again after college. He reached Double-A ball, but then real life arrived: marriage, a family, a job.

But even as he got older, we could see his athleticism and competitiveness. His golf clubs would sit untouched in the basement for almost an entire year, but then, on a whim, he'd join a friend for a last-minute round and shoot 80—and do it with a maddening ease.

He played baseball into his thirties and then switched to fast-pitch. We'd go to his games and shag foul balls. Get enough of them, and you got free candy or a sno-cone.

My mom says I got my competitiveness from my dad. Makes sense. He had lettered in baseball, basketball, and football at East High School in Youngstown. He wasn't an "every kid gets a participation ribbon" kind of guy. You had to earn your victories. You had to learn from your defeats.

We had a ping-pong table and a bumper pool table in the basement. Dad gave no mercy wins. If you played him, you got his best. "Gosh, let them win, will you?" my mom would plead after he beat me again in ping-pong or pool.

"No," he'd say. "He'll learn. He'll get better."

And I did. We all did.

My mom (Evelyn Rochford was her maiden name) went to Ursuline High, which later became Mooney's longtime rival. She had first noticed Dad when he played in a basketball game at Ursuline. He was class of 1953, and she was class of 1954. They began dating when she was a senior in high school and he was a freshman at Youngstown State. They married on Valentine's Day in 1956.

Boom Boom—Ray Mancini—lived over on Cambridge Street. A year younger than me, he would later become the World Boxing Association lightweight champion of the world. When we were kids, we'd run some rope around the fat part of four trees and create a makeshift boxing ring. Or we'd rope off part of our basement and determine matches by weight and height. Three rounds, and may the best man win. We'd box, but nobody ever messed with Ray. No, no, no. We weren't that stupid.

Yeah, the Bengal bouts in the cellar... I was one of the smaller guys, but my father taught me how to throw punches straight. I had fast hands, hit pretty good. I was strong. Nobody's used to getting hit at that age. But that was my sport.

Now, football, I was a running back. We used to do those drills, and Bobby used to break us. He used to hurt guys. That was no bargain.
—Ray Mancini

I was a problem child, no doubt about it. If there was a fight, I was in it. Middle child...in the middle of every brawl. I fought up, and I fought down. I didn't care if you were older or younger, bigger or smaller, I'd fight you. An hour couldn't pass in our house without some sort of brawl involving us boys.

Bob had an ornery side to him. Very competitive. Kind of intense. There was something different about him, beginning even with his hair. We had fair hair, but his was dark. For a time — when he seven, eight, nine years old — he thought he might have been adopted.

He was three years younger than me, but we had our battles. One time, we were wrestling in the basement — and we were going at it hard. There was nothing brotherly about it. I wanted to put him in his place. He wanted to put me on my back. It got heated enough that our mom opened the basement door and yelled, "Stop it! Now!"

Usually that would have done it. But not this time. We didn't stop. Bob wouldn't let us. He had a drive about him that was noticeable, almost palpable. I played football and basketball. So did he, and he was better than me at both. He was willing to put in the work. He was the kind of kid who got up early and ran his miles, even if we were on vacation.

—Ron Stoops Jr.

Typical middle child . . . looking for his spot, looking for attention. By far the most intense of any of us. When he got an idea in his head, he would fight with anyone about it.

Bobby was the instigator. He was always in trouble. He was just stubborn. My mom always says he was difficult from the time he was an infant.

But if one of us got in a fight with a neighbor, Bobby would be the first to come to our defense. Whoever it was, he'd tell them, "You don't mess with my brothers and sisters."

—Kathy Stoops Kohowski

Our parents taught us to look out for one another. They also taught us the value of a dollar. Money? Who had money? My dad was almost oblivious to it. He didn't think the way people do now. He would have thought a 401(k) was some sort of uranium isotope. Retirement accounts? Investments? Mutual funds? Stocks and bonds? Not my dad. My mom would ask him about life after retirement, and he would say with all the conviction in the world, "Don't worry. God will take care of it."

Our house had cost $16,200. We never owned a new car. My parents' combined income: $38,500. The most they ever made was about $48,000 a year. We were a five-figure family that lived a million-dollar-quality life. We had neighbors who became lifelong friends. We had sports. We had family. We were like the Baileys in *It's a Wonderful Life*. We weren't consumed by what we didn't have. We were safe. We were happy. More money wouldn't have made us any happier.

I think about that even today. I was paid very well as the head coach at Oklahoma, but my saving grace is that I know how little I really need. Growing up in a family where we pinched pennies until Lincoln gagged for air taught me that. Extravagant houses and the most expensive cars are like cotton candy—big and impressive until you realize it's mostly just wisps of sugar and air, nothing truly substantial.

When I was a kid in the 1960s, the steel industry was the heartbeat of Youngstown and the surrounding Mahoning River Valley. It was generational... institutional. The region once produced about a fifth of the country's steel. At night, the Youngstown sky was a muted orange with the glow of the flames from the mills. When we crossed the Center Street Bridge to go to my grandparents' house on the east side of town, we could see the steam rise from the Mahoning River as its waters cooled the mills' molten metal.

My dad had worked in the mills on his summers off from college at Youngstown State. The men there had looked after him because he was a local athlete and such a hard worker. They'd tell him, "Hey, kid, we'll cover for you—go study for an hour."

We lived in a boom town. It had two department stores: McKelvey's (with its distinctive vertical red neon sign; my mom worked there when she was in high school) and Strouss's. Homeownership was at record levels. The city budget needed rivets to keep it from bursting with prosperity. There were so many public and parochial schools in the area that we never had to bus more than twenty minutes to play a football or basketball game.

Yet Youngstown was never a pretty city. No one will ever mistake it for Carmel or Santa Fe. And the Mahoning River isn't the Danube. We were a steel town and proud of it—and proud of the people who worked in its mills. We were a city of mutts: Italians, Irish, Germans, Poles, Slovaks, Greeks, those of Middle Eastern descent. The Warner brothers, who were sons of Polish immigrants and later became Hollywood studio legends, grew up in Youngstown.

I'm mostly of Irish descent—my mother's parents were Irish; my dad's side was mostly English—but when I close my eyes, I can still smell the homemade breads and pierogies that some of the Polish women of our congregation brought for after-Mass meals.

Ours was an unapologetically industrial city. Its skyline boasted more smokestacks than skyscrapers. Thousands of Youngstown working men always carried two items in their wallets: a driver's license and a union card.

If you lived in Youngstown, you were probably a Cleveland Browns fan. Pittsburgh and the Steelers were actually closer (by about ten miles), but the Browns were Ohio's team. The Bengals didn't even exist until 1968, and they might as well have been in Brazil. We didn't acknowledge the Bengals.

I wasn't a Browns fan. I loved the Kansas City Chiefs. When we played ball in the streets, I was Otis Taylor, Len Dawson, or Ed Podolak. I wore Podolak's number, 14, in grade school. I ended up playing college ball at Iowa—Podolak's school—and was issued number 41. Same numerals, different order. (Years later, I would meet Podolak—a thrill.)

My second-favorite team was the Steelers. They won championships. They were an hour and change away and also from a steel town. Even their helmet logo was inspired by the Steelmark insignia of U.S. Steel.

There was something about football that always appealed to me. It was a no-excuses game. Either you made the tackle or you didn't. Either you made the block or you didn't. Caught the pass or didn't. It was a sport with grass stains, not gray areas. I liked the finality of it, the clarity of the scoreboard.

I played basketball, too. Loved to shoot. Loved to defend. You know the scene in *Hoosiers* where Gene Hackman wants his player to guard an opponent so closely that he knows what kind of gum the kid is chewing? I would have been that player.

But you couldn't hit and tackle in basketball. And I liked to hit.

Dad was the defensive coordinator at Cardinal Mooney, but he also worked with the offensive tackles and tight ends. He first coached Ronnie. Then I was next, followed later by Mike and then Mark.

Dad and head coach Don Bucci were institutions at Mooney. You could make more money in the public school system—and the public schools had a pension plan and better benefits—but my dad wanted to be part of the new Catholic school in town.

The high school welcomed its first class of 610 freshmen and sophomores in 1956. In 1959, my dad joined the faculty and coaching staff. Seven years later, when Bucci was hired as head coach, Dad became the defensive coordinator. During their twenty-two-year partnership, they helped bring four state championships to Mooney.

They were more than coaching colleagues; they were friends. The Bucci family would meet our family for vacations at a lake cabin. But even during the summer, our fathers would talk football. Dad took care of the defense, Bucci the offense.

There were no special favors granted to the Stoops boys. My dad judged each player by his performance, not his last name. He treated every player with respect, toughness, fairness, and a matter-of-fact nature that we saw at home and on the field. You always knew where you stood with my dad, not only as a father but as a coach and teacher.

My dad had a habit of casually asking other Mooney teachers how the Stoops children were doing in their classes. And, just as casually, a teacher might mention that I had been late with an assignment or maybe a little too social in class.

Before I knew it, I would be staring at the steely, unforgiving eyes of my father. I'd get a brief, stern come-to-Jesus talk. There would be no more assignments turned in late. There would be no extracurricular chatting with Tina in typing class.

Bobby was at the top of the food chain in high school. Very confident. Handsome. A very good athlete. The rest of us went through a more awkward stage.

High school was a breeze for Bobby.

—Kathy Stoops Kohowski

23

Secretly, I loved that my dad didn't play favorites. In fact, at times he was much, much tougher on us than on our teammates. I understood his reasons. He never wanted to be accused of cutting us a break. It was ping-pong and bumper pool all over again: earn it.

I was a cornerback but also played wide receiver and tight end at times. My jersey number for the red and gold of Mooney was number 80. Mike wore it after I left.

There are nuances to each position — nuances that are occasionally lost on a sophomore tight end who maybe thinks he knows more than he does.

As a tight end, you had to learn the three-block technique, which is simple enough: you and the offensive tackle block down (in essence, a double-team block) on whoever is lined up on the outside shoulder opposite the offensive tackle. But if that defensive player moves inside at the snap and leaves that gap, then your job is to find and block the linebacker. Got it?

During one practice my sophomore year, my dad called for the three-block technique. One problem: the guy lined up on the outside shoulder of the tackle moved to another spot at the snap of the ball. Before I could find the linebacker . . . he found me. I went airborne and landed flat on my back. Got my ass kicked. That's when I heard my dad blow the whistle, glance at me as I staggered up from the ground, and then give me a little smirk.

He knew that I knew I hadn't been in the right position, that my stance was too high, that I was a perfect target for the linebacker.

Now fast-forward to my junior season. I'm at tight end . . . and a three-block technique moment. But this time I put the linebacker on *his* ass. I hear the whistle and see my dad, and he has that same smirk of a year earlier. But he knew that I knew I'd done it right this time.

If there was a football soundtrack to our lives on Detroit Avenue, it came from the clackety-clack noise of Dad's 16mm film projector. One turn of the switch brought the projector's lamp to life. Another turn activated the motor. This was old school. This was pre-Betacam tape, pre-DVD, pre-digital, pre-HD, pre-AVID system, pre-XOS, pre-DVSport, pre-iPad . . . pre-everything.

Though this was just game film, to my dad, it was his lifeblood. He would set the projector on our kitchen table, aim it at the front of our white refrigerator, attach the metal reels to the arms of the projector, thread the film through the sprockets and gate, and settle into his chair. Then, using a notepad and colored pens, he'd analyze the film's every frame.

Clackety-clack forward. *Clackety-clack* reverse. Back and forth. Back and forth. You could almost hear the projector motor and the clicker begging for mercy as Dad carefully and methodically noted formations, plays, jersey numbers, tendencies, tells, strengths, weaknesses, field position, techniques, and pursuit angles. He analyzed who hustled and who didn't, presnap positioning, pass blocking, run blocking, blitz pickup, footwork, leverage, route running, ball delivery, and mismatches.

The average football fan watches where the ball goes. My dad taught us how to *see* the game; there's a difference. That's how you understand the game and your opponent.

How many hours did we sit at that table with my dad? Had to be in the hundreds. The whirring sound of that projector is still ingrained in my memory. How many times did we open and close that refrigerator to pour a glass of milk or grab a bite to eat during those sessions? My dad would patiently pause the projector until he got his viewing screen back. How many times did we repair a torn piece of game film with Scotch tape?

Even when a Mooney alum offered to buy my dad a desktop computer in the 1980s—that way, he could log all his game film information on a hard drive or disk—my dad politely said no. He had his own way of doing things. A computer would have changed that.

We didn't realize it at the time, but watching these films with Dad was our version of Advanced Placement courses in football. It was an education. It was a revelation. For the rest of my playing and professional life, I would study game film using the principles my dad had taught me: Pay attention to detail. Identify a strength. Find a weakness and then exploit it.

Friday was our game night, but Saturday was reserved for college football. Ohio State and Woody Hayes dominated all things college football in our state. And the streets of Youngstown were empty during the annual Ohio State–Michigan game.

I liked Ohio State well enough, but I didn't go to bed humming "Carmen Ohio." Watching the tuba player dot the *i* in Script Ohio wasn't a life-changing moment for me. If anything, we were a Notre Dame or Michigan house—Notre Dame because we were Catholic; Michigan because we had a cousin, Ed Moore, who had played linebacker and defensive line for the Wolverines. And Big Ed Muransky ended up playing there, too.

The truth is, *my* team wasn't located in Columbus, South Bend, or Ann Arbor. It was eleven hundred miles away in Norman, Oklahoma. Though Ohio State football was a religion in my town and state, I preferred the sermons given by Rev. Barry Switzer and his Oklahoma Sooners. It was the triple-option attack. It was the Selmon brothers. It was an attitude, a swagger, an aura. Switzer, with those squinted eyes, those awful 1970s-era coaches' pants that the bootlegger's son somehow made look cool—he would even fire up a cigarette on the sidelines.

Woody Hayes wore a baseball cap and schoolteacher glasses. He rolled up his pants legs. His offenses were brutally efficient and powerful—they left bruise marks on defenses. They were the epitome of Big Ten football: three yards and a cloud of dust. But OU and Switzer played fast. They played fearless. They wanted to run around you, through you, past you. They wanted to score as many points as the scoreboard lights would allow—and then some. They wanted to cut your still-beating heart out of you, have a laugh at your expense, and then keep running to the end zone. It wasn't personal—it was business. And they were in the business of beating anyone and everyone. They were so good, they could fumble six times and still beat you by fifty.

OU running back Joe Washington wore silver cleats. So during my freshman year at Mooney, me and my teammate Jerry Williams painted *our* practice cleats silver with red Adidas stripes. (Jerry and I were part of the starting backcourt for the Mooney basketball team, too.) Years later, when I met Joe, I told him about my silver cleats. He just laughed. His are displayed prominently in a glass case in the lobby of the Switzer Center at OU... mine disappeared into obscurity.

I might have been the only guy in Youngstown who appreciated the OU-Nebraska Thanksgiving game as much as the Buckeyes versus That Team Up North. I loved watching Greg Pruitt run the ball and Tinker Owens catch the ball. I loved the arrogance of the OU offense.

On the day before a Mooney game, we'd sometimes pretend we were the Sooners running the option, with me as OU quarterback Thomas Lott. Maybe one of us would wear a bandana just for fun. I'd squat down lowwww under center, my chin resting on the center's butt. Everything was exaggerated and in slow motion.

At the snap of the ball, each of us would slowly begin the choreographed football dance that is the triple option offense. It was like we were watching it in the film room. Halfway through the play, someone would yell, "Replay!" and we'd slowly retrace our steps, as if someone had hit the reverse button on the projector's clicker. Back and forth we went. I wish Switzer could have seen us. Or maybe not...

I weighed 155 pounds as a junior, 165 pounds as a senior. But I played bigger. Like I said, I'd fight up, and I'd fight down.

Forty-plus years ago, the rules of football were different. If a wide receiver came across the middle, you could hit him. As a defensive back, that's what you dreamed about: hitting a receiver the moment the ball touched his hands. I wasn't the biggest or fastest player, but I could hit.

There were also no comprehensive recruiting services in the mid-1970s. No ESPN.com 300 rankings. No Rivals.com. No 247.com. No Scout.com. In fact, there were no dot-coms at all. No internet. No cell phones. No texting. Fax machines were exotic. An emoji? What was that?

This is incomprehensible for today's kids. They grow up on i-things: iPads, iWatches, iPhones. The difference in the technology of my youth and theirs is astounding, mind-boggling. We didn't have desktops or laptops at Mooney. Nobody did. The first desktop computer was still in its infancy then. Laptops didn't exist. Instead, we had typewriters. Harry Joyce was my typing teacher (and also my dad's partner in their summer house-painting business).

We had two phones in our house—one in the kitchen and one in the basement. They were rotary phones. (For you millennials, a rotary phone has a dial for selecting each digit of a phone number, used in a circular motion by hand. Amazing!) Did we have an answering machine? Not just no, but *hell* no! And if you wanted to use the phone, you had to battle seven other people for a line. It was first-come, first-serve.

We started with a black-and-white TV. And by that, I don't mean the exterior of the television was black and white; I mean the picture itself was in only black and white. We didn't get a color TV until years later—and it only got three channels: ABC, CBS, and NBC. I repeat: three channels.

Our TV was tuned to whatever channel featured a comedy program. My dad was a man of few words but also a man with a full laugh. We grew up watching Carol Burnett, Benny Hill, Flip Wilson, *Laugh-In*, Red Skelton, Bob Hope, Dean Martin, Johnny Carson, and whatever sitcoms were on during prime time.

We watched Cleveland Indians baseball in the summer (Dad, Mark, and Mike were huge fans; I wasn't), and after our season was finished, it wasn't unusual to find my dad watching the Browns in the winter. Sometimes I'd walk in and Dad would have a hockey game on TV. I'd ask my mom, "Why's Dad watching hockey?"

She'd shrug. "It's sports," she'd say.

Our source for local news was the Youngstown *Vindicator*. You were having a good day as a high school player if you made it into its sports pages.

My dad was a man of the arts—as much as a coach in Youngstown, Ohio, can be. It wasn't unusual to find him plopped on the couch, listening to his favorites: Frank Sinatra, Bing Crosby, Dean Martin, or Neil Diamond. He also loved the symphony.

My parents didn't drink alcohol—OK, maybe my dad had an occasional glass of wine or half a beer after a long day of painting houses. But that was it. And yet we had a bar in our basement. Since it was the loneliest bar in America, we used it as a fort of sorts. When our cousins visited for a holiday or birthday, the Stoops boys would take positions behind the bar, and the cousins would crouch behind a table we'd turned on its side. Then we'd start firing plastic bowling pins at each other. My dad's trophy collection behind the bar took a beating, what with the bowling pins crashing against it and the knotty pine walls.

We were the children of a coach, but most of all, we were the children of a teacher. My dad was an educator, and he believed deeply in the value of a college diploma. For us, going to college was a given. My brother Ron had already moved on to Youngstown State, which was less than four miles from our front door. My sister Kathy was at Bowling Green. I was next on the Stoops education assembly line.

When I was a freshman, Bobby was a senior. He was the most popular kid in his senior class. All the girls wanted to date him, and all the boys followed him. Even though he had a strong personality and went after what he wanted, he also had a kindness about him.

Bobby definitely had an edge to him. I would say him and Ron were very competitive. With Mark being the youngest, he was probably the son who would try to make everybody laugh. Mike was very quiet but had the same kind of competitiveness.

—Reenie Stoops Farragher

College wasn't a certainty or even a priority for a lot of my buddies in Youngstown. At the time, the mills were often the first option out of high school. Maybe their dads or grandfathers had worked in the mills. You thought you could depend on always seeing that orange glow at night. The nation and the world needed steel, right? It was a job for a lifetime—or so we all thought.

And then came September 19, 1977: Black Monday.

Without warning, Youngstown Sheet & Tube Company closed the Campbell Works mill. In a moment's time, five thousand people lost their jobs. It was the beginning of an economic tsunami—except nobody realized it then. Or maybe they didn't want to admit it.

I was just a high school kid, but I knew our city's entire identity was based on steel. It was who we were.

There was a domino effect of concern and then despair. First, Sheet & Tube shut down. Then another fifteen hundred workers were laid off at Sheet & Tube's Brier Hill Works. Then U.S. Steel pulled the plug on Youngstown Works and another thirty-five hundred jobs. Republic followed with its own closings.

Eighteen years later, Springsteen would write a song—"Youngstown"—about the rise and fall of our city because of those steel closings. He even referenced the Jeanette blast furnace of the Brier Hill Works.

I remember a kind of pall over the town. None of the parents in our neighborhood worked in the mills, but some of them had older sons who had suddenly lost their jobs. We felt such sympathy for all those people. It was alarming; how was this going to impact everybody?

Imagine an entire city getting sucker punched economically, psychologically, emotionally. Fathers and mothers wondered how they were going to pay their mortgages, put food on their tables, send their children to college. Local businesses were suddenly worried about their own futures.

There was talk of an employee takeover of the mills, but that was fantasy. My hometown—and the people in it—would never be the same again. In 1960, when I was born at St. Elizabeth Hospital on the south side, the Youngstown population was about 167,000. Three years after Black Monday, it was about 115,000. In 2017, it was about 65,000.

It was a big-time steel town until our graduation year, and then some of the big mills went dark. That's when the downturn started.

For a lot of kids in this town, you figured when you graduated from high school, you could always do what your dad did: work in the mills. There were forty thousand jobs, a lot of work: aluminum manufacturers, the blast furnaces, metal stamping. It was a fairly vibrant area, and then...

—Ed Muransky

I was a high school senior in 1977. I drove a beater: a very used Ford Gran Torino that I had bought from Ronnie. I knew I wanted to go to college and play football. But now I had to find a college and football team that wanted me. Ohio State wasn't interested. Oklahoma wasn't interested. Lots of schools weren't interested.

I was a five-foot-eleven, 165-pound defensive back. Do the math. Maybe that's why I've always had a soft spot for players on the fringe, for guys who were ignored or dismissed because of the so-called measurables. I was one in high school.

One of the few schools that recruited me was Youngstown State. YSU is where Ron Jaworski played in the late 1960s, early 1970s. Cliff Stoudt played there when I was growing up. So did Kevin Statzer, Robby Robson, Jim Ferranti, and Bob Davie. They were good players, and they had distinguished careers there. YSU is the program built for the bar bet, "What coach and program invented the penalty flag?" The answer: Youngstown coach Dwight Beede—the penalty flag made its debut in 1941.

YSU is where Jim Tressel would lead the Penguins to four national championships and two second-place finishes between 1991 and 1999. YSU is also where Mark Mangino got his degree and later became an assistant coach...where Mark Dantonio was once a defensive coordinator... where Bo Pelini is now the head coach. But I wasn't sure YSU was where I wanted to spend the next four years of my life. And if I needed a reminder, Snake provided it.

During my recruiting visit, the YSU coaches took me through the Beeghly Center, a combo facility for varsity sports, intramurals, and campus recreation. There were some pool tables in the middle of the facility back then, and Snake and a handful of our mutual buddies were there shooting a game. My escort, a YSU coach, saw Snake and decided he might have an ally there. So in a tone that might have been a little too confident, a little too smug, the coach said, "Tell Bobby he needs to stick around and play for us."

Snake didn't even look up from the pool table. "No he don't," he said.

Snake knew that it was time to get out of Youngstown. We loved our hometown—still do, and always will—but with the steel mill closures, it was no longer a place of optimism or opportunity.

I took another recruiting trip, this time outside the city limits: to Southern Illinois in Carbondale. The Salukis were a I-AA program (an FCS program in today's college football designation). I had buddies from Mooney at SIU, so it became an option when the coach offered me a scholarship.

The only Division I program (or FBS program now) to offer me a scholarship was Bowling Green, which was about three hours west of Youngstown. It wasn't Ohio State, but it was a Mid-American Conference program with pedigree and a history of good coaches (Doyt Perry, Don Nehlen, and, decades later, Urban Meyer, Dave Clawson, and Dino Babers).

I made my official visit to Bowling Green to see the campus and the facilities and to meet the head coach, Denny Stolz, who had been hired in 1977. Unlike the assistant coach who had recruited me, Stolz had never seen me in person. And when he did see me, you could tell he wasn't impressed.

Shortly after I returned home, the offer was rescinded. The assistant coach, to his credit, was honest with me and my father. He said I wasn't what Bowling Green was looking for. In other words, I wasn't what Stolz was looking for. You could tell the assistant coach felt terrible about relaying the bad news.

I understood. I wasn't an imposing physical figure. I didn't give stopwatches goose bumps with my forty-yard-dash time. Stolz had taken one look at me and probably decided I was too skinny, that I wouldn't hold up.

I thought, *Now what do I do?*

I could have stayed home and played for Youngstown State. It would have been comfortable, familiar, convenient. My family and friends could have watched me play. That front door on Detroit Avenue would always be open to me.

I could have gone to SIU. From a football standpoint, SIU was basically a rural version of Youngstown State but with an Illinois zip code.

I would have been fine. But I'm not sure I would have been happy. Then again, I didn't have many choices. And I'm not sure YSU or SIU were too worried about my happiness level.

And then, there was a football miracle...

In early January 1978, University of Iowa coach Bob Commings offered me a scholarship. He was a Youngstown guy. He had played at East High School, where my dad had also played.

Most of Commings's assistant coaches must have thought he was out of his mind. But I was from Youngstown, and that counted for something with people who knew the city, the work ethic, and the quality of players from Mooney. What I lacked in physical talent, I compensated with the Youngstown in me. And it certainly helped that Bucci and my dad—both of whom college recruiters and coaches respected for their honesty—vouched for me. I was feisty. You weren't going to intimidate me. You hit me with a two-by-four, I'll go find a crowbar and hit you back. It was the Youngstown way.

Underdeveloped, underrecruited, undersized, but he had a pretty good-sized chip on his shoulder.

> —Dan McCarney, Iowa graduate assistant coach
> 1977–1978; assistant coach 1979–1989

Maybe that's what Commings liked about me. Maybe he knew he could take a leap of faith with a coach's son from Youngstown. Maybe he remembered his own career as an undersized, 180-pound MVP offensive guard on the 1957 Iowa team that won the Big Ten championship and Rose Bowl. Maybe someone had showed him game film of our 34–0 win against Struthers High School in 1976. Struthers is where Commings used to coach in the late 1960s. Or maybe it was this simple: he saw a little bit of himself in me.

Iowa was everything YSU and SIU weren't. That's not a criticism of those two programs, but the differences were obvious: Iowa was a Big Ten school with a Big Ten campus and Big Ten opponents. Iowa City was far away from Youngstown — a ten-hour drive — but I wanted to play football at its highest level. I was a 165-pound, two-time All-Steel Valley selection who didn't know any better.

And here's the kicker: you know who was thrilled for me when he heard the news? The assistant coach who had recruited me to Bowling Green.

So hand me a pen. Give me the National Letter of Intent. I wanted to sign it before Commings changed his mind.

I was going to be a Hawkeye and play football. Me, the instigator. The pain in the ass. The third child of Ron and Dee Stoops.

I was going to a place I had seen once in my life. I was leaving Snake and the rest of my friends, my family, my hometown, those smokestacks. I was doing the *Star Trek* thing: boldly going where no Stoops had gone before. I was going to cross three state lines, defy the football odds, and step into the great unknown of Iowa black and gold.

Chapter Two

Iowa City

The drive from Youngstown to Iowa City was long, solemn, and sobering. With each mile marker, I separated myself from what was familiar and moved closer to the unknown.

Excitement was replaced by a mixture of dry-throat nervousness and a seventeen-year-old's naive confidence. The romance of the road trip was eventually overwhelmed by reality.

With a full tank of gas in an uncle's borrowed Cadillac, the past and present slowly disappeared from view as we made our way from Detroit Avenue to South Avenue to Interstate 680 and then took one final look out the car window at proud but wounded Youngstown; at that grimy, polluted Mahoning River; at all that I knew and had ever known.

There were four of us—six, if you counted my clothes and stereo—Dad, Mom, me, and Kathy. Mom and Kathy had their best faces on, shining with support and optimism. Dad gripped the steering wheel, the law-abiding high school coach determined to drive all 241 miles of the Ohio Turnpike without nudging the speedometer needle much past the mandated 55 miles per hour. The Caddy's V-8 barely broke a sweat.

I smiled at my memories of the last eight months. After my senior season of football, I had decided to try out for my dad's Mooney baseball team. It had been a great plan—except for the part where I wasn't very good at the game. I hadn't played baseball in years, and it showed. I'd dive out of the way of soft curveballs and then freeze as a fastball tailed toward my ribs. The experiment lasted only several weeks before I told my dad that maybe I should transition to running hurdles for the track team in the spring. You could see the relief in his face. "Good," he said, "because I thought I was going to have to cut you."

I spent my final high school summer working out, doing everything I could to add a pound or two to my frame. Even when we went to the lake for vacation, I'd load weights into the car and make sure I brought along plenty of protein powder for my daily drinks. The stuff tasted like a combination of chalk and cardboard, but I would have eaten tree bark if it'd put a few pounds on me.

During the ten-hour drive west, Youngstown began to feel like an afterthought. Every exit sign we passed made it more real: Cleveland and Lake Erie to the north, Sandusky, Toledo. Ohio became the Indiana Toll Road. We eventually passed the exit for Notre Dame, and soon Indiana became Illinois. Interstate 80 took us to the Mississippi River, and across it lay the blank page of Iowa. It wouldn't be long now.

I'd never seen so much green. Youngstown had muted my color spectrum. Urban and suburban were replaced with rural and agricultural.

Dad checked the map. We saw the signs of the little towns: Springdale, West Branch. We crossed the Iowa River and into my new home, Iowa City. This was foreign land, a new world to the occupants of the Cadillac.

We got there on a Saturday. Mom, Dad, and Kathy left on Sunday. Football practice started on Monday.

It was devastating. It was heartbreaking.

I remember him standing there. He was just standing there outside of the hotel as we got ready to leave. He was confident. He kept saying, "I'll be fine. Don't worry." But it was hard. He was the first one of us to really leave home. In those days, no one left Youngstown.

—Kathy Stoops Kohowski

I later found out that my mom cried as they headed back east. My dad, true to his personality, said little.

I didn't have time for tears. I was a true freshman parachuted into a Big Ten university with an enrollment of 22,990. I wasn't a five-star recruit. I'm not sure I had any stars next to my name. But by the grace of Coach Bob Commings, I was there to play football.

When I arrived in the fall of 1978, Iowa was a football wasteland. The Hawkeyes hadn't finished above .500 since 1961. They hadn't been ranked in the *Associated Press* poll since 1960. They hadn't played in a bowl game since 1959. They had been on network television just three times in the previous seven seasons. During that period, their record was a combined 19–57–1 (later nudged up to 20–56–1 when a loss to UCLA was reversed because of an ineligible Bruins player). Commings was Iowa's third head coach since 1970.

All the football players were housed in the Hillcrest dormitory, an aging, no-frills, West Campus residence hall built in 1939. It had a view of the Iowa River and was a nine-minute walk to the stadium—even less to our football facility.

We lived in the basement and the first and second floors of the North Wing. A few baseball players and wrestlers were mixed in, too. At Iowa, football players had to live in the dorm during their entire careers. Regular students lived in the South Wing.

My first roommate was from New Jersey, but he left after the first semester. He couldn't handle the culture shock of going from Newark to the new world of Iowa City.

Over the years, I also roomed with defensive back Tracy Crocker, linebacker Todd Simonsen, offensive tackle Bruce Kittle (decades later, I hired him for my OU staff), and offensive tackle Tim Hanna.

As the season approached, I saw a sign outside an Iowa City construction site. Someone had spray-painted something on a large piece of plywood. It read, "Go Hawks! Beat Somebody!"

The program was in disarray. I had come from a successful high school program where there was a culture of winning. At Iowa, the cumulative effect of years and years of losing had created an attitude of resignation. Team morale was nonexistent. You could sense it the first time you walked into the locker room.

The roster, however, wasn't without talent. And it's not like they *wanted* to lose games. But football inertia had set in. Losing almost had become comfort food to some (but not all) of the upperclassmen.

I would join the ranks of the miserable soon enough. It turned out that the coaches wanted to redshirt me in 1978. I would practice but never play.

Didn't they know I had run hurdles to get in condition? Lifted weights on vacation? Drunk cardboard shakes?

During one of our first practices during fall camp two-a-days, we did a tackling drill. It wasn't complicated: you were supposed to hit and then drive through a single padded dummy on a tackling sled. We called them "popsicle dummies" since each was on a stick of sorts.

I watched as player after player tackled a popsicle dummy and then tipped it over at the completion of the hit. When it was my turn, I ran full force into the dummy—with perfect form—and it barely moved. I couldn't tip it over. I couldn't really budge it much.

I heard the snickers and the chuckles. *Look at the Stoops kid. He can't even tackle a dummy.*

A few days later, we had a live tackling drill. This time, I put one of our top running backs right on his own back. There weren't any chuckles this time. I might have been a true freshman, but I wasn't intimidated by my surroundings, by the Big Ten, or by my low status on the depth chart. I was young, but I was always trying to get better.

But nobody, it turned out, seemed too interested in Bobby Stoops in 1978. I was a scout team guy. Nearly invisible. An afterthought.

Meanwhile, our team descended into its familiar hell. We began the season with a September 16 win at Kinnick against Northwestern. We wouldn't win again until November 18. A week later, after a loss at Michigan State, our 2–9 season was mercifully finished—and so was I.

I wanted out of Iowa. Or maybe a better way of putting it: I wanted to go back to Youngstown. I was homesick. I was sick of not playing. I was sick of losing. I missed my friends. I missed my Gran Torino. I missed my hometown, my mom's cooking, my sisters, the brawls with my brothers.

As part of an emergency squad—to be used only if the team ran out of players at a certain position—I dressed for every home game with the other redshirts. But even then, we weren't really part of the team. We dressed in the practice-field locker room and then had to walk across the street to the stadium like outcasts. Once we got there, we weren't allowed into the varsity locker room. Instead, we sat outside in the stairway area. It was humiliating.

During that season, I almost appeared in one game. In fact, the coaches actually put me in the game to return a punt. There was a momentary issue with our regular punt returners, and during the confusion, they sent me in.

I sprinted out there, took my position, and waited for my Iowa debut moment. But it never came. There was a penalty on the play, and the other team kept possession of the ball. Back to the bench I went, my redshirt year safe.

Each week I would call home and hope my mom would answer the phone. She had a sympathetic ear and voice.

I probably would have brought him home. It would be in the evening, maybe after practice, and he would call me. He'd kind of break down a little bit, and I'd cry a little bit.

Bobby would say, "Dad knows a lot of coaches. I'll go anywhere else. I just want to go to a college that's closer to home."

I'd tell him, "Just believe in your dad. Stick it out for one year. You owe it to your dad."

And then Ron would see me on the phone, and he knew. He would say, "Is that Bobby? Give me the phone."

—Dee Stoops

It was tough love from my dad. It wasn't, "Oh, I hope you're OK. You feeling sad? Aww."

No, none of that. It was, "You're not coming home."

—Kathy Stoops Kohowski

My dad was not sympathetic.

"Bobby, we agreed you could play at that level," he would tell me. "You have to stick around. You'll stick it out for a year, and we'll talk about it when you come home."

Our season had ended with that dreadful 42–7 loss at Michigan State on November 25. Two days later, Iowa president Willard Boyd, athletic director Bump Elliott, and the Iowa Board in Control of Athletics met for three hours. The board voted, 16–1, to fire Commings.

I had been at Iowa for four months, hadn't played a down, had witnessed nine defeats in eleven games, and now had lost the only major college coach to offer me a scholarship. When we were dismissed for Thanksgiving break, I headed home to Youngstown to once again make my case to my dad.

We were working out in the yard one day. He had just mowed the grass, and I was helping him sweep the sidewalk. A couple of neighbors came down and chatted with us. That's when I brought up the Iowa thing again and explained all the reasons that it was best that I transfer.

After the neighbors left, my dad looked at me in that dad sort of way. You know the look. I remember his response word for word.

"You know what," he said with a hardened edge to his voice, "you're going to end up like all these other chickenshits who go off to school and come back and amount to nothing." Then he walked away.

The decision had been made. Not by me, but for me.

There was no more talk of leaving Iowa.

—Dee Stoops

On December 9, 1978, Iowa hired Hayden Fry from North Texas State.

I'd never heard of him, or it. As it turned out, Fry didn't know anything about Iowa, or me. Years later, he'd tell interviewers he'd had no idea where the school was located.

But those three events — my dad's refusal to let me leave Iowa, the firing of Commings, the hiring of Fry — were defining moments in my life. I just didn't know it at the time.

I always will be indebted to Bob Commings. Without him, I'm not sure where I'd be. I obviously wouldn't have been at Iowa. His belief in me and the Youngstown work ethic got my foot in the Hawkeye door.

Bob died of cancer in 1992. I think of him often. He was my football guardian angel. He gave me the biggest break of my life.

Fry was no angel. He was all Texas. All US Marine. All business. But in time, I would learn that Hayden Fry also was all heart.

I'm not sure Iowa or the Big Ten had ever seen anybody like Fry. Before he was fired in 1978 for punching a Clemson player during a bowl game, Ohio State's Woody Hayes was bigger than life. So was Bo Schembechler at Michigan. But Fry wasn't intimidated by reputations and personalities. He wasn't intimidated by anything or anybody.

Fry had been born and raised in Odessa, Texas. I've been there. It's in the Texas Panhandle, a place with a long history of oil fields, hard living, and high school football at the highest, craziest levels. Fry played quarterback for Odessa High in the mid-1940s.

When Fry was only fourteen, his dad had died in a car accident. To help his mom make ends meet, he worked part time as an oil-field roughneck, where one of his jobs was to overturn rocks and then kill any rattlesnakes he found.

Through the years, I heard and read more stories about Fry: that he'd majored in psychology while a backup quarterback at Baylor...that he'd earned a master's degree in behavioral psychology...that he had become a Marine Corps captain and hand-to-hand combat instructor... that he had been a football coach at Odessa High and, in 1962, when he was only thirty-three, had been hired as SMU's head coach...that he had defied the bigoted and racist norms of the time in the Southwest Conference by signing the SWC's first African American scholarship player, Jerry LeVias. LeVias (and sometimes Fry) were subjected to vile hate mail and death threats. Later, when LeVias became an All-American wide receiver, Fry would icily observe: "Every time he scores a touchdown, all my good friends thought he became whiter and whiter." Vintage Fry.

I remember a story in the *Los Angeles Times*, where Fry said he had always wanted to coach "at someplace that was the 'University of.' I would've gone to the University of Iowa–Jima."

Given the state of our program at the time, "Iowa-Jima" might have beaten us. But Fry changed that. He changed everything.

We got new uniforms with a new helmet logo. And for once, Iowa reminded me a little bit of Youngstown. That's because our uniforms looked almost exactly like those of the Pittsburgh Steelers, my boyhood second-favorite team. Our helmets now featured something called a Tiger Hawk. I know this much: it looked a lot better than our old logo, Herky the Hawk.

Fry came in and rejected the narrative that we were losers. He was aware of the history, but he simply wouldn't accept the premise that the program was doomed. He projected strength and confidence, even when there was no reason for it. He had a badass mustache, and he wore highway patrolman–style sunglasses—even indoors. And only Fry could get away with wearing white pants and cowboy boots—and look cool in them. He had that swagger going on before almost anyone did, with the exception of OU's Switzer.

Fry had all sorts of down-home sayings. And he'd say them in that high-pitched Texas drawl of his.

"The sun don't shine on the same dog's rump every day."
"High-porch picnic." (a big, fancy party)
"We'll take what the other team gives us. We'll scratch where it itches."
"I don't want any egg-hunters." (undersized players)
"We're going to win, and we're going to look good doing it."

Little by little—and I mean little—his attitude trickled down to his assistant coaches, his staff, and us, his players.

I had the greatest psychological advantage of all time. They hadn't had a winning season in seventeen years. I took over a team and inherited young men known as losers, tails between their legs. But they were determined to win.

Same thing with my assistants. I never hired an assistant in my life unless I was completely convinced they were motivated to become a head coach. There's a reason why I was successful: I surrounded myself with winners.
—Hayden Fry, Iowa head coach, 1979–1998

If coming to Iowa was the biggest break of my life, then the hiring of Fry and his defensive coordinator, Bill Brashier, was number two on the list. They arrived with no preconceived notions about the roster. To the previous regime, I was the too-small, too-slow defensive back who needed to redshirt. To Fry and Brashier, I was an unopened package, a mystery—like every player on the roster—who deserved a new and fair evaluation.

During the off-season, I vowed to make an impression on the new staff. When it came time for those first spring practices, I played like my hair was on fire and began working my way up the depth chart.

He was not an impressive-looking player. If you were going to judge him on a forty-yard dash, he would be way down the line. But when we first saw him on the field—some kids have it, some kids don't. It's hard to explain what "it" is, but you know it when you see it.

When we came in from that first practice, I said, "Hayden, I want to tell you something about this Bobby Stoops. This kid was not talked about by the old staff at all. In my opinion, he looks like the best one out there."

He had been overlooked by the other staff. It doesn't happen a lot, but it happened with him.

—Bill Brashier

I had a staff meeting, and I asked Bill Brashier, "Did you have anyone in the secondary that surprised you?"

He said, "Coach, you wouldn't believe it. There's a guy named Bobby Stoops. He was chasing a receiver up into the stands just to hit him." And we were practicing in shorts that day.

—Hayden Fry

By the beginning of the 1979 season, my redshirt freshman year, we had those new uniforms, new paint in the visitor's locker room (Fry had ordered the walls to be painted a soothing pink for our opponents), and new instructions on how to emerge from the locker room (Fry didn't want us bouncing off the walls; he wanted us to jog onto the field and exude an air of confidence). He also had a new starting safety: me. I had gone from obscurity to the starting lineup.

The Fry/Stoops era began with a loss at home to Lee Corso and his Indiana team. The following week, we went on the road to my teenage dream school: Oklahoma.

Can you believe it? In only my second game ever, I was going to face Switzer and the Sooners.

OU was ranked third in the country. We weren't ranked in anybody's poll.

They had 1978 Heisman Trophy winner Billy Sims. We didn't. They had quarterback J. C. Watts, All-American linebacker George Cumby, and a total of nine players who would be chosen in the 1980 NFL Draft. We didn't.

I couldn't wait for the game. To me, it was the coolest thing ever. How many times do you get to measure yourself against the very best? How many times do you face a Heisman winner and a legendary coach (Switzer, by the way, had reported to Fry on the 1961 Arkansas offensive coaching staff)—and face them on an Owen Field where so many great players had been?

Our team bus made its way onto Jenkins Avenue toward Memorial Stadium. As I looked out the window I kept thinking, *I'm in Norman, Oklahoma.*

It wasn't a grass field back then. The artificial turf was as hard as a marble countertop, and it had a crown like the roof of a Volkswagen Bug.

OU won the game, but they had to work for it. We knocked Watts out of the game for a while. We recovered five Sooner fumbles. We scored first and only trailed, 7–6, going into the fourth quarter.

Sims ended up with a touchdown and 106 yards, but it took him twenty-three carries and the whole game to get them. There's even a photo of me as I'm making a beeline toward Sims. In it, I'm jumping over a guy trying to get to Billy. He slipped past me on that one.

Years later, not long after I got the job at OU, Billy and I talked about that game and that photograph. "Hey, Coach," he said, "if it was a game of tag, you still wouldn't have gotten me."

He's probably right.

We lost, 21–6, but you would never have known it when we got back to the locker room. We had played OU hard and tough. We were feeling good about ourselves...until Fry walked in. He wasn't interested in moral victories. He wanted to win.

Afterward, he addressed the media. One of the reporters there that day was eighteen-year-old Berry Tramel, who was only a few months removed from high school graduation. He was working for the Norman *Transcript.* Years later, Berry would cover my OU teams for the *Oklahoman.*

Said Fry, in part, to the reporters, "Men, I just told the football team what's wrong with this ballclub. We get our ass kicked and get complimented.

And if I see one guy that's got a smile on his face, I'm going to bust him right in the mouth.

"I didn't come to Iowa to lose, and I don't think these kids enrolled in school at Iowa to lose. These kids have been babied, pampered, petted, and complimented so much when they lose that it makes me sick."

The following week, we played Nebraska at Kinnick and lost, 24–21. The Cornhuskers were ranked number five or six, depending on the poll, but this time, our postgame locker room didn't include any smiles. Fry was right; we were tired of moral victories. We wanted actual victories.

We won four of our next five games and finished the season 5–6 overall and 4–4 in the Big Ten. It was a baby step forward for our team.

Late in the season, during a home loss against Purdue, I sustained the first of at least a half dozen concussions I had while playing for Iowa. A flanker named Mike Harris came across the middle of the field. The ball was thrown. Iowa's number 41 collided with Purdue's number 41.

In twenty-six years in the Big Ten, he was one of the most physical players I'd ever seen. He would light your world up, knock you back where you came from. He didn't want to give up a yard of plus-yardage after contact.

He played big. Whatever weight he was, I'm sure we jacked it up for the game program.

You have to remember, it was different then. You weren't going to get thrown out of the game for some of the hits that are illegal now: clothesline hits…you could throw some violent hits back then. Coming across the middle, it could get violent.

The Purdue flanker came across the middle. Big collision. Both of them went down, but the flanker stayed down. They took the flanker to the hospital. But it was a legal hit.

—Dan McCarney

I've seen replays of the tackle. I don't remember much about the hit. You could tell I was out on my feet moments after contact. As I crumpled to the ground, my body was limp. I was unconscious as I hit the turf.

Today, that hit would be illegal. And it should be. But in 1979, the rules allowed for that type of helmet-to-helmet collision. Coaches and players weren't educated on the dangers and cumulative effects of those kinds of hits. We saw the ball, we hit whoever caught the ball—or tried to catch it.

My style of play had always been physical. I could do three things particularly well: coordinate a defense from my safety position, be in position to make a play, and hit you.

I was later told that the collision not only broke Harris's jaw, but that its impact had required doctors to wire the bones together. Afterward, my teammates started calling me "Jawbreaker."

This was football in 1979 and for the decades that followed. We didn't know better. Football and football-specific medical research hadn't intersected yet.

I was raised and coached by a defensive coordinator. I played safety. Mike played safety, joining me at Iowa in 1980 and redshirting. Mark played safety and arrived at Iowa in 1985.

The Stoops-to-Iowa City pipeline was no coincidence. Barry Alvarez, one of our defensive assistants, had been born and raised in western Pennsylvania, so Fry assigned him that half of the state, as well as Ohio. Alvarez became a regular at our house as he recruited Mike and Mark.

He wasn't the only one. Earle Bruce, who succeeded Woody Hayes in 1979, tried to get Mark to sign with the Buckeyes. He told my mom, "Don't hold it against me, Mrs. Stoops, that I didn't get your other boys here. I know your feelings are toward Iowa, so I'll understand."

Nick Saban, who was the defensive backs coach at Michigan State, also was a regular visitor to Youngstown. He knew my dad and my uncle Bob, who was also a coach.

One day, Nick and my uncle Bob went to a local bar/restaurant to grab something to eat and talk football. They had their notepads out and were totally engrossed in diagramming plays and schemes. As they were drawing their Xs and Os, a guy came into the bar, flashed a gun, and robbed the place. The register was cleaned out.

The cops came and started interviewing everyone in the bar. The bartender pointed at Nick and my uncle Bob and said, "Don't even bother with those two. They never got their heads up from their notepads."

And it was true. Nick and my uncle didn't have a clue what happened. Sound like Nick?

Nick recruited Mark. Needless to say, he wasn't pleased when Mark canceled his official visit to East Lansing after deciding on Iowa.

Mike got to Iowa City just in time to watch our program take a step back in 1980, and it was a painful one at that. We lost four of our first five games (including a 57–0 loss at Nebraska), three of our last five games (including a forty-five-point defeat at Purdue and a thirty-four-point loss at home against Bruce's Buckeyes), and finished 4–7.

Even more frustrating, during that season, I tore my right anterior cruciate ligament, which essentially stabilizes the knee joint, and then reinjured it during spring ball of 1981. If I underwent reconstructive surgery, I would miss that entire season. That was a deal-breaker for me. I decided against surgery and instead chose to strengthen all the muscles around the knee.

I can't explain how I did it, but I did. My knee somehow still functioned at an acceptable level without a working ligament. I was never fast to begin with, so it's not like my speed was significantly reduced. As long as I played where my knee was in a flexed position, I could control it. Weird but true.

Without the burden of surgery—and the yearlong rehab it would have required—I settled into my usual nonschool routine. Each summer, I would split my time between Iowa City and Youngstown. One time I drove the Gran Torino back—or, at least, I tried. I made it as far as Toledo. Then the water pump broke, and then something else quit working. What usually was a ten-hour drive became a three-day ordeal.

I ended up junking the car and buying a used 280Z from Snake. It was great as long as you didn't mind driving with a rusted-out floorboard. If you went through a puddle, water would splash up and into your lap.

Years later, my brother Mark would buy it from me. Sucker.

Summer was my time to recharge, to hang out with friends, to train a bit, and to make some money. Nowadays, football programs are much more structured during the summer. Players stay on campus, train, and take classes. That wasn't the case back then.

Once I got home, I became part of my dad's house-painting crew. He and a fellow teacher at Mooney, Harry Joyce, used this all-cash business to supplement their modest salaries. I had been part of the summer crews since high school. So had Ron Jr., Mike, and later, Mark, as well as any of our neighborhood buddies in need of a job.

We would start at 7:30 a.m. and paint until 5:30 p.m., sometimes later. I'd get home at six, go for a run, and then lift weights in the garage. I'd eat dinner and then head out with my buddies, sometimes until 2:00 or 3:00 a.m. Rather than go upstairs and sleep when I got home, I'd put on my paint gear and then crash on the couch. Sure enough, at 7:30 on the dot, I'd feel my dad kick my foot and say, "Let's go."

My mom would have our lunches made and packed. She'd fill up a grocery bag each day with sandwiches, cheese bread, chips, and sodas.

For a college kid, the money was good: five or six bucks an hour, maybe more if we finished the job a day or so early. And we weren't getting taxed on it (sorry, IRS). Dad would collect the cash at the end of a job, divvy it up, and then take something off the top. He was barely breaking even. "That's for your lunches," he would say.

As in all things involving my dad, each job had to be done as professionally and perfectly as possible. It didn't matter if the sun was beating down on us for ten hours each day or if we had to climb that ladder ten, twenty, thirty feet to reach the eaves and paint them just so. We carefully cleaned the brushes at day's end. We folded the tarps with precision. The goal was to get through the entire day without hearing my dad say, "If you're going to do it half-ass, then don't do it."

When I'd get back to Iowa City late in the summer, the coaches would sometimes arrange jobs for players. A week here, a week there. With my background as a part-time painter, I got on the house-painting circuit with several of my teammates, including Andre Tippett and Reggie Roby. Mike was sometimes part of those crews, too.

Tippett was an All-American defensive end who went on to become a fixture with the New England Patriots and eventually was inducted into the Pro Football Hall of Fame. Roby was our All-American punter, one of the best I've ever seen. He also had a long and distinguished NFL career, but he died much too early at age forty-three. They were the stars. I, apparently, was expendable.

We had them paint the coaches' houses. Bobby had done it with the whole Stoops crew in Youngstown, so he knew how to cut an edge, how to paint trim.

Of course, we didn't want Andre or Reggie getting hurt, so we said, "Bobby, you can go up on the ladder." And we'd have Reggie and Andre doing the trim around the basement windows. We wanted them on the ground.

—Barry Alvarez

When we reported to training camp in 1981, nobody in the media was predicting any sort of breakthrough for our program. We had won nine games in two years under Fry. We were better—we knew that much— but it wasn't as if the rest of the Big Ten was losing sleep over the Hawkeyes.

There was a different attitude, a different atmosphere in '81. The players on defense, I don't know if you want to call us demented or socially unacceptable, but we thought we were tougher and meaner.

Bobby's nickname was Blinky. He would get so intense, so fired up after tackles that he would start blinking really fast. He would hit you so hard you couldn't see straight. We were constantly trying to make sure he was all right.

Our first-team defense terrorized our scout team. At practices, if our scout team offense completed a pass, even crossed the line of scrimmage, there would be a melee. There was automatically a fight—somebody was going to be taken out. It was horrible. We really did feel bad about beating up people.

We felt like we had a good team. Anything was possible. But we ain't done nothing yet.

—Mark Bortz, Iowa defensive tackle, 1979–1982

Reggie, Andre, Bortzy, Simo, Crocker, Brad Webb, Mel Cole, Pat Dean, and Lou King were all part of that 1981 defense. So was I, thanks to my decision not to undergo reconstructive knee surgery during the off-season. Had I done it, I would have missed one of the great years in Iowa football history. That was the season we quit being losers.

We faced Nebraska in our opener. That meant Tom Osborne on the sideline, Roger Craig at I-back, and the usual top-ten ranking for the Cornhuskers. A year earlier, Nebraska had buried us, 57–0, in Lincoln.

One of the newspaper wire services dismissed our chances outright. Its prediction: "The Huskers have to look for quarterback Jeff Quinn's replacement this season, but that's all they have to worry about in their match with Iowa."

Another wire service picked seventh-ranked Nebraska to win, 31–10.

Is that right? Actual final score: Iowa 10, Nebraska 7. Nonbelievers 0.

We lost to Iowa State the next game, but then we upset number-six UCLA, 20–7, at Kinnick. Bortz recovered a fumble in the end zone for a TD. We held the Bruins to just seven first downs and 121 total yards.

Something unusual happened: we snuck into the top twenty-five rankings at number eighteen. We beat Northwestern, then Indiana, and then traveled to Ann Arbor for a game that helped redefine the way we thought of ourselves and how the rest of the country thought of our program.

October 17, 1981 . . . number-twelve-ranked Iowa at number-five Michigan.

Michigan had begun the season not only as the favorite to repeat as Big Ten champions but to win the national championship. The Wolverines were the preseason number one but were upset in Madison by unranked Wisconsin in the opener. The next week, they beat the new number one, Notre Dame, and were on a four-game win streak when we got to the Big House.

Even though we were ranked twelfth, few outside Iowa City gave us much of a chance. In fact, I'm not sure many people *inside* Iowa City thought we'd actually win. Las Vegas didn't; we were underdogs. An Iowa team hadn't beaten Michigan since 1962 and hadn't won in Ann Arbor since 1958.

Michigan had won the Big Ten and the Rose Bowl a season earlier. It would win the Big Ten again in 1982.

But on that day, in front of 105,915 fans—the largest crowd of my playing career—we left a bruise mark on Michigan's football ego and positioned ourselves for the unthinkable: a run at the Big Ten title and the Rose Bowl berth that came with it.

We were tired of hearing about the great Bo Schembechler (Iowa was 0–8 against him), about the mighty Michigan Men, about how intimidating the Big House could be, about their loaded roster, about the decades-long Michigan win streak against Iowa, about the Big Two (Michigan and Ohio State) and the Little Eight (the rest of the teams in the Big Ten).

During the game, I got into a tussle with running back Butch Woolfolk. Woolfolk, whom Schembechler said was the greatest back he ever coached, was Michigan football royalty and would later go on to a successful NFL career.

We held him to fifty-six yards. A game earlier, he had rushed for 253 yards against Michigan State.

After a tackle, I pushed Woolfolk. Or maybe he pushed me. We started chirping at each other, and that's when I heard the familiar chuckle and laugh of Big Ed Muransky, my Youngstown buddy who was now an All-American offensive tackle for the Wolverines.

That might have been my favorite moment in college football. Bobby Stoops was at strong safety, and Butch Woolfolk put his hand on Bobby's throat and face.

Bobby is grumbling, and he has his back to me as he tries to get back at Butch. I put a bear hug on him — he doesn't know who it is at first — and he's trying to fight me. I pull him aside and say, "Butch does that all the time. C'mon, let's have some fun."

— Ed Muransky

We had fun. We won, 9–7, and suddenly Iowa City loved us. There were no more "Beat Somebody!" plywood signs seen in town. We were undefeated in the Big Ten, our defense was the conference's best, and we were gaining national respect.

Representatives from the Orange, Fiesta, and Cotton bowls had come to Michigan Stadium expecting to spend their postgame congratulating Schembechler on a victory. Instead, Schembechler told reporters after his team dropped to 4–2 overall and 2–2 in the conference, "Our bowl chances? Zero to none...To hell with bowl games."

That's not how we felt. For the first time in years, Iowa fans — and we—were thinking about the possibility of a winning record, of a postseason game, and maybe in the back of our minds, the Rose Bowl.

But that didn't last long. We lost our next two conference games, then beat Purdue at home and Wisconsin in Madison (I recovered a fumble that later led to a score) to move into second place. Guess who was in first place? Michigan—the team the experts had left for dead after we'd beat them a month earlier.

The Wolverines had won four conference games in a row to climb to 6–2 in the league, 8–2 overall. We were 5–2 and tied with Ohio State. If Michigan beat the Buckeyes at the Big House the following week, the Wolverines would win the conference title and go to their fifth Rose Bowl in six years. Iowa had been to a grand total of two Rose Bowls since 1889.

"Our destiny is now in our hands, and we're elated to be here," said Schembechler to reporters.

We needed a mini miracle. We needed Earle Bruce and Ohio State to upset Michigan in Ann Arbor. Then we needed to beat Michigan State at home. If that happened, we'd finish tied for the conference lead with the Buckeyes and receive the automatic Rose Bowl berth because Ohio State had played in Pasadena more recently than Iowa.

President Ronald Reagan was on our side. Reagan, a former Davenport and Des Moines radio sportscaster in the 1930s, publicly said he was rooting for us. And within the Big Ten, I'm guessing there might have been a little Michigan fatigue. Everyone loves an underdog, right?

It was freezing that day. The snow had to be plowed off the field before kickoff. But we didn't feel the cold. We couldn't wait to play.

On the first Michigan State play of the game, I recognized a formation the Spartans liked to use whenever they wanted to run a flat route to their tight end. Sure enough, they ran the route, and I came up to make the hit with all the power my little ass could generate. I hit Al Kimichik just perfect—right under the chinstrap—and the ball went flying. Tippett scooped it up, ran eight yards, and our offense scored a couple of plays later.

About midway through the second quarter of our game against the Spartans, we heard a murmur in the stadium. Fry left the sideline and found a fan in the stands with a radio. He asked, "What's the score of the Ohio State–Michigan game?"

"It's 14–9," said the fan.

"Who's leading?"

The fan froze.

Fry tried again. "How much time is left?"

"Less than a minute," stammered the fan.

"Who has the ball?"

"The team that's ahead."

At exactly 6:14 left in the second quarter, the stadium public-address announcer ended the suspense. Ohio State had beaten Michigan.

That's all we needed to know. We forced five turnovers; Phil Blatcher, playing in his last home game, rushed for a career-high 247 yards and scored twice. We won, 36–7.

The game had gotten chippy at times. There was a fight near one of the sidelines, and players came off the bench. A Michigan State player started charging toward me, but I raised my hands as if I wanted no part of the skirmish. He hesitated but then took another step forward, so I popped him under his face mask on the chin. The refs, who were busy trying to restore order, never saw it.

As the final minutes ticked off the clock, fans showered the field with rose petals and chanted "Rose Bowl...Rose Bowl!" Some even tore down one of the goalposts while the game was still being played at the other end of the field.

The fans enveloped us. They were grabbing at our jerseys, patting us on the shoulder pads, hugging us in jubilation. Could you blame them? It was Iowa's first conference title since 1960.

I grabbed Todd Simonsen, who had just played his final game at Kinnick. We celebrated like little kids. As more fans poured onto the field, Simo said, "Follow me," and we worked our way through the crowd and into our locker room.

It was snowing rose petals that day. We had a pile of them in the locker room. Someone took a photo of Mike and me each holding a rose. Fry showed up at his postgame press conference with a long-stemmed rose in his hand and a cloth rose taped to his forehead. A writer from the *Gazette* wrote that there were so many roses, it looked like "a gangster's funeral."

Afterward, Michigan State coach Frank Waters said we had the best defense in the country. I wasn't going to disagree with him—we led the Big Ten in every meaningful defensive statistical category. We were a rough crew.

And to give you an idea of how grateful Iowa fans were to Ohio State, they sent thank-you notes to Bruce (a former head coach of rival Iowa State!) and bombarded his office with thank-you calls. One Hawkeyes fan called Bruce's home at 2:00 a.m. to express his gratitude.

One season you're crap, and the next season, you're going to the Rose Bowl. Back then, you could dream about playing in the Rose Bowl, but it was out of nowhere that it showed up.

—Mark Bortz

My only regret is that my parents weren't there to see it in person. My dad had a Mooney game that Friday night, so they weren't able to leave Youngstown before the snowstorm made the roads too dangerous to drive. But Dad did watch the game on TV, and afterward, I got a phone call. He had seen me punch the Michigan State player. "What the hell were you doing?" he asked. But he couldn't stay mad at me too long.

During the course of my Iowa playing career (and Mike and Mark's too), my parents came to as many home and road games as they could. In the spring, my dad and Ronnie would drive out for my spring game.

For years, they took the family car. For the 613-mile trip to Iowa City, they would load up after the Friday night Mooney game, be on the road by midnight, and get to campus by mid-to-late morning. Then they'd leave first thing Sunday for Youngstown.

I loved to see them after the games. I could see the pride in the faces of my brothers and sisters, but especially in my dad's. He didn't live vicariously through me; he was secure in who he was. But as a coach, he knew the work it took to succeed in football. He appreciated that. Sometimes, at Coach Fry's invitation, he'd come into our locker room after a game. He'd find a place in the corner of the room. He didn't want to get in anyone's way.

After our game, we'd meet up in my dorm room. We couldn't afford to go to a fancy restaurant, so we'd eat picnic style on the floor or bed. My mom would bring homemade sandwiches or heat up a batch of chili or spaghetti for all of us.

My whole family did make it to the Rose Bowl, thanks to the generosity of Eddie DeBartolo Jr. Mr. DeBartolo is a Youngstown and Mooney man, and he knew my father and our family well. He also knew how little a high school teacher and coach earned in salary.

By then, Mr. DeBartolo was the owner of the San Francisco 49ers, and his teams would win five Super Bowls during his stewardship. Right after we clinched the Rose Bowl bid, Mr. DeBartolo called my dad and said he was going to pay for all the flights and hotel expenses for my family. He also said he wasn't going to take no for an answer. I'm forever grateful for that gesture of kindness.

As it turned out, my family probably would have had more fun going to the Rose Bowl parade than to the game itself.

During our first defensive series of the game, I hyperextended my right, non-ACL knee while lunging to make a tackle. It caused my femur (thigh bone) to go one way and my tibia and fibula (shin bones) to go the opposite direction. I don't recommend it. The injury tore cartilage and chipped my femur, though we didn't know that at the time.

While I was getting examined by the team doctor, my brother Mike took my place in the lineup. I got my knee taped up and clearance to return in the second quarter. By the fourth quarter, my knee had swollen to the size of a cantaloupe, and I had to come out of the game again. To make matters worse, Washington beat us, 28–0.

Still, it was a season to remember. In only his third year at Iowa, Fry had led us to a Rose Bowl appearance. He had revived and rebuilt a program that some had thought was beyond help. It remains one of the great coaching achievements certainly in Big Ten history, and as far as I'm concerned, one of the great college football achievements of all time.

In 1982, my fifth and final season as a player at Iowa, we again finished 8–4 and defeated Tennessee and the great Reggie White in the Peach Bowl. Our quarterback that year was a redshirt freshman from Wheaton, Illinois, named Chuck Long.

Late in the season, my parents drove to Iowa for our game against Wisconsin. We beat the Badgers in the afternoon of November 13, and afterward, we all walked back to my dorm room, ate dinner there, and then turned on CBS and watched Boom defend his lightweight championship at Caesar's Palace in Las Vegas. This was going to be neat—our neighborhood buddy on national TV.

The challenger was a South Korean fighter named Duk-Koo Kim. We had never heard of him. Nobody had, really.

It was a brutal fight. As each round passed, it was obvious that Kim didn't stand a chance. Every time we thought the referee would stop the fight, Kim would somehow battle back. It wasn't until the fourteenth round, when Ray sent Kim to the canvas with a series of devastating punches to the body and face, that the fight was finally called.

The aftermath of the bout was tragic and well documented. Kim was removed from the ring on a stretcher, slipped into a coma, and died four days later.

Ray is our lifelong friend. We grieved for Kim, and we grieved for our friend, who had stepped into the ring to compete, to defeat the man in the other corner. He had boxed to the best of his abilities and had done nothing wrong. But a life was lost in that fight, and Ray was blamed for it. The ref was blamed for it. Boxing was blamed for it.

Father Tim O'Neill, who had been our religion teacher when Ray and I attended Cardinal Mooney, was with him after the fight. What could you say? What could anyone say? How do you make sense out of accidental tragedy?

I've read Mark Kriegel's book on Ray called *The Good Son*. I've seen the ESPN documentary that aired in 2007. To this day, Ray remains a friend—and always will be. I rooted for him in all his fights, and he rooted for me—at Mooney, at Iowa, and every stop along the way.

In 1982, I was named one of our team captains, earned first-team All–Big Ten honors, honorable mention All-American, and was voted team MVP. All this from a player who was all but ignored in recruiting, who wanted to transfer from the only major program that gave him a chance, and who played without an anterior cruciate ligament for the final two seasons of his career. Some things you can't make up.

Bob Commings gave me that chance. My dad saved me from myself. Fry and Brashier rescued me from the scout team and believed in me.

The truth is, had I left Iowa when I wanted to, I wouldn't have the life I live today. I would never have become the head coach at Oklahoma. It's a lesson I've never forgotten, and it's one that I conveyed to my own players — that it's OK to be uncomfortable, that sometimes life is supposed to be difficult...really difficult. That's what makes the accomplishments even sweeter.

By sticking it out at Iowa, I got to play more football with Mike, who became an All-American selection. I got a Big Ten championship ring. I played at Kinnick and in front of Iowa fans who to this day still appreciate and cherish the memories of those early Fry teams.

I played at some of the greatest stadiums in the country: Oklahoma, Wisconsin, Michigan, Ohio State, Nebraska (the fans treat the visiting team with so much respect and class), and, of course, the Rose Bowl. I played against some of the best coaches the game has seen (Schembechler, Hayes, Osborne, Johnny Majors, Terry Donahue, Don James, and Coach Switzer). I played in front of my dad, my mom, and a revolving cast of family and friends. I was the luckiest guy ever.

What happened there with him at Iowa is nothing short of a miracle. He almost came home.

—Kathy Stoops Kohowski

I gave all that I had. I hit people as hard as I could.

On November 3, 1979, in that game against Purdue, the Boilermakers flanker got the worst of it. I broke his jaw fair and square. But by the time I finished playing at Iowa, I was a walking, sometimes limping, medical chart. That's football.

I can go down my list of injuries, just like any player can. It's an occupational hazard.

I played my redshirt junior and senior seasons without an ACL. In all, I would have three separate arthroscopic procedures to clean up that knee.

During the 1982 season, I played with an injury to the sesamoid bones in the big toe of my right foot. You don't want that one, either.

The sesamoid bones are embedded in the tendon of the big toe. Mine were a mess. They were cracked. The only way I could play was to undergo a series of painkilling shots before each game. The team physician would come into the locker room and insert the needle in the bottom of my arch and then into the top of my toe. It was a full minute of agony. It felt like my toe was in flames.

The guys in the locker room would turn away; they couldn't handle the sight of that long needle going into my toe.

That was the same season I played with a broken thumb on my left hand. During the week, I wore a boot on my right foot and a cast on my right hand. I looked like I had been in a car wreck. One day during class, a professor looked at me, shook his head, and said, "You won't be able to play Saturday."

I said matter-of-factly, "Oh, no, I'll be able to play."

And I did. I got those shots in my foot, and they taped up my thumb and encased it in a rubber cast. Our athletic trainer, Ed Crowley, who had lettered at Purdue and played on its 1967 Rose Bowl champion team, was my MVP.

He'd hobble around all week. He'd practice, but he'd look terrible.

On game day, he'd get the happy shot. He'd look at us and say, "That feels a lot better." He'd have a big smile on his face. He was ready to go.

—Mike Hufford, Iowa tight end, 1980–1983

I sustained at least a half dozen concussions at Iowa, the kind where I was knocked out from running full speed into people. During that senior season, I collided with someone, saw stars, and then saw nothing. I woke up in the middle of the field. Crowley came running out.

"Whattya say, Ed," I said groggily. "It happened again, didn't it?"

I had shoulder surgery, too. I cracked a windshield with my forehead when the driver of the car missed a turn, hit a guard rail, and sent me hurtling toward the dashboard (I stupidly wasn't wearing a seatbelt). Doctors had to tie off an artery that had slightly ruptured.

As I got older, the injuries caught up to me. I had to get a screw inserted into my right big toe. Issues related to my right knee began to affect my hips. About three and a half years ago, I had a hip replacement. So I know what it's like to be wheeled into surgery.

If you gave me the choice between those injuries and playing football versus no injuries and no football career, I'd take the injuries. Would I play again? Absolutely, in a heartbeat. To this day, some of my fondest memories involve that game, those fields, those teammates, and those opponents. Some of my best friends are guys I played football with.

You can't put a price tag on the sense of accomplishment, of actually being in the arena. It helps define your character, your being, who you are. When you compete at that level and are willing to sacrifice for the good of the team, in my eyes, it's a spiritual thing. You find out so much about yourself through struggle, through adversity, and through competition. There's honor in that.

I'm a big believer in a speech that Teddy Roosevelt gave in 1910. He said the credit belongs to the person "who strives valiantly...who at the best knows in the end the triumph of high achievement, and who at the worst, if he fails, at least fails while daring greatly, so that his place shall never be with those cold and timid souls who neither know victory nor defeat."

You don't have to agree. We all make our individual choices. But I didn't want to be a cold and timid soul.

After we beat Tennessee in the Peach Bowl, I sat in the locker room and knew I had played my last game of football. It was strange to take off my helmet, my shoulder pads, to cut off my ankle and wrist tape and know I was doing it for the last time.

I wasn't sad. I sat there thinking that I was just a kid out of Youngstown who hadn't known what was coming next in life—and then everything turned out great. I had had so much fun. I had been coached by the best, played with the best.

Chuck Long walked by.

"Took you until the last game of our season to finally get it, didn't it?" I said.

I smiled when I said that. I knew—everyone in that locker room knew—that Long was going to be a great player. He would later lead Iowa to the 1986 Rose Bowl and finish second to Bo Jackson in the 1985 Heisman Trophy balloting.

Long would eventually play in the NFL. And later, he would coach for me at OU. But the NFL was never an option for me. When NFL scouts attended our games or visited our football facility at Iowa, I knew they weren't there to see me. One time, when the scouts were around, I half-jokingly asked Bortz, "Hey, how about if I slide an extra five- or ten-pound weight plate into my shorts to help me on the scale?" I was realistic enough to realize I had no prayer to play professionally. My body simply wouldn't allow me to play anymore.

After the Peach Bowl, it was time for some R and R. Me, Mike, and a couple of buddies drove from Atlanta to Miami, Naples, and Tampa and then back toward the Midwest. We made it as far as Cincinnati. My longtime girl-friend was going to school there. We crashed at her place, and the next day, Mike and my Iowa buddies left for Iowa City. I decided to stay an extra night.

While I was there, I called Snake. He said that if I could get to Akron that night—which is where he was living at the time—he had an extra ticket for the Bob Seger concert in Cleveland.

Goodbye, girlfriend. Hello, Seger.

The drive from Cincinnati to Akron usually takes less than four hours. But I didn't have a car. I didn't have any money.

I grabbed a tennis racket out of my girlfriend's closet and a steak knife out of her kitchen drawer. I taped a sign to the tennis racket that read, "71N." That's I-71 North, the interstate running from Cincinnati to Akron.

I stuffed the grip of the racket into my duffel bag, but the face of the racket—and that I-71 North sign—was on the outside. The steak knife was for protection in case I got in trouble.

I didn't have as much as a dollar when I began hitchhiking that morn-ing. One guy picked me up and explained that someone had helped out his son when the kid was thumbing his way from Ohio to Alaska. Another dude tried to pick me up in his van. Sorry, not happening.

It took me eight hours, but I made it to Akron. True to his word, Snake had that spare Seger ticket. We drove to Cleveland and saw a great concert with my boys.

My football life was done. I didn't have to worry about winter condi-tioning drills. Or spring practice. Or injections in my toe. I had my memo-ries, my rings, and my jerseys from the Rose Bowl and Peach Bowl. I still have those jerseys.

Eventually, I bought myself a very used Kawasaki 650 motorcycle and tooled around Iowa City on it. The bike was cheap transportation, and I liked cheap. That's why I usually hung out at the Iowa City honky-tonks and dive bars like Tuck's Place (since closed) instead of the trendy, upscale places. Tuck's played Seger, Springsteen, Mellencamp—something with a soul—not Joe Cocker/Jennifer Warnes ballads or overwrought songs about total eclipses of the heart. The beers were cold, the bar tab low.

By February of 1983, my sort-of girlfriend was still in Cincinnati, and I was in Iowa City. The geography thing was taking its toll on the relationship. We were a couple in name only. At the time, I was just going to classes and finishing up my requirements for my business management degree.

One night, I was at the Fieldhouse, which is a bar in the downtown district of Iowa City. It was almost closing time, and I noticed this beautiful blonde walk past me. I did what all dudes do: I tried to pretend I wasn't really staring when, in fact, that's exactly what I was doing. Guys know; it's an art form.

After last call, everybody spilled out onto the sidewalk. That's when I saw the girl again. I walked up to her, tapped her on the shoulder, and said, "Where's the party tonight?"

I believe in destiny and fate. When I was in ninth grade, I decided to follow a player from the Iowa football team. I told my mom I was going to follow one player, because that would make it easier to follow a team that lost a lot and that also wasn't on TV.

I came down that morning and opened the sports page, and I saw Bobby's picture in the paper. He was a freshman. I said to my mom, "He's cute. I'll follow him." Truth is, it was that simple.

My mom said, "You know he's older than you, and you'll probably never meet him."

"I know," I said.

When it came time to pick a college—Northern Iowa or Iowa—I put together a list of pros and cons. On the pros list, I had Bobby. I know; it's so sad.

And then I met him. Isn't that weird that it came true? I swear I wasn't stalking him.

—Carol Stoops

We got to talking. She was there with a friend, and they were going to walk home from the bar. I said, "I'll walk with you guys."

I'm thinking, "Oh, my God, he talks just like Rocky Balboa." He had a big neck and sounded like Rocky.

—Carol Stoops

As we were starting to leave, I glanced back and saw that one of my roommates, Todd Simonsen, was literally in the middle of a fight. I didn't even think twice; I left the girls at the corner and ran back to help my buddy. By the time we got done rolling and scrapping around, I went back to find the ladies. But they were gone.

I didn't know the blonde's name. I hadn't had a chance to get her number. I thought she had told me she was a freshman, but I had no way of getting in touch with her. She'd made it clear, though, that she wasn't going to wait around on me, hadn't she?

It was hard to be mad at Simo; he'd needed a wingman. But I sure wished I'd had time to at least get the girl's name. Instead, I was flat out of luck.

That, however, was about to change.

In ways I'd never expected.

Chapter Three

Opportunity

In the spring of 1983, I still had a football neck. A football neck comes from years of weightlifting and wearing a six-pound helmet for hours at a time. It's a great thing...until you have to wear a dress shirt and tie.

On this particular spring day, my oversized neck was having a fist fight with my dress shirt. The collar was hanging on for dear life, and the button was losing the battle. Don't even ask me about the pitiful tie knot I had clumsily jammed together. It was too big and lumpy. All in all, I looked as if I'd dressed in a dark closet.

I was on my way to the IMU—the Iowa Memorial Union—for a series of job interviews. A bunch of different S&P 500 companies—Coca-Cola, Procter & Gamble, Johnson & Johnson, General Electric, etc.—had come to campus and set up shop in the student union for interviews with graduating seniors. I was only a month or so away from getting my degree, so I had signed up.

I made the rounds, answered questions, and hoped my top shirt button wouldn't pop off. After the interviews, I went to the football offices, and McCarney and Alvarez were there. They saw me in my shirt and tie and started laughing. "You don't need to be going over there," Alvarez said. "You need to stick around with us and be a coach."

I had thought about it, of course. My dad was a coach. And as a player at Iowa, for me it wasn't enough just to hear we were going to run a certain kind of pass coverage or use a certain kind of blitz package. I wanted to know *why* we were going to do it. The why was the most interesting part. And my defensive coordinator and mentor, Bill Brashier, was always great about answering all my questions. He's really the guy who got me started.

OPPORTUNITY

I didn't know what I was going to do after graduation. A desk job at a corporation wasn't very appealing, and the thought of wearing a coat and tie each day was scary—but that's what you did back then: you got your degree, went to work for a big company, and started up the corporate ladder. I just didn't know if I wanted to climb that first step.

After the knee injury, it wasn't going to happen with Bobby and the NFL. It wasn't going to be the same. Had he stayed healthy, maybe? I just hoped and prayed he would get into coaching.

—Dan McCarney

I said, "You're a coach—what the hell you doing with those interviews? You're a natural coach. Get into what you know best."

—Barry Alvarez

After graduation, I stuck around for the first few weeks of the summer. I was out at a bar again with my buddies one night, and sure enough, who did I see after closing time? It was the blonde girl.

I tapped her on the shoulder and repeated my line from February: "Where's the party?"

She turned around and sort of glared at me. "We're going nowhere," she said and turned away.

I tried again. "I've met you before," I said.

"No, you haven't."

I knew I'd screwed up back in February by leaving the ladies at the corner so I could join the fight. Now she was making me pay.

"You don't even remember me, do you?" she said.

"Well, uh, sort of," I said.

I asked her if I could walk her home. She thought about it and finally said yes. She was renting a room for summer school at the Delta Tau Delta fraternity house. She was sure of herself. I'd never encountered anyone like her. We talked the whole way home.

"You have the smartest mouth of anyone I've met," I said.

Her name was Carol Davidson, and she was from Cresco, Iowa.

I had made a scrapbook of my freshman year at Iowa. I had Bobby's picture in there and thought, "Well, I had met him in February, but he's gradu-ated, so it wasn't meant to be. That's over."

And then our paths crossed again. We ended up talking for hours that night, just sitting in the parking lot of the frat house.

One of the questions he asked was, "Do you like Bob Seger?" I said yes. I saw him the next night.

—Carol Stoops

I was going back to Youngstown and didn't know if I was ever returning to Iowa. My future was up in the air. I told Carol, "Look, if I come back, I'll call you. If I don't, then have a great life."

About a month later, Coach Fry offered me a job as a graduate assistant coach. The moment he asked was the exact moment I knew that's what I really wanted to do. From that day on, it was like I never had to work again.

In the time it took me to say yes, I had moved from the outside to the inside, from the locker room to the coaches meeting room. What a break. What luck I had.

I had met Carol, lost Carol, and then met Carol again. I had thought I was probably going into the private sector, but now I was going into coach-ing. (By the way, I never got a job offer from those corporations. Must have been the tie.)

Late that summer I called Carol from Youngstown and left a message for her at the frat house. But I didn't leave a number. This was pre-Google, and she didn't know my dad's name, so she couldn't find me through direc-tory assistance. So she called the only Bob Stoops listed in Youngstown: my uncle Bob. But she was so embarrassed that she had called the wrong house that she didn't leave a message.

Early that fall, when I reported for my Iowa coaching duties at camp, I gave her a call. "I came back," I said.

Our first date, he borrowed Bruce Kittle's Chrysler, brought a bottle of wine and a blanket, and we had a picnic near the river. He was very sweet, and we had a great time.

OPPORTUNITY

When I got back to my dorm, I called my mom and said, "I met the guy I'm going to marry."

—Carol Stoops

We started dating. Meanwhile, I was working on my MBA and beginning to learn the coaching profession as a grad assistant. In the history of college football, you'd be hard-pressed to find a better staff than the one Hayden Fry assembled in 1983.

There was Fry himself, of course, a Hall of Famer.

Among the others on that staff:

Alvarez was our linebackers coach. He went on to become a Hall of Fame head coach at Wisconsin.

Bill Snyder was our offensive coordinator and quarterbacks coach. He went on to become a Hall of Fame head coach at Kansas State.

Kirk Ferentz was our offensive line coach. He replaced Fry in 1999, and I have no doubt he'll be inducted into the Hall of Fame.

Brashier was our defensive coordinator, one of the best defensive coaches ever.

McCarney was our defensive line coach. He later became a head coach at Iowa State and North Texas. A pro's pro.

Don Patterson coached a handful of different positions. He later was named the head coach at Western Illinois.

Del Miller was also a longtime Iowa assistant who became a head coach at then–Southwest Missouri State.

And then there was me, the rookie GA.

We all respected one another. We all respected the job each of us did. Hayden was very demanding. There was never any second-guessing.

I've had people say to me, "With all those future head coaches, I bet there were some interesting staff meetings." Let me make something clear: there was no confusion about who was in charge.

—Barry Alvarez

From 1978 through 1991, there was always a Stoops at Iowa.

I was there as a player from '78 to '82, then as grad assistant from '83 to '84, then as a volunteer assistant from '85 to '87.

Mike played there from '81 to '84; then he was a GA in '86 to '87, and then a volunteer assistant from '88 to '91.

Mark arrived in '85, played until '89, and then became a GA from '90 to '91.

With the exception of the two years that Mike and I overlapped as players, a Stoops always wore jersey number 41 (Mike wore number 2 during his first two seasons). My mom and dad were sitting in the Michigan Stadium stands watching Mark play in 1987 when the public address announcer said, "On the tackle, number forty-one...Stoops."

Sitting next to my mom that day was an elderly Michigan fan who had followed the Wolverines for years. And for years, he had seen a Stoops make tackles against his maize and blue. This time he turned to my mom and said, "There's that number forty-one again. Isn't he *ever* going to graduate?"

In '85, Bob and I drive from Youngstown to Iowa to report for camp. I'm a true freshman, he's a volunteer assistant. We drive those ten hours, get to campus, and he pulls up to Slater Hall, where I had been assigned.

He says, "Here's your dorm. Good luck. I'll see you."

Then he drove away.

I had two duffel bags, and they had all my earthly possessions in them. I remember looking around and seeing all these people moving into their dorms. They had fridges, TVs, CD players. All I had were my clothes. That's the first time I realized I came from a humble background. It took me about five minutes to move in.

I called Bob two or three hours later. "Hey, I've got to be at this place for a meeting soon. Do you know where it is?"

Bob said, "I don't know. Figure it out." Click.

That's the honest-to-god truth. "Figure it out." That's how he is, very matter-of-fact. He doesn't mean anything by it. He had to figure it out when he first got to Iowa. He was making me do the same.

—Mark Stoops

OPPORTUNITY

Graduate assistants and volunteer assistants didn't make much money. I was always scraping by. I loved what I was doing (I ran the scout team defense against Snyder's offense), but at some point, I was going to need a full-time job.

As a GA, I received the equivalent of a scholarship. It paid for my graduate classes and room and board but not much else. Paying the bills often was a challenge.

Bernie Wyatt was our defensive ends coach and recruiting coordinator. He was a Jersey guy Fry had retained from Commings's staff. Near the end of each month, I would sheepishly knock on his office door and ask if I could borrow money to get through the next. Wyatt would dig out his wallet, find a folded hundred-dollar bill in the deep recesses, and give the bill to me. Once I got my next scholarship check, I'd pay him back. He would take my bill, fold it up, and slip it into his wallet until the end of the month, when I'd come calling again. Sometimes he wouldn't accept my repayment.

Complicating matters — but in a good way — was my relationship with Carol. We were crazy about each other. By then, I was twenty-seven, and Carol was student teaching.

We had been together for more than four years. I didn't know it at the time, but shortly after we had started dating on a regular basis, Carol had had a conversation about me with a longtime buddy of mine who had moved to Iowa City from Youngstown. In so many words, she had wondered if there was a future for us together. "Carol," said my buddy, "I'm going to tell you this: the day Bobby asks you to go to Youngstown with him, that's when you'll know he's serious about someday marrying you." I knew none of this. But in 1982, I took Carol home for my sister Kathy's wedding.

Carol wasn't prepared for the full Stoops family experience. She had come from a small town in Iowa with a population of about four thousand. She ran track, played golf, was captain of the cheerleading team, played saxophone in the band, and was a great student. She was the youngest of three girls in a family that was small, quiet, and orderly.

The Stoopses were not a small family. We weren't all girls. We definitely weren't quiet.

When she walked in the front door of 865 Detroit Avenue, Carol had no idea what she was getting herself into. We were used to the bedlam; she wasn't.

Anybody who has grown up in a large family knows that it's every man and woman for him and herself. If Reenie poured a glass of water, one of the boys would just walk by, take it, drink it, and say, "Thanks, Reen."

Carol was proper, polite. She stayed in Reenie and Kathy's room on the first floor. One time, she was sitting at the kitchen table with a freshly opened bottle of soda pop. One of my brothers came by, took a big swig from it, and kept walking. That sort of thing didn't happen in Robert and Bernice Davidson's house in Cresco, Iowa.

One morning during her visit, she was sitting at the kitchen table eating a bowl of cereal by herself. Snake walked in the back door. "I'm Snake. Where's Bobby?" he asked. "Upstairs?" A startled Carol just nodded, and up he went.

With limited bathrooms in the house, you had to be aggressive. Carol would patiently wait outside a bathroom, only to have one of the Stoops kids dart in front of her the moment the door opened. My dad watched with a bemused look and then said, "Carol, you just have to charge in there and hold your ground."

Carol was a huge hit with my family and friends. I knew she would be. She was exposed to all things Youngstown, and after the initial shock wore off, she fit right in.

One day in January of 1988, I was sitting at a campus bar called Joe's Place. It was happy hour, and I was there with my buddy and fellow GA Bruce Kittle. Bruce had been married for a couple of years. Out of nowhere, Kittle asked, "You ever thought of being married?"

"Sort of," I said. Which really meant, "Not really."

"Well, it's not like you're trying to chase girls anymore. What are you waiting for?"

"Yeah, you're right," I said.

Suddenly, it hit me: I needed to marry Carol.

When I had woken up that same morning, the thought of getting engaged wasn't anywhere on my mind. It wasn't until the exact moment that Kittle suggested it that it all made perfect sense. It just felt right.

I called Carol and asked her to meet me at Bo-James, a burger place on campus. I didn't have an engagement ring, but that didn't matter. Nothing mattered except one thing.

Carol got there first. In fact, I was late—and Carol wasn't happy with me. We ordered a couple of burgers, and in the middle of the meal, I just blurted it out. "So do you want to get married, or what?"

Carol's eyes grew wide. I think she had been expecting me to ask her to pass the ketchup. "I can't believe you said that," she said.

"Yeah," I said, "so you want to get married?"

She got teary eyed. And then said yes.

I'm not exactly Mr. Romance. The first-date picnic project had been a stretch for me. And I'll be the first to admit that a wedding proposal in the middle of a burger place wasn't storybook romantic.

When Carol asked me when I wanted to have the ceremony, I said as soon as possible. We decided to lock in a summer wedding date. We told Mike that night, and then everybody else. The reactions usually included, a "What took you so long?" They were right. What *had* taken me so long?

Then came another thunderbolt. Shortly after our engagement, new Kent State head coach Dick Crum called and asked if I'd be interested in interviewing for a full-time assistant coaching job. Interested? I was over the moon.

Crum was from Boardman, Ohio, which is basically a south suburb of Youngstown. He had been an assistant at Boardman (where Ron Jr. would later become a teacher and assistant coach) and then at nearby Warren G. Harding High School before becoming a head coach at Mentor (Ohio) High School. From there, he joined the college ranks and became a head coach at Miami of Ohio, North Carolina, and then Kent State. The runner-up for the Kent State job? Kent State alum and Michigan State assistant coach Nick Saban. How'd he turn out as a head coach?

Of course, I almost screwed up the whole thing. On the day I was sup-posed to fly from Cedar Rapids to Cleveland and then drive to Kent for my interview, I took Carol out for a late-morning breakfast. We were halfway through the meal when she asked, "By the way, what time's your flight?"

"Oh, I've got plenty of time," I said. "My flight doesn't leave until 1:10."

"You sure?"

I pulled the ticket from my pocket...and nearly fell off my chair. The flight left at 11:10 a.m., not 1:10 p.m.! The plane was already in the air.

I called Coach Crum, owned my mistake, apologized, and said I'd catch the next flight. So much for making a good first impression.

Once I got there, though, the interview went well and Crum later offered me the job. With the blessings of Fry, I accepted the position as the outside linebackers and defensive ends coach. It was a no-brainer. A full-time coaching gig...a $3,000 raise (from $15,000 as a volunteer assistant to $18,000 on Crum's staff)...and Kent State was only forty-five minutes west of Youngstown.

Still, it was bittersweet to wave goodbye to Iowa. I had come there as a seventeen-year-old freshman from a different world. During the next ten years, I would find myself, my future wife, and friends for life. I owed so much to that place, to that school, and to those people.

I got to Kent in time for spring practice and in May returned to Iowa City to load the rest of my belongings and all of Carol's stuff. The U-Haul truck was crammed with hand-me-down furniture. That's all we could afford.

Having dated me for nearly five years, Carol knew something about the time demands on a football coach. Even as a lowly Iowa GA or volunteer assistant, I was at the football office late into the evenings. She was an athlete, loved sports, and understood the commitment involved. Plus, she was an independent person. It's not like she was unable to function without me. She had always understood that coaching was more than a nine-to-five job.

We rented a great little apartment in a lovely retirement community in Kent called Silver Oaks. It was about a mile from the football office.

The wedding was in Carol's hometown of Cresco. The hordes from Youngstown soon descended on it. There was only one little motel there, and we took it over. We called it "the Dorm."

The rehearsal dinner was a picnic at Carol's home. There were basketball courts across the street, and we set up a volleyball net in the backyard. Everybody was there: all the Stoopses, Iowa wrestlers we had met, my teammates, friends from Iowa and Youngstown, Carol's friends and family. It was great.

OPPORTUNITY

We got married on July 16, 1988. Mike was my best man. And this time, I had a ring to give Carol.

Their wedding was so much fun. My dad had such a good time. He was out there playing basketball with the kids, playing hoops with Bob and all his friends—everybody who was there for the wedding.

Carol and Bob, they're just meant to be together.

—Reenie Stoops Farragher

The day after the wedding, we drove to Chicago for our honeymoon. The plan was to spend the week there and then drive to Youngstown for a reception with all those who couldn't make it to Cresco.

As we made our way down Michigan Avenue to our hotel, I put my left elbow on the ledge of the open car window. A jolt of pain shot through. I looked; I had a tiny nick on my elbow. But the pain intensified with each hour. My elbow was bright red. Then the redness spread from my armpit to my wrist. Something was terribly wrong.

Carol rushed me to the Northwestern Memorial Hospital. I could barely sit in the reception area. The pain was unbearable and getting worse. Even the slightest touch to the area caused my knees to buckle. Compared to any of my football injuries, surgeries, and needle injections, this was by far the worst pain I had ever experienced.

They pumped an IV in me and said I was suffering from cellulitis, which is a bacterial infection that is life threatening if it goes untreated.

I spent our entire six-day honeymoon in the hospital. I could barely get out of bed. My temperature was 104 degrees at one point.

The doctors finally released me from the hospital on the day of my reception in Youngstown. Their wedding gift: another IV.

Chapter Four

Tragedy

Life was good. Carol was substitute teaching about four times a week in different grades at various schools in nearby townships. I was coaching outside linebackers at Kent State and loving it.

Best of all, I was back home, or close to it. In forty-five minutes, I could sneak over to Youngstown, play pickup basketball with my buddies, and knock down a couple of beers afterward. I was able to spend quality time with my dad and mom. Dad was still the defensive coordinator at Cardinal Mooney, still coaching baseball, still painting houses, still a lean 185 pounds with a thirty-four-inch waist, playing fast-pitch softball at age fifty-four (and still outplaying guys fifteen years younger), still sitting at the kitchen table breaking down game film. It was reassuring to see that little had changed.

At Kent State we were a program in transition. It was Crum's first season, and after opening wins against my hometown Youngstown State and then Akron, we had lost three in a row going into our Saturday, October 8, 1988, home game against Ball State.

The game that really mattered to our family that week didn't involve me and the Golden Flashes. Instead, it was all about Mooney's big Friday-night rivalry game at Boardman Stadium: father versus oldest son — my dad on the Mooney sideline and Ron Jr. on the Boardman side of the field as a second-year assistant coach. The Cardinals and the Spartans had been playing each other for decades. A year earlier, Mooney had beat Boardman, 7–6. This was supposed to be another close game.

After the Mooney game, the plan was for my dad and mom to pack up the used Chevy van they had purchased earlier in the year and drive to

Iowa City. Mark had a home game on Saturday against Wisconsin. A week earlier, my dad had driven a van full of family and friends to Mark's game at Michigan State.

I wanted to sneak over to Boardman for the Friday-night game but couldn't get away. Kathy was going to go, too, but it was a chilly, dreary, rainy night, and her kids weren't crazy about getting soaked. She decided to listen to the game on the radio.

Mike was still in Iowa as a volunteer assistant coach. Mark was in his dorm room. Fry always locked down the dorm the night before a home game so the players could get their rest.

Reenie, fresh out of nursing school, was in the Boardman Stadium stands with her husband and my mom. Mom wondered how Dad felt. Earlier in the day, he had mentioned that he was a little nauseous... probably just a case of jumbled nerves from having to coach against his son.

We all have our memories of what happened next.

It was late in the game, fourth quarter. I was up in the press box, and somebody came in and said, "Your dad isn't feeling well."

I got this horrible feeling. I sensed right away that this was serious. I ran down the stadium steps and across the field, and there was my dad in his coaching clothes, laid out on a stretcher. He was conscious but pale and expressionless.

Just as I got down there, Mooney scored. I hugged my father and said, "There you go, Dad, you can relax now. You just tied the game."

I don't know why I said that. I was just trying to make him feel OK.

—Ron Stoops Jr.

I always went down to the field a few minutes before the end of every game to see Ron. I liked to go down to the gate where the team came on and off the field.

I went down there, and a few moments later, Sister Jane Marie Kudlacz, who was the Mooney principal, rushed up to me. "Dee, I was looking for you," she said. "Ron doesn't feel well. He's sitting on the bench."

My knees went down. By this time, he was lying on the bench. His color looked terrible. Oh, my Ron.

Ronnie was down from the box, and he put his arm around me. Reenie was there. She was a nurse, and when she saw him, she just said, "Oh, Dad." We were all scared.

—Dee Stoops

This was so out of character for my dad. He was never sick. He never complained.

I wanted him immediately out of there. There were some policemen there who were friends of mine. They got the ambulance over to where my dad was. The police kept saying, "He'll be fine, he'll be fine." They didn't think it was serious.

My dad was talking a little. Mooney had won the game in triple overtime, so people told him about the score. They put him in the ambulance. I got in the front seat, and the doctor and the paramedic were in the back with Dad. They closed the door, and we were off to the hospital. They tried to do what they could.

By the time we got to the hospital, they weren't giving us any hope.

—Reenie Stoops Farragher

I was putting the kids to bed. My sister-in-law's father called me. He was at the game. He said, "They took your dad in an ambulance. He didn't feel well. They said he's OK, that he should be fine."

For some odd reason, I knew. I looked at my husband and said, "He's dead."

—Kathy Stoops Kohowski

He had a massive heart attack on the way to the hospital.

—Ron Stoops Jr.

When we all got to the hospital, we were extremely worried. You put two and two together that it's not good.

We called Bobby. He had a funny feeling in his stomach, too. After all, Ron was not a smoker, not a drinker.

Not long after—I forgot who came out to talk to us—but they said they did everything they could.

TRAGEDY

Bob and Carol drove in and made it to the hospital.
That was a hard night.

— Dee Stoops

It was late Friday. I was getting ready to go home. Somebody got the news to
a friend, and the friend told me.
 It's hard. That was hard to deal with.

— Mike Stoops

I was twenty-one. We didn't stay in a hotel the night before a home game,
but we did have security on our dorm floors. At about eleven or twelve that
night, I heard a pretty hard knock on the door. It was Mike. He came over to
tell me the news.
 He and I were sitting there talking, crying. We got on the phone with
Mom and family back home.

— Mark Stoops

I was in the team hotel but had never thought to give anyone from my family, including Carol, the name of the place. After all, we were only there the one night.

Ronnie had called our apartment looking for me. He told Carol that Dad had collapsed on the field and that we should come to the hospital as soon as we could. Carol contacted another coach's wife, got the name of the hotel, and they patched her through to my room.

I instantly had a bad feeling. As Carol and I were driving back, it was as if I already knew the outcome.

When we pulled into the parking lot at the hospital, Ronnie was waiting outside. I walked across the lot, and as soon as I saw his face, I knew what he was going to say.

It didn't take long for word to spread about my dad's death. By the time we got back to my mom's house, there were probably fifty people already there. The number kept growing.

I was numb. We all were. A few hours earlier, my dad had been on a football sideline, doing what he loved best. In an instant, he was gone at only fifty-four. It was surreal to think of him in the past tense.

The wake was at Rossi Brothers funeral home, and the visitation lines stretched out the front entrance. My dad was dressed in his Sunday best.

Coach Fry, who on a game week had flown into town for the service with several other Iowa assistants and staff members, presented my mom with the same number 41 Iowa jersey that I, Mike, and Mark had worn during our Hawkeye careers. Shortly before they closed the casket for the funeral Mass, my mom gently placed the jersey next to my dad. Then I slipped my 1981 Rose Bowl ring off my finger and placed it in the coffin with him. I wanted him to have it forever.

My mom said, "Bobby, you'll want that ring and the memories that go with it."

"No, Mom," I said. "I got it because of my dad."

St. Dom's was standing room only that day. So many people came to pay their respects that the line stretched around the block. The Iowa contingent sat in the choir section. Muransky came back for the funeral. The pews were filled with those whose own lives had somehow been touched, however lightly or heavily, by my dad in his fifty-four years.

When it came time to drive to the cemetery, the procession of cars stretched as long as the eye could see.

My dad would have been embarrassed by the attention. We weren't a family that sought the spotlight or were even comfortable in it. But we appreciated the respect and love paid to my dad that day, and the days, months, and years after his death, too. He had been an iconic figure in our community. A teacher. Coach. Businessman. But to my mom, he was a husband. To us, he was a father.

At the funeral, someone had read a poem by Al Williamson, a Mooney alum who later became a Mooney teacher. It ended with, "Old Ron's been promoted, and it only makes sense. God needs him now—to run His defense."

To this day, I'm convinced that God had arranged for my Kent State job offer, sending me home to be with my dad. Because of that, I had been able to be around him right up until the day he died. That couldn't have been a coincidence, right?

Bobby had so much respect for his dad, and a little a bit of fear. He revered his dad.

That was a gift, him being there for at least that year near his dad.

A guy came up to me at the service. He said, "You a Stoops?"

"I'm married to Bobby," I said.

He said, "I was there at Mooney when Coach Stoops was the baseball coach. I was a pitcher. He was my favorite coach. He was my favorite teacher."

That's how people were about Bobby's dad.

—Carol Stoops

That was heartbreaking. The whole town was heartbroken.

—Ray Mancini

Earlier that fall, my boss, Kent State defensive coordinator Chris Smeland, and I had made the drive to Youngstown. We had just finished our own late-afternoon practice session and had decided to jump in the car and catch the end of a Mooney practice. We wanted to take a look at several possible recruits.

Chris was anxious. "We're not going to get there in time," he said. "Practice will be over."

"Nah, you don't have to worry about that," I said.

Chris didn't know my dad and Don Bucci. When I played there, we were famous for our four- and five-hour practices.

By the time we got to Mooney, the sun had almost set. The practice field was nearly dark, but there were my dad and Bucci—and the entire team in full pads—assembled on the cinder track and blacktop near the edge of the field. They were using the dim lighting from an adjacent Mooney school building to continue practice.

At the time, Smeland had spent most of his playing and early coaching career in California, Nevada, and Colorado. I turned to him that night and said, "Coach, this is how we do it here at Mooney."

"Here." The Midwest...Ohio...Youngstown.

My dad taught me and my brothers about football. But he was more than a coach. He was more than just football.

He loved to compete. The act of competing, of giving your best against the opponents' best, gave him joy. I've always loved the purity of that thought.

He loved the relationships he built with assistant coaches and his players. It was a very personal thing with him. He stressed the value of loyalty. And loyalty has been a string running from the start to the finish of my own life.

I witnessed my dad's ideals, and I became a version of him. In their own ways, so did my brothers and sisters. Those are the things that matter most to me, too. The fame, whatever that is, means nothing to me. Fame doesn't last, but friendships do. Memories do. The bond between a coach and player, or between a father and son . . . it stands the test of time. That's what my dad gave me—and much, much more.

Who knows what would have happened if my dad hadn't ordered me to stay at Iowa. What if he hadn't said those twenty-five words to me that day in our front yard? Where would I have transferred? Would I have achieved the same success? Would I have returned home as a chickenshit and amounted to nothing?

I'm glad I didn't find out.

My mom was now a widow. We were now a family without a dad. I remember stopping by the house not long after the funeral. "How you doin', Mom?" I asked.

"Bobby, I'll fake it 'til I make it," she said.

It was one of her favorite sayings.

Last October 2018 was the thirty-year anniversary of my dad's death, and for a long time, it was difficult for my brother Ron to walk into Boardman Stadium. And to this day, he says one of the hardest things he ever had to do was look into the faces of Mike and Mark when they got off the plane from Iowa for my dad's funeral.

I try not to live a life of regrets, of what-ifs. To me, it's a waste of time. When people ask me—and they mean well—if I wish my dad had been alive to see my accomplishments, I tell them that I truly believe he *has* seen them all. Seen us win games and championships. Seen our families grow. Seen us try to honor his legacy by honoring what he and my mom taught us. He's seen it, and he's been able to enjoy it in ways we can't comprehend.

Do I wish he had been on the sidelines with me during those national championship games, or sharing those moments in the locker room after a victory? Of course. But in the end, the thing that hurts most is that he wasn't able to be with my three children. Or to get to know Carol better. But these are wishes, not regrets.

Ray Mancini once told a reporter that I felt like my dad still talked to me at times, that I could feel his presence, that he had a hand on my shoulder to guide me.

I know what Ray was trying to say. No, I actually never heard my dad's voice—it wasn't like he was visiting me. But in certain situations, I know exactly what he would have felt or said. I know what sort of advice he would have given me.

In 1993, my dad was inducted posthumously into the inaugural Cardinal Mooney High School Athletic Hall of Fame. Included in the induction class that year was DeBartolo Jr., the man who had underwritten my family's trip to the Rose Bowl.

I was inducted in 1996; Coach Bucci in 2001, Mike in 2002, Mark in 2004, and Ron Jr. in 2012. We're all honored to have our awards included on a wall of plaques that begins with my dad's.

There's also a Ron Stoops Award presented each year to the Mooney baseball and football players who best exemplify my dad's qualities. The practice facility is also named after him.

I miss him every day. But right after his funeral, I did something that I think he would have wanted, even expected me to do.

I went back to work.

Chapter Five

Extraordinary

Iowa fans think that Hawkeyes football was in bad shape when Fry took over. It was. But nothing—and I mean nothing—compares to the Kansas State football program when Bill Snyder left Iowa for Manhattan at the end of the 1988 season.

Snyder was forty-seven. There were people within the Big Eight Conference who weren't sure he'd make it to forty-eight if he took the Kansas State job. They said he was nuts.

Well, I guess I was nuts, too, because I left Kent State to become his defensive backs coach.

There are lost causes, and then there was Kansas State football thirty-plus years ago. You had to see it to believe it.

Sports Illustrated called Kansas State "Futility U...America's most hapless team...home of the worst major-college program." When K-State and Kansas played (KU was having its own struggles), it was mockingly called the "Toilet Bowl." Harsh words directed at college players doing the best they could under tough circumstances.

At the time, K-State was the only Division I-A program with more than five hundred losses. It was the kind of program that forced out its head coach after two games of the 1985 season. There were stories that some K-State fans threw oranges at the players during the 1987 season.

Everyone on the Iowa staff knew it was only a matter of time before Snyder became a head coach. But nobody could have predicted that Kansas State would be his first—and last—head coaching job.

Steve Miller was the Kansas State athletic director. The story goes that he wanted Snyder to interview for the job, but Snyder said he wasn't interested. Miller kept asking until Snyder told him to quit calling.

Miller didn't give up. He said to forget about a formal interview; the job was Snyder's if he wanted it. To prove the point, he told Snyder the school would wait for his answer, even if that meant waiting until Iowa played its New Year's Peach Bowl game against North Carolina State. After that, Snyder could come to Manhattan, check out the school and the program, meet Jon Wefald, the school president, and then make a decision. Snyder said he'd take a look.

Fry helped prep Snyder for the visit. They had such trust in each other. You have to remember that Fry is the one who first hired Snyder as quarterbacks and wide receivers coach at North Texas State in 1976. Most head coaches would have looked at Snyder's resume—at the time, he was the offensive coordinator and *swimming coach* at Austin College—and moved on to the next guy. Not Fry. He looked beyond the obvious, as did Snyder.

Snyder arrived in Manhattan with a wish list of conditions that needed to be met before he'd consider the offer: recruiting budgets, facility upgrades, assistant coach salaries...that sort of thing. It was the kind of list you make when you're hoping to get a yes on half of its requests.

Well...Kansas State said yes to all of it.

Before he made his final decision—and this was so Bill Snyder—he walked around the Kansas State campus during the visit and stopped perfect strangers to ask them about the community and the university. He didn't identify himself—he was just a middle-aged man asking about the school.

Snyder would say later that it was freezing cold that day, but every stranger he stopped had offered him a warm smile and a few minutes of their time. He was struck by their friendliness but even more by how much they supported the university. The responses of those strangers helped convince him to take the job.

It was not a job for the weak. One early potential candidate had told the St. Louis *Post-Dispatch* that "I'd rather go back to Vietnam" than coach Kansas State.

When Snyder got there, K-State hadn't won a game in its last twenty-seven tries. The loneliest place on campus was its football trophy case. It had one piece of hardware: a "runners-up" trophy from the 1982 Independence Bowl. At the time, that had been the Wildcats' first and only bowl appearance since the school had first fielded a team in 1896.

The facilities were awful. You could see the open seams in the stadium artificial turf.

And the roster was a disaster. Of its 113 players, only 65 were scholarship players (compared to 95 in most programs). Almost half of all the players were true freshmen or redshirt freshmen. *Sports Illustrated* pointed out that the best players in the state—stars such as Barry Sanders, Rodney Peete, and Keith DeLong—had bolted to out-of-state programs. Another indication of our talent level—or lack of it—was that in four of the previous six seasons, no K-State players had been chosen in the NFL Draft. In two of those six seasons, the only Wildcats picked were a fifth-rounder, a tenth-rounder, and an eleventh-rounder. And this was during the era of twelve-round NFL drafts as opposed to the current seven rounds.

Support for the team was threadbare. By the last home game of the 1988 season, only 10,850 people had bothered to show up—and capacity was 42,000. *SI* said that only 2,700 of the 19,301 students at KSU bought season tickets in 1988. The school only had 7,200 season ticket holders in all. And of the 13,000 Kansas State alums in the Kansas City area, only 200 donated money to the program.

One writer, Mark Wangrin, put it perfectly. He said that "few people even cared enough to be apathetic."

It wasn't a surprise that some KSU officials had discussed the possibility of downgrading the program to Division I-AA—or shutting it down altogether and moving the other sports programs to the Missouri Valley Conference. There was talk that the Big Eight might drop KSU. We knew the reality: if we didn't fix the program, there was a good chance that we might be the last staff ever to coach football there.

Like I said, there was bad. And then there was *really* bad.

Snyder was coming to Kansas State with impressive credentials. He had been a key part of our turnaround at Iowa. He was a Fry disciple. And as Iowa's offensive coordinator, he had overseen an attack that was number one nationally in passing efficiency and number three in passing yardage over the previous five seasons.

Kenny Mossman, who was the K-State sports information director at the time of the hiring (and later our media relations director at OU and now a senior associate athletic director there) told me about the introductory press conference. While Mossman and Snyder were walking to the interview room, Kenny could barely contain his happiness. As they were about to enter it, Snyder paused, looked at Kenny, and said in his soft deadpan, "I'm glad you're so excited about this."

I'll forever be indebted to Dick Crum for giving me my first full-time job. He's a great, great guy. He was awesome to me. But even though Kansas State football was in ruins at the time, it wasn't a difficult decision to take the leap of faith with Snyder. Plus, it was a bump in conference strength, and it doubled my salary—from $20,000 to about $40,000.

Coach Crum understood. He couldn't have been more supportive.

I was twenty-eight when I got to Manhattan, which is in the Flint Hills, about two hours west of Kansas City. I had never been there, but it didn't take me long to realize what an underrated place it was. The full-time population was less than forty thousand then, but I thought the town, with its Aggieville area, and the school were fantastic.

K-State paid Snyder $85,000 in salary that first year. It was the best money it ever spent. The first thing he did was address the football culture.

When it came to morale levels, KSU was in negative integers. The cumulative effect of all its losses had beaten the players and the fan base into submission. Wefald would later tell the *Kansas City Star* that he'd once given a speech at the Rotary Club of Kansas City and said he expected the Wildcats to be "competitive" under the new coach—and by competitive, he meant winning four games a year.

The audience burst into laughter.

The mood permeated the entire school. Its teams thought they were losers. That's what happens in those situations. So many people want to project the negative. They want to keep you down, convince you that something can't be done. It's human nature; people like to pile on.

I get it. Sometimes it's easier to lose and then justify the losses with excuses. Snyder was the players' fourth head coach in five years, the thirty-second in just ninety-three years. They had been conditioned to believe that nothing would make a difference.

I never doubted Snyder. It never crossed my mind that we wouldn't win. That's the real truth. Maybe I was naive, but I knew we would win even when everyone else tried to tell us we wouldn't. We heard it all: we wouldn't be able to recruit anyone to K-State...we'd never be able to beat the powerhouse programs in the league—Oklahoma, Nebraska, Colorado...we were committing career suicide.

But Snyder did at K-State what Fry had done at Iowa (and what I would do at Oklahoma). He identified the problems. He identified methods to solve the problems. He instituted changes. And he never wavered from his beliefs.

It sounds simple, but it takes discipline and trust to stay true to those core philosophies, especially when you don't have instant success and the outside world is questioning your every decision.

Snyder's default position was to outwork everyone else. Sleep was an inconvenience. He supposedly once asked a doctor if sleep was medically necessary to sustain the body. Again, typical Snyder.

Taking time to eat a meal was an annoyance for him. Had it been his choice, I'm not sure he would ever have gone home.

Snyder made it clear during his introductory news conference that losing, and even mediocrity, would no longer be accepted. "The time seems right at Kansas State," he said. "Kansas State has the opportunity to achieve the greatest turnaround in the history of college football."

As for our upcoming 1989 season, he told *SI*, "We will be as good as we can be, and we will not be 0–11."

Dana Dimel was on that staff. He had come to K-State as a junior college transfer and suffered through losing as a player. When Snyder got the job, Dana was a graduate assistant. Snyder promoted him to assistant offensive line coach.

Dana would later become the head coach of Wyoming in 1996. He hired my brother Mark, who would live in Dana's basement. And Dana later worked with my brother Mike at Arizona.

My first impression of Bob was that he had a lot of confidence. He had that northeast Ohio bravado to him.

EXTRAORDINARY

We were about the same age, but even at twenty-seven, I remember coming to work and thinking, "I don't know how I'm going to get the energy today." One of our other assistants, John Latina, had a minivan, and about five minutes before practice started, we'd sit in there and try to get the energy for our usual three-hour practices, which became legendary.

Coach Snyder believes in one way: outworking everybody. That's one thing about Coach Snyder—it's one of his strongest attributes—his consistency. It's an important trait for a leader.

But the hours? Unbelievable hours.

—Dana Dimel, Kansas State graduate assistant,
assistant coach, 1987–1996

This was a Bill Snyder workweek:

Monday—8:00 a.m. to 11:30 p.m., with two staff meetings, one at 8:00 a.m. and one at 11:00 a.m.

Tuesday—8:00 a.m. to 11:00 p.m.

Wednesday—8:00 a.m. to 10:30 p.m. (This was the *easy* day. You thought you were catching a break by working only fourteen and a half hours.)

Thursday—8:00 a.m. to 11:00 p.m.

Friday—9:00 a.m. to 10:00 p.m.

Saturday (game day)—7:30 a.m. to 6:30 p.m.

Sunday—10:30 a.m. to midnight.

Bill Snyder actually brought me in and told me not to be seen on the golf course (during the off-season). He said it wouldn't be good for people to see his assistant coaches out on the golf course.

—Dana Dimel

The hours were draconian. Snyder would even schedule 1:00 p.m. staff meetings in the summer. He worked us hard—but then again, there was a lot of work to do. And nobody worked harder than Coach Snyder. No matter how early you got to the football facility parking lot off Kimball

Avenue, Snyder's car was almost always there. And no matter how late you left, his car was usually still there.

The totality of what he had to fix is why he felt like he had to outwork it. It was darkness to darkness in many cases. They worked holidays. Football was going to be the dominant aspect of your life.

Bill had regard for family—I'm not saying he didn't—but the nature of the K-State program at the time...people forget how completely inept the football program was.

— Kenny Mossman, Kansas State sports media
relations director, 1983–1991

Every second of his day was dedicated to improving K-State football. To him, anything was possible. He was driven by what he called a "what-have-you-done-for-me-lately world," and he was fine with that. It was fair to be judged that way, because "there's always going to be a tomorrow."

It wasn't unusual for Snyder to ask a player, "Did you get better today?" He once instructed one of our offensive linemen, who was right-handed, to learn how to eat and write left-handed; it would help him play left offensive tackle better, said Snyder. He would have defensive linemen tie their hands together during drills to promote better technique.

One of his favorite sayings: "If you take care of the little things, the big things will come."

He was meticulous, almost obsessive, about perfecting the fundamentals. On the first day of practice, the legendary John Wooden used to show the players on his national champion UCLA basketball teams how to properly put on their socks, how to correctly tie their shoes. The little things...

Wooden developed the Pyramid of Success, a fifteen-step structure of championship philosophies. Snyder outdid Wooden by one. He had a sixteen-point "goals for success" program. Different coaches and sports, but same ideals.

Snyder cared about his players. He would drop them notes of encouragement and make sure he sent cards on their birthdays. He didn't feel the same way about the media. He closed our practices to reporters (just as Fry had done at Iowa). They howled in protest.

Snyder did another Fry-like thing: he changed the KSU helmet logo. He called the university art department and enlisted the help of Tom Bookwalter, a part-time teacher who was a renowned illustrator and graphic designer. Bookwalter designed the Powercat logo that has become synonymous with K-State football.

When we walked into Coach Snyder's office, he would have department-store-type mannequins outfitted with our new helmet and uniform designs. He liked to look at them each day and determine if any tweaks should be made. They are essentially the same designs that K-State uses today.

But new helmet logos can only do so much. During our first spring practices, we had only four defensive linemen, and two of them were walk-ons. We had to take breaks during the team sessions so the four of them could recover physically.

The program was such a wreck that it had lost an entire recruiting class before we even got there. They had signed a lot of at-risk guys, some low-character guys, and some junior college kids. They had guys flunking out. The roster was in dire shape.

We lost our first three games of the 1989 season, which meant the winless streak had grown to thirty. We were blown out at Arizona State, lost by two points to Division I-AA Northern Iowa at home, and then got beat at home by seventeen against Northern Illinois.

Even with the losses, we'd try to convince the team, "See? We're getting better. Hang in there. Believe."

I know moral victories don't count in the standings, but we took what we could get. Positive was better than negative. Negativity, that feel-sorry-for-yourself stuff, just pulls you down.

I'll admit there were times when my own belief was tested. I didn't doubt Snyder or his methods; instead, I wondered when we were going to finally break through. We were working so hard. Our team, which was vastly undermanned, was working hard, too.

Based on what we did at Iowa, I knew success was in our future. But when?

On September 30, 1989, we played North Texas State—Fry and Snyder's old program—at home. NTSU was tied for number one in the D-IAA rankings.

We trailed, 17–14, with ninety-one seconds remaining in the game and the ball on our own fifteen-yard line. First play: a sack.

But then we began to move down the field. A pass completion here. A penalty there. Another sack. Three completions. Two incompletions.

There were four seconds left, the ball at NTSU's twelve-yard line. Last play. Could it be?

Backup quarterback Carl Straw dropped back and got hit a split second after he threw the ball to the front corner of the left end zone. The ball somehow dropped into the waiting hands of wide receiver Frank Hernandez, who had been questionable to play that day because of an injury.

I've seen the replay dozens of times, and it never gets old. Our radio play-by-play announcer at the time, Mitch Holthus, lost his mind when Hernandez caught the winning TD with no time on the clock. Can't say that I blamed him.

His screaming call was one for the books:

"He got it!

"He got it!

"He got it!

"Touchdown Kansas State!

"Touchdown Kansas State!

"Touchdown Kansas State!

"Kansas State wins!

"Kansas State wins!

"What it is…

"What it is… it's a big, big, big, big, big, big touchdown!"

Holthus called it "one of the best moments in this school's history… and tomorrow, when you open up the paper, for the first time in thirty-one football games, Kansas State will be on the left side of the column."

The left side… the winner's side.

The Streak was done.

What fans were there (it wasn't a full house that day) stormed the field. On the way to the locker room, I saw the students carrying the goalposts. They carried them all the way downtown.

It was elation. It was relief. Our players were hugging, crying, jumping around. It was as if they had to remember how to celebrate.

The coaches' wives, some of them with tears in their eyes, made their way to the field. I was so happy that I picked up Carol and swung her around in the air. I had never done that before...and haven't since.

There was a tradition at K-State: when you won a game, you rang a victory bell located just up from the end zone. That bell hadn't been heard in nearly eleven hundred days. Two of our offensive linemen, Chad Faulkner and Paul Yniguez, ran up there and rang that bell silly. I'd never heard a sweeter sound.

After the game, most of the assistant coaches found a little bar and celebrated together. That night, the whole community celebrated. Losers? Not that day.

All we had heard was, "You can't win at Kansas State." But guess what? We had just won. To this day, that game remains one of my favorite victories—and that includes the national championships at Oklahoma and Florida, the national championship games, the Big 12 championships... any of them. It's one of my all-time favorites because I have never been anywhere where a school, a team, and a community needed a win more than Kansas State.

Snyder said we wouldn't finish 0–11, and he was right. We finished 1–10. The week after we beat North Texas State, we were forty-five-point underdogs to Nebraska and lost by fifty-one. Later in the year, we lost at OU by twenty-three, to Colorado by forty-eight. But at least we were no longer the owners of the longest active winless streak in college football.

Given our situation, Snyder made two important decisions that helped shape our program for years to come. One, he softened our nonconference schedule. The Big Eight (and later, the Big 12) was tough enough for us. In the previous ten years, K-State had played nonconference games at Auburn, LSU, Washington, Arizona State, South Carolina, and Iowa. It was like driving your car over your own foot. By dialing down the schedule, Snyder gave the program a chance to compete. You could call them cupcake opponents, but back then, nobody was a cupcake to us. We were usually the dessert for other programs.

The second defining moment was Snyder's decision to emphasize the recruitment of junior college players. They became the backbone of our program and helped stabilize our roster. We had all sorts of success stories with those players.

By the end of our first year there, everyone on the staff was a mini-Snyder. We knew what was expected of us, and we did it. There was almost a perverse pride in the number of hours we worked.

We finished 5–6 in 1990 but were still getting crushed by the Big Three: Nebraska, Oklahoma, and Colorado. That's how we judged ourselves: were we closing the gap between us and them?

The gap began to shrink in 1991, when we lost in Lincoln by only seven, lost to CU by just ten, at Oklahoma by twenty-one, and finished 7–4 — the most victories by a K-State team since 1954. (We were ineligible for a bowl game because two of our wins were against I-AA programs; you needed six I-A wins to qualify.) That was the season that I was promoted to co-defensive coordinator with Jim Leavitt, and Mark Mangino was hired as our run game coordinator. It was also the season that an undersized linebacker from Salina, Kansas — one of those juco transfers we recruited — began making an impact. His name was Brent Venables.

My brother Mike joined our staff in 1992 as a defensive ends coach. Venables was an honorable-mention All-Big Eight selection. Our record took a step back at 5–6, but we finished the season with only a fourteen-point loss to the Cornhuskers in, of all places, Tokyo.

Coach Snyder had agreed to play the game in Japan because he wanted the team to experience something approximating a bowl game. K-State hadn't been in one since Jesus had walked the earth.

This would never happen today, but we actually shared a plane with Nebraska for the flight to Tokyo. Coach Snyder, always looking for an edge, even arranged for our team to sit on a certain side of the plane. Nebraska would get the other side. His thinking was, our players would be on the side where the sun wouldn't shine through the windows and disrupt their sleep. I did notice, however, that Nebraska's players simply pulled down their window shades.

Still, you had to admire Snyder's attention to detail. I could be the same way.

Bob would draw up cards of opponents on Sunday nights during the season. He'd have more than one hundred cards spread out on his desk and floor — this was before computers were so prevalent — of the offensive plays and for-

mations the other team would use. If you walked in and accidentally kicked them, he'd get nervous.

He coached intense. I thought he did a great job keeping it simple for our defense: crowd that box, played man to man—played a lot of bump and run.

— Mark Mangino

Everyone knows he used to paint houses in Youngstown. But he came over and helped me paint my house in Manhattan.

We're finishing the west side of the house, but the clouds roll in, and it looks like it's going to rain. Just as we get done, the clouds open, there's five inches of rain in two hours, and it washes all the paint off my house. My basement is flooded with what appears to be milk.

Bob? He came over the next week with a couple of players, and we painted the house again. That's him. His dad was probably that way, too. When you paint a house, you got to take care of the brushes. You've got to do the job right.

— Matt McMillen, Kansas State associate
athletic director for development, 1987–1997

There's no question that 1993 was the breakthrough year. We tied Colorado, and we beat Oklahoma for the first time since 1970.

During that game against Colorado at home, there was a critical, late-game play.

I was on the headset with Snyder. "Coach, what do you think?" I asked.

"Bobby, that's why I pay you good money," he said.

He was right. That *is* why he paid me. Plus, it was unfair to ask him to jump in and make the call. "All right, then. I'm coming after them," I said.

We stopped Colorado on the play.

We entered the *AP* top twenty-five for the first time since 1970 after that game. It also ended an eight-game losing streak to CU. During that time, the Buffs had outscored K-State, 363–38. In many ways, it was another turning-point day in our program.

We won nine games in 1993, a school first. We beat thirteenth-ranked Oklahoma, the first time we'd defeated a top-twenty-five team since

1970. Our offense was fast and formidable; our defense was physical and aggressive. We appeared in a bowl game and won, a school first. We beat a Joe Tiller–coached Wyoming team in the Copper Bowl, and fifteen thousand KSU fans made the trip to Tucson, almost five thousand more than who watched the final *home* game of the 1988 season. There were thousands of fans at our team hotel for a pregame pep rally. It was incredible.

Best of all, we could put an actual winning trophy in the lonely trophy case, another school first. Everything was a first when it came to Snyder and KSU.

That first bowl game we won was the greatest thing ever. It was exciting, one of my most memorable moments.

Me, Bob, and Jim Leavitt sat in a hot tub back at the hotel after the game. Venables, who was a grad assistant, was there, too. We were having some celebratory drinks, just having fun. To be able to go and win a bowl game was just so great.

—Mike Stoops, Kansas State assistant coach, 1992–1998

That Copper Bowl would be the first of eleven consecutive bowl appearances for K-State under Snyder. We had it going. Nine wins and the Aloha Bowl in 1994. Ten wins and the Holiday Bowl in 1995.

It was in 1994 that Notre Dame contacted me about becoming the defensive backs coach. It would be the second time my name had come up as an assistant coach there, but only the first time I was aware of.

Barry Alvarez, who was on the Notre Dame staff in the late 1980s, would tell me years later that he had tried to convince Lou Holtz to hire me when I was just breaking into the business. Holtz had told Alvarez I was too young and inexperienced.

This time I had a few bona fides. And I was interested. After all, it was Notre Dame and Coach Holtz.

I had heard Barry Alvarez talk about Bob all the time, and about the Stoops brothers, how tough they were. If Barry Alvarez says they're tough, you can take it to the bank.

They brought Bob in. He was very impressive. He met with Coach Holtz and the staff, and when he left, it was like, "Man, he's just one of those guys who's got it."

I showed him around the weight room, talked to him a bit. I thought we had him.

They offered him a job at Notre Dame, and he turned it down. It blew me away.

He's in Manhattan—and I'm not trying to put Kansas State down or trying to be disrespectful—but he turned down Notre Dame. He said it didn't feel right to him.

—Jerry Schmidt, Notre Dame assistant strength and
conditioning coordinator, 1989–1994

I came very close to taking the job. The fact that it was Notre Dame really intrigued me.

I think highly of Bob Davie, and he would have been great to work with. But in the end, I wanted greater control of my own career path. I would have gone from co-defensive coordinator—and making our defensive calls—to a secondary coach. I know it's Notre Dame, but I thought it would be better to develop as a coordinator. Plus, we were building something special at Kansas State.

I called Bob and thanked him for the offer, but I told him I wasn't going to take the job. Not long after that chat, I received a phone call from Coach Holtz. It wasn't a very pleasant conversation.

Coach Holtz and I have a great relationship now. But on that day, I think he wanted to drop me from the top of the Golden Dome.

The difference between Notre Dame and Kansas State wasn't apples and oranges; it was apples and zucchini. We were recruiting and developing players. We didn't get five-star recruits at Kansas State—not even close. But we started churning out players who became All-Americans, all-conference, and/or NFL draftees. Guys such as free safety Jaime Mendez, cornerback Chris Canty, punter Sean Snyder, wide receiver Kevin Lockett, quarterbacks Chad May and Matt Miller, defensive tackle Tim Colston, kick returner Andre Coleman, linebackers Percell Gaskins and Chuck Marlowe, and cornerback Thomas Randolph, to name a few.

In 1993 we finished twentieth in the final *AP* poll. We were nineteenth in 1994 and seventh in 1995. In 1995 we also recorded our first victory against an *AP* top-ten team in twenty-five years—and only the second such win in school history.

All of this was fantasyland stuff for us. When we first got to K-State in 1989, we had *hoped* we might have success one day. Thanks to the leadership of Coach Snyder, we were confident we could do it. We believed we could win.

Our program was no longer a laughingstock. We were a hard out. But we still had work to do. With Bill Snyder, there was always more work.

Chapter Six

HBC University

It was an accident, really. I just happened to be watching the November 25 game between Steve Spurrier's third-ranked Florida Gators and Bobby Bowden's sixth-ranked Florida State Seminoles in Gainesville on Thanksgiving weekend. This is when FSU-Florida was must-see football.

Our 1995 regular season had ended on November 18, so I had a little time to relax with Carol before our recruiting and Holiday Bowl prep work began.

Florida beat FSU. The next week I saw them easily beat Arkansas in the SEC Championship. I was aware of Spurrier and had followed him and read about him but had never met him. I was always impressed with the way he coached his teams, though.

From the outside looking in, he had an interesting blend of confidence, unfiltered honesty and humor, and a dose of humility and self-deprecation. You could tell he was a character, what with that white visor he threw around and the way he said exactly what was on his mind during those TV interviews. He had won everywhere he'd coached in college: at Duke, where they didn't win before him and, for the longest time, didn't win after him, and now at Florida, where he always seemed to be collecting some sort of coaching award and the Gators always seemed to be winning SEC Championships and playing in big bowl games.

As the Gators pulled away from Arkansas, I told Carol, "I don't know Steve Spurrier, but he's really got it going on down there at Florida. He's killing it."

In the national championship game, Nebraska did to the Gators what I had seen it do to a lot of teams in the Big Eight: steamroll them. Counting their 62–24 win against the Gators, the Cornhuskers had four games that season when they'd scored sixty or more points.

They had also beaten us by twenty-four earlier that season, but in my time at K-State—even during our first few years there, when we were clinging to respectability—we had never given up sixty-plus to them. Of course, we didn't beat them during my time there, either.

Five days after the national championship game, I was in New Orleans for the annual American Football Coaches Association convention. I was walking one way, and Coach Spurrier walked by me the other way. I sort of did a double take when I saw him and said to myself, "Wow, that's Steve Spurrier." He was sort of a rock star in our business. But I didn't think to stop and introduce myself.

One afternoon in February, I was in my office at the K-State football facility. I wasn't the kind of coach who constantly updated his resume and kept track of job openings around the country. I liked Kansas State. Carol liked it. We had been there for seven years and had worked so hard to position the program for consistent success. I wasn't in a hurry to leave.

What I didn't know in February of 1996 is that Florida had an opening for a defensive coordinator.

My first year at Florida was 1995. We got our brains beat in by Nebraska in the national championship game. We had a good team, but we had a defense that needed somebody.

Jeremy Foley asked me, "When you were at Notre Dame, did anyone stand out to you?"

I said, "Yeah. Bob Stoops came in to Notre Dame and turned us down."
— Jerry Schmidt, Florida strength and conditioning coordinator, 1995–1998

We got whacked by Nebraska. I think [Spurrier] was frustrated with [defensive coordinator] Bobby Pruett, who ended up taking the head coaching job at Marshall. Steve promoted [Ron] Zook, but Zook left a month later to take a job with the [Pittsburgh] Steelers.

Jerry Schmidt mentioned Bob Stoops's name while we were talking in the weight room. I got Kansas State's stats and handed them to Steve and said, "Here's a guy you might want to look at."

I had never met Bob, never heard the name. But they had really good defenses at K-State. Steve took it from there.

— Jeremy Foley, Florida athletic director, 1992–2016

Heck, I'm going to call this guy, Bobby Stoops, and see if he's interested in coming to Florida. I called out there. I called Coach Snyder — I don't know how many times — but they wouldn't put me through to him. He wouldn't get on the phone with me.

The third time I called, I said to whoever answered, "Tell Coach Snyder I'm going to call Bobby Stoops. I'm going to try to hire him for defensive coordinator."

I called the secretary for the assistant coaches and asked for Bobby Stoops. "Tell him Lawson Holland is calling." Lawson had coached at Oklahoma State the year or two before and now was with us. Bobby knew him.

— Steve Spurrier, Florida head coach, 1990–2001

When the phone rang, I was talking to one of my players. The secretary had told me it was Lawson Holland.

I picked up the phone. "Hey, Lawson, how you doin'?" I asked.

"This isn't Lawson," said the caller. "This is Coach Spurrier. I want to talk to you about this D-coordinator job we have here at Florida. I used Coach Lawson's name because I didn't want your secretary yelling down the hall saying, 'Coach Spurrier's on the line!'"

Like a lot of coaches, Lawson and I pulled jokes on each other all the time about job openings. I'd thought this was another one of his pranks.

I didn't say anything for five seconds. Then I realized it really might be Coach Spurrier.

Coach explained that Jeremy Foley had asked him which team had the number-one defense in the country. Spurrier had guessed Bill "Brother" Oliver, who had just left Alabama for Auburn. Foley told him it was Kansas State and that Jim Leavitt and I ran that defense but that I made the calls. It's true: we were number one in total defense and number two in scoring defense and pass defense.

Coach started talking about the job and what the pay would be, and he asked what my defensive philosophies were. We talked again that day and the next day.

After those conversations with Coach, I decided it was time to talk to Carol about Florida's interest. Carol was a big hitter with Mary Kay, a worldwide cosmetics company based in the United States. She was extremely successful, and when you called our house phone, there was an option to leave a message specifically for Carol and her Mary Kay business.

Before we sat down at the dinner table—and I hadn't told her a thing about any of my discussions with Coach Spurrier yet—she hit the play button on our message machine. One of the last messages was from none other than Steve Spurrier: "Carol, I don't need any Mary Kay products, but I would really like to talk to you and Bobby."

Carol took a step back, pointed at the message machine, and said, "That's Coach Spurrier."

"Yeah," I said, "that's what we've got to talk about."

We talked that night about Florida, about Kansas State, about what we had built in Manhattan, about making a move, about the pros and cons of becoming the defensive coordinator at UF. The more I thought about it, the less sure I was about leaving K-State.

The next night, I started hemming and hawing to Carol about the possible move. "I'm not sure I want to do this," I said.

Carol, who had never questioned my football job instincts, looked at me as if I'd just said, "I wish Coach Snyder worked us harder."

"Bobby," she said, "if you don't take this job, I think you need your head examined. If you don't take this job, you won't take any job."

Carol pushed me out of my comfort zone. All my life, I've been pulled and pushed from comfort to bigger and better things. I was pushed to stay at Iowa, and it had turned out to be the biggest break of my life. And now Carol was pushing me out of my comfort zone at Kansas State. I thought, *You know, you're right—I'm thirty-five, and we've been here seven years. Maybe it's time.*

The next day, Coach Spurrier offered me the job.

"That sounds great, Coach," I said. "I want the job. But don't you think we should at least meet in person, see if we get along?" He agreed.

Carol and I flew to Gainesville that Friday. We met Steve and his wife, Jerri. We spent time with Jeremy. We talked to everybody, saw everything. And we loved every minute of it.

We got back to our hotel room, and we were like two kids on Christmas morning. We were pinching ourselves about it. We sat on the hotel bed and said, "Could it really be *this* good?" And it really was that good.

I accepted the job on Saturday and the next day flew to Youngstown for the annual Athletic Hall of Fame banquet at Cardinal Mooney in honor of my dad. I was one of nine inductees in the HOF Class of 1996.

When I got back to Kansas State on Monday, Coach Snyder wanted to see me. I had told him earlier that I was going to Florida to meet with Coach Spurrier and UF school officials.

When we talked that day, Snyder said that Kansas State now was prepared to double my salary and match Florida's financial package.

Wait...what did he just say?

For K-State, that was a commitment. Even though the KSU assistant coaches' salary pool had increased over the years, it still wasn't at the level of Florida or other top-twenty-five programs.

I didn't want to seem ungrateful or unappreciative, but as Coach Snyder outlined K-State's counteroffer, I couldn't help but think, *If I was worth that salary to some other school now, why wasn't I worth it to Kansas State before I went to Florida? Why didn't you pay me that to begin with? Pay me what I'm worth.* "Coach, I gave them my word," I said. "I can't go back on my word."

I had loved my years at Kansas State. But it was just time to go.

Working for Snyder had been an honor and an experience. If you could survive the early years of K-State and the demands of Snyder, you could survive anything in our profession—and I mean that in the most complimentary way. There was a precision to his coaching and to his organization. I wouldn't have left if it hadn't been Coach Spurrier, Florida, and a defensive coordinator position that I no longer had to share with another coach. It was great working with Jim Leavitt, but eventually, you don't want a "co-something" in front of your title. (Leavitt also left KSU after the 1995 season to become the first head coach at the University of South Florida.)

I pride myself on my honesty, so I would be less than honest if I didn't say I was disappointed by Coach Snyder's actions when it came to Coach Spurrier's initial phone calls.

Snyder was protective of his staff. He had hired them. Developed them. And he wanted to keep them. But his actions confirmed what I had always thought: a head coach should try to help his assistants to move up. I had been loyal and hardworking and had never lobbied for another job. But to me, an assistant's success reflects positively on a head coach. The more branches on a coaching tree, the better.

Before it became public that Bob was going to be our new coordinator, Coach Spurrier was at my dad's house in Tampa. He was playing in the pro-am at a Seniors Tour event. It was a Tuesday thing, and I was caddying for Coach.

The group in front of us was playing with Jim Colbert, who was a pretty good PGA Tour player in his day and had also won a Champions Tour major. He was a proud Kansas State alum.

We catch up with them on one of the tee boxes, and Colbert sees Coach and congratulates him on playing in the national championship. He says, "Damn shame you don't have a defense like we do at K-State."

After they left the tee box, Coach Spurrier says to me, "Wait until he finds out I just hired his defensive coordinator."

It was the first time Coach Spurrier went out of his comfort zone to hire a coach. He only hired coaches he knew or followed. Steve didn't know Bob at all.
—Jamie Speronis, Florida graduate assistant, senior administrative assistant, director of football administration, 1988–2001

He wanted to see the game from somebody else's perspective. Steve Spurrier certainly gave him that. He had Hayden, then Bill, now this.

It was time to go somewhere else. Florida was on a different level.
—Kenny Mossman

At the time, I was Florida's fourth defensive coordinator in seven years under Coach Spurrier. I was going to install a four-to-three defense that was much different from what Florida had used in the previous few years. We were going to be aggressive, drop players in and out of the box, blitz, and implement a claustrophobic type of bump-and-run man coverage. Nebraska had used elements of that same design to beat the Gators in the national championship.

Not a lot of teams were using those types of coverage techniques. They're popular now, but not so much back then. Wide receivers generally don't like physical play. We wanted to crowd the receivers, challenge them on every route they ran.

At K-State, we not only were number one in total defense, but we limited offenses to the lowest number of plays in the nation. Fewer plays for Gator opponents would mean more opportunities for Coach Spurrier to run more plays. He liked that.

He ran the offense; I ran the defense. Our defense had worked in the Big Eight, and I was confident it would work in the SEC.

And then I faced Coach Spurrier's offense.

I got to Gainesville in late February. I quickly installed our defense during spring practice, and in March we had our first scrimmage. Ones versus Ones. My guys against Coach Spurrier, quarterback Danny Wuerffel, running back Fred Taylor, and wide receivers Jacquez Green, Ike Hilliard, and Reidel Anthony.

"All right, Bobby, here we go," he said.

The ball was placed on the thirty-five-yard line. Three plays later— boom, boom, boom—the ball was in the end zone.

"All right, Bobby, let's spin it around," he said.

The ball was put on the thirty-five going the other way.

Three plays, another touchdown.

We went Twos versus Twos. Same thing. More touchdowns.

We blitzed. We faked blitzes. We told our corners to crowd the receivers. We tried everything.

I was the new, supposedly hotshot defensive coordinator, and my defense couldn't stop anybody. I was shaken. I rocketed my visor off of somebody's helmet. As I watched Coach Spurrier's offense score at will, I wondered if I really belonged here...if my defensive philosophy would actually work.

Then I heard Coach Spurrier yell from across the field. "Hey, Bobby!" he said in that clipped sort of way of his, "You think we're gonna be able to force a punt this year?"

My face turned red with anger and embarrassment.

After the scrimmage, Steve walked over to me, put his hand on my shoulder, and said, "Don't worry about it, Bobby—you're not going to see anybody like us this year. Keep doing what you're doing."

And he was right. The "Fun-n-Gun" offense was virtually unstoppable.

After our first week of practice, we had a staff meeting. Coach Spurrier was fired up about the team.

Coach went around the room. Then he got to Bob. "Bobby, what do you think so far?"

Bob said, "Coach, we're the biggest bunch of pansies I've ever seen in my life. Coach, we have got to hit."

Because of that, Coach switched the way we practiced. We had a laid-back night practice on Monday but then went full pads on Tuesday and Wednesday. That was Bob insisting that we get tougher. He brought a level of toughness that we had never had.

—Jamie Speronis

I survived that first spring. The other assistant coaches were so accepting of me, as were the players. Carol and I bought a house. In fact, my brother Mark, who had taken a job as a defensive backs coach on Leavitt's USF staff, drove over from Tampa and helped paint it.

In July, we had our first child: Mackenzie Rae Stoops. She had been born five weeks premature, and it had been a difficult pregnancy for Carol.

Speronis came by the hospital to see how everyone was doing. When he walked in the room, we had birthing videotapes and books all over the place. It was like we were cramming for a final exam. With our move to Florida and Carol going into labor early, we had never had a chance to go through any formal classes. We hadn't had time even to buy a crib or a car seat. We were scared and didn't know anything.

Speronis shook his head and said, "Bobby, it's a little late to worry about this."

Coach Spurrier sent along his regards. He always said that whenever an assistant coach had a baby, it was good luck for the Gators.

Carol and I couldn't believe our luck. For starters, we saw each other more. That's because a Florida off-season was much different from a Kansas State off-season. There were no mandatory 1:00 p.m. summer staff meetings. Nobody discouraged us from playing golf. In fact, Coach Spurrier was usually the first one on the tee box.

We played one time at a local Gainesville course with Speronis and a couple of NBA refs that Jamie knew. I wasn't a great player, but on a long par 5, I reached the green in two shots. I was staring at an eagle, or at the very worst, a birdie.

Instead, I four-putted for a bogey.

I'm not proud of this, but after my fourth putt, I helicoptered my putter some twenty or thirty yards off the green and toward our golf cart. It spun around and around, and just as it was about to hit the ground, I saw a squirrel dart directly into its landing path. It hit the squirrel flush, and the squirrel staggered back, dazed.

One of the NBA refs said, "Bob, you've got to take that squirrel out now."

I couldn't believe it. First, I had four-putted after reaching the green in two. Then I had hit a squirrel—and was going to have to put it out of its misery?

I started to walk toward the injured squirrel. As I got closer, the squirrel came to life—like someone had given it smelling salts—took a look at me and then ran off. Suddenly, I had never been so happy to make a bogey.

When I got to the office the next day, there was a squirrel doll sitting on the middle of my desk. It had a bandage on its head and tiny ears, and there was fake blood smeared on its body.

I put the squirrel on an office shelf. Later that fall, my mom came to visit. "What is this squirrel doing here?" she said.

I think she thought I'd killed it and had it stuffed. By the way, it was the last time I ever helicoptered a golf club.

* * *

My Gators coaching debut took place in The Swamp against then–Southwest Louisiana (now called University of Louisiana at Lafayette). In the Florida media guide, which was thick enough to crush a small dog, I was now referred to as "Bob," not "Bobby."

We returned two fumbles for touchdowns and two interceptions for touchdowns in the 55–21 win. That next day, Coach Spurrier knocked on my office door, stuck his head in, and said, "Bobby, I bet you we'll outscore you next week."

We played another home game, this time against Georgia Southern, a Division I-AA program with a funky, flex bone option attack. It wasn't an offense you saw on a regular basis. It was a ball-control offense designed to shorten the game, to keep things close.

The final score wasn't close—62–14—but there were times during the game that Georgia Southern used up large chunks of the clock. They converted a handful of fourth downs to maintain possession of the ball—and keep it out of the hands of Coach Spurrier, who got more frustrated as the game went on.

Not long before the end of the first half, he got on the headphones and started chiding me. "Just let 'em score, Bobby," he said. "We'll score a TD and get it back."

Later, he asked one of our players what defensive coverage we were in. The player told him, and Coach said something about us being in a bad coverage.

We scored a defensive touchdown before the game was done, but we also gave up 311 yards to Georgia Southern. I wasn't happy about that, but I was absolutely furious about what Coach Spurrier had said to me during the game.

It was that triple-option stuff, hard to get them off the field. Steve got frustrated, and I remember after the game that Bobby was not happy.

I asked, "You OK, Bobby?"

He said, I'm going to talk to the Head Ball Coach. That's not going to happen again."

He went to the elevator on the other side of the weight room. I never followed up.

—Jeremy Foley

I left the locker room after the game. I found Carol—she was feeding our baby daughter—and I said, "Let's get out of here." Usually we'd hang with the other families, but I wasn't in a mood to be social.

"What's wrong?" asked Carol.

"It isn't good. Let's get out of here."

I walked up to my office to get my things before heading home. Coach tapped on the door. "Bobby, don't let that bother you," he said. "It's all right." He thought I was upset about the 311 yards.

"No, Coach, it isn't all right," I said. "I'm not going to work that way. I'm not going to have someone pester me, agitate me during the game. If you want to offer something constructive, I want it. But I'm not going to work like this."

And then I left.

The next morning, Coach came to my office again and acted as if what had happened during Saturday's game was no big deal. But it was a big deal to me. I'd never had a coach look over my shoulder and second-guess me during a game. It was a big enough deal that I told Coach, "I'm not worried about me finding another job."

"Nah, nah," he said, "we don't need to do anything like that." Then, about what he had done—telling me to let the other team score and asking players about coverages—he added, "It won't happen again." And it never did. From that day on, we had nothing but a great relationship. In fact, we couldn't have had a better one.

With the Georgia Southern episode behind us, we began preparing for Tennessee. We had a bye week before we played at Knoxville, and already the media and fans were calling it one of those game-of-the-century types of deals.

We were ranked number four. They were ranked number two and had preseason Heisman favorite Peyton Manning. Tennessee had just expanded its stadium, and everybody knew that UT coach Phillip Fulmer wanted nothing more than to beat his nemesis, Spurrier. Florida had won four of the last five meetings, including a 62–37 win in 1995. The game was going to be on national television. The winner would have the early inside track to the SEC Championship and maybe a national championship.

If it had been Coach Snyder, we would have worked the entire bye week, including the weekend. But Coach Spurrier had a different way of dealing with those situations.

This was going to be my first big game at Florida, so I wanted to have everything buttoned up early. If that meant grinding through the bye week, I was fine with that. But Coach Spurrier had other plans. He said we were going to the beach.

Sure enough, we headed to Crescent Beach for a bye-week break. Instead of using every waking minute of extra time preparing for Manning and Tennessee, I was floating in the Atlantic with Coach Spurrier.

"Bobby, you think Phil Fulmer is in the ocean today?"

"No, Coach, I believe he isn't. I'm having a hard time believing I am."

Coach Spurrier was fabulous. He was the best. He just exuded such confidence and assuredness, and it rubbed off on the players and assistant coaches. You knew that any time you went out there, you were going to win. He was demanding, but he also made sure it was fun. He knew the right time to take a little break, to relax.

The more time I spent with Coach, the more I realized that we were very similar. My demeanor was closer to his than to that of any other coach I'd known. I'm my father's son, so I always shared traits with him, but Coach Spurrier was a scrapper, always in the middle of it—just like I was as a kid.

He valued family time. So did I. It wasn't unusual to see the kids of the assistant coaches running down the hallways of the football offices. He encouraged us to take our kids to school in the morning, to make time for dinner with our family each night.

He wanted us to work smart. It wasn't about how many hours you put in but about what you accomplished during those hours.

Snyder had had his way of doing things, and it was successful for him. But as I watched Coach Spurrier, it was obvious that there was another way to coach and win. You didn't have to guard your desk. You didn't have to have long meetings just so you could say you had a long meeting. More wasn't always better. At Florida, less *was* more.

When we landed in Knoxville for the Tennessee game, our players and staff reflected Coach Spurrier's easy confidence. The media was calling it the biggest game in Tennessee history, and nobody from the Tennessee program, which had won eleven games in a row, was disputing the description.

I had never seen so many people — 107,608, to be exact — shoehorned into a stadium. At the time, it was the largest crowd in college football history. It didn't matter that we were playing in the rain. It wouldn't have mattered if there were lava flows coming out of the Neyland Stadium scoreboard.

In less than twenty minutes, we led, 35–0, including a defensive touchdown (our sixth of the season). We forced three turnovers in the first 19:54 of the game and six in the first half.

With about ten minutes left in the second quarter, Manning found Peerless Price wide open on a seventy-two-yard touchdown pass. Coach Spurrier was instantly in my ear. "Bobby, what the hell are we doing?" he asked.

But Coach Spurrier later found out that Teako Brown, our starting safety, had taken himself out of the game and put in a backup on his own. The backup was out of position on the play. I hadn't wanted to say anything to Coach about it. It wouldn't have been fair to Teako or to the backup.

Manning threw on almost every down in the second half, and the Vols scored twenty-nine straight points.

What mattered in our 35–29 win were the turnovers we caused and the sacks and near sacks we used to pressure Manning. We made a great quarterback look ordinary at times. Against Peyton, that was no small thing. We also held UT to the sixth-fewest rushing yards in SEC history at the time.

When Nebraska was upset at Arizona State that night, we moved from number four to number one — and we stayed that way until we played number-two Florida State and Bowden in Tallahassee on the last game of our regular season.

I did not know him until he came to Florida. But I tried to learn everything I could about him.

Bob would walk the corners right up to the receiver's face and then handle you the whole time you ran your routes. We weren't used to that. It was the first time we faced a press defense. We had to really change our pass patterns once he came in there.

I thought he presented the toughest defense when I was coaching at Florida State. Him, and the other was Jimmy Johnson at Miami. You had your hands full when you coached against them.

— Bobby Bowden, Florida State head coach, 1976–2009

We were undefeated, and then we weren't. Warrick Dunn rushed for a career-high 185 against us. It was our first regular season loss in twenty-eight games.

The FSU fans tore down the goalposts. We got off the field before the police started using pepper spray to disperse the crowd.

Our national championship scenarios now relied on others, which is the worst feeling in the world. We needed to beat Alabama in the SEC Championship and then hope Texas, a twenty-point underdog to Nebraska, could win the Big 12 Championship. Their Big 12 game would be played at noon on December 7, ours later that night.

I knew all about Nebraska. I didn't like Texas's chances.

Final score: Texas 37, Nebraska 27.

Final score: Florida 45, Bama 30.

Bowden wasn't happy about it, but we had a rematch in the Sugar Bowl.

Shortly after midnight of our SEC Championship win, I stood in a corner of our locker room at the Georgia Dome and made a phone call to Minneapolis. Nobody except Coach Spurrier knew it at the time, but I was supposed to fly to Minnesota that Sunday morning and meet with school officials about becoming their next head coach.

I didn't want to go. I called my Minnesota contact and said I was canceling the trip. At the time, the school had yet to name a replacement for university president Nils Hasselmo. Hasselmo was going to retire in June 1997, but his successor hadn't been announced yet.

The Minnesota official asked me to reconsider. He said it was important that I follow through on the trip, that it would make the school look bad if I canceled at the last minute.

Against my better judgment, I said I would be there.

We flew back to Gainesville, and the coaches and wives met at our favorite hangout, Napolatanos, to celebrate. Carol and I got home at about 5:00 a.m. and regrouped and packed, and then we headed to the airport, where Minnesota officials had a private plane waiting for us.

There was snow on the ground when we landed, and it was forty-five degrees colder in the Twin Cities than it had been when we left Gainesville. We had Mackie bundled up in a puffy down onesie. Carol's sister, who lived in Minneapolis, met us at the airport and took care of Mackie for the day.

Athletic director Mark Dienhart was the point man. They gave us the tour of the town, campus, and facilities and even took us to the governor's mansion in St. Paul. Carol spent part of the day with Dienhart's wife touring the Twin Cities and looking at potential neighborhoods for houses.

Minnesota was starved for a winner. It hadn't won as many as seven games or been to a bowl game since 1985. It was looking for the secret sauce: how to turn a perennial loser into a winner. I had been part of turnarounds at Iowa and Kansas State, and it certainly helped to have been the defensive coordinator on Coach Spurrier's staff.

Minnesota's people indicated that I was their first choice, but I told them that the circumstances made me uncomfortable. They had an outgoing school president, but they didn't have an incoming one yet. I needed to talk to *that* person before I could make an informed decision.

Don't get me wrong; it was a job with potential. Minnesota was a Big Ten school in an urban area. It was *the* state school. Alvarez had used the same reasoning to take the Wisconsin job in 1990, and by his fourth season, he had the Badgers in the Rose Bowl. If you could do that at Wisconsin, you could do it at Minnesota.

But the more I talked with Carol and Coach Spurrier, the more I realized this wasn't going to work. I think I knew it before I got there, and I definitely knew it during the interview. "You're thirty-six. We're not going bad; we're going to play for more national championships," said Coach Spurrier. "If it isn't right, then wait for the right job, the one you really want."

I agreed. Plus, I wanted to be around him longer. I wanted to learn more from him. I had only been at Florida for ten months. I felt a loyalty to him and Jeremy for bringing me to this great program, accepting me as a late addition to the staff, making me part of this fantastic football journey.

I didn't want to be a one-and-done assistant coach. What, we win the SEC Championship, we're going to play for the national championship in the Sugar Bowl, and I'm just going to bolt at the first head coaching opportunity?

I thanked Minnesota for its interest but said that I was no longer a candidate.

I didn't know about it at the time—we were shoulder-pad deep in our prep work for the Bama game—but two days before the SEC Championship, the St. Paul *Pioneer Press* reported that Coach Snyder had been in "extensive and highly confidential talks" with Minnesota about the job. According to the paper, Snyder had turned down a big-money offer a weekend earlier.

To this day, I don't know if that's true. Dienhart has never said so publicly, nor has Coach Snyder. If it is true, it was a smart move by Minnesota to try to hire him. He had a Big Ten coaching background and impeccable credentials. I would have tried to hire him, too.

But it doesn't matter. I wasn't leaving Florida for Minnesota.

Coach Spurrier entered that national championship game with a 2–5–1 record against Bowden while at Florida. He had played in one previous national championship game, and his team had been humbled.

But was he tight? No, of course not. He had a four-year starter at quarterback who had just won the Heisman Trophy. He had devised a way to counteract FSU's pass rush: use the shotgun snap on every play. He had revenge on his side.

We never trailed in the game. Florida State got as close as 24–20 in the third quarter, but then we scored twenty-eight consecutive points. It was like that spring practice scrimmage all over again, except this time, FSU defensive coordinator Mickey Andrews played the part of frustrated me.

Florida had its first-ever national championship. It was only fitting that Coach Spurrier was the guy to do it.

For me, it had been a twelve-month period like no other. I had left Kansas State, seen my defense torched in my first-ever Florida scrimmage, welcomed my first child into the world (Coach Spurrier was right about Mackie being good luck), confronted my new head coach, bobbed in the ocean with my new head coach, withstood and savored the pressure games, seen my players step up to every challenge, recovered from a crushing loss to our in-state rival, and been part of an SEC Championship win and then a national championship effort.

Life was good. It was better than good.

But here's a confession: after we won that national championship and Carol and I got back to the hotel room just as the sun was rising, I had a sinking, sad feeling. I remember thinking, *It's over.*

To me, the best part had been the chase. Now that we had won, tomorrow was going to be boring. I liked the fight, the pursuit, the battle of it all. I was almost disappointed that the journey had ended.

Of course, if you believe in fate and destiny—and I do, to a great extent—then August 23, 1997, is a date that deserves mention. We had just finished a scrimmage (our season opener wasn't until the following week against The Citadel) and had filed into the locker room.

There was a game on TV. I instantly recognized the uniforms: it was Oklahoma. The Sooners were playing—and getting their tails kicked—by Northwestern at Soldier Field. The final score was 24–0.

I shook my head sadly, tapped the screen, and told the other coaches in the room, many of whom had no idea how powerful OU football had once been, "That is a crying shame. That is a sleeping giant right there. Oklahoma is a sleeping giant."

Nobody seemed too interested in my assessment. But they had no sense of Big Eight and Big 12 football history. Or maybe they hadn't painted their cleats Joe Washington silver when they were high schoolers.

Life as the defending national champions (but this time without Wuerffel) went well in 1997 until, as the number-one team in the country, we lost at LSU and then, two games later, to Georgia. But we ended the season with a win against FSU and, later, a Citrus Bowl victory against Penn State.

Between the win against FSU and the bowl game, the coaches hit the road for recruiting. Recruiting never has a start or finish. It seemingly goes on forever.

I had been on the road for about a week, long enough for Texas to interview and hire Mack Brown from North Carolina. I walked into the house, dropped my bags, and expected to be greeted with a warm welcome. Instead, I found Carol in front of the TV, and she didn't look happy. "Bobby, how could you not have told me we were going to Texas?" she asked, making no attempt to hide her disappointment in me.

"Texas?" I said. "What are you talking about?"

"They just said on TV that you're taking a job with your good friend Mack Brown," Carol said.

I started laughing. "I don't even know Mack Brown. I've never talked to him."

"Well, that's not what they just said on TV."

The wife of one of our coaches had called Carol earlier in the day and said, "I can't believe you're going to Texas."

"What? Why would we do that?" Carol said.

"Because they're going to pay you $650,000," said the coach's wife.

Then Jeremy Foley had called the house and told Carol, "Please have Bobby call me before you two commit to go anywhere."

I had to talk Carol off the ledge. This was the first time we had ever experienced a rumor that was so detailed, so public, and so untrue.

Once I had convinced her the story was completely false, the phone rang. It was Coach Spurrier. He was in Tampa on a recruiting trip. "Hey, Stoopsy," he said, barely able to contain his laughter. "I heard you're going to Texas with your good friend Mack Brown."

He knew it wasn't true. Nothing against Mack Brown or Texas, but I wouldn't have left Florida for a lateral or lesser move there. Once again, it just goes to show that you can't believe everything you see or hear.

And shortly after that nonsense, I got a call from the legendary Frank Broyles, a former coach and then–athletic director at Arkansas. He had just fired Danny Ford, and he needed a new head coach. Would I be interested in interviewing for the job?

I don't know why, exactly, but I politely turned down the request. I wasn't sure I would be a good fit at Arkansas. But, knowing what I know now, that was probably a foolish decision. In retrospect, I should have taken a look at it. But I was happy at Florida. It was paying me more than I ever could have expected, and I had one of the best bosses in the business. Plus, we had a team that could win it all in 1998.

As it turned out, 1998 was a what-could-have-been season. We lost at Tennessee early but worked our way back to number four in the polls headed into our final regular season game, this time at Florida State.

Going into the November 15 game at FSU, undefeated Tennessee was ranked number one in the *AP* poll, and Coach Snyder and K-State were ranked number two, followed by undefeated UCLA.

If we beat the Seminoles, we still had a tiny chance of playing for a national championship. And wouldn't it be something if we somehow ended up playing Kansas State?

Instead, we lost. No back-to-back titles for the Gators.

Two days after our loss to the Noles, I heard the news about one of my football heroes: Coach Fry, at age sixty-nine, was calling it quits.

After thirty-seven seasons, three different schools, 420 games, 232 wins, and seventeen bowl appearances, Coach Fry walked away from the football—and the program—he loved. He did it with tears in his eyes.

It had been a tough season for Coach Fry. Iowa had finished 3–8, which was his worst record in twenty years with the Hawks. There had been injuries and a rough finish where Iowa had lost six of its last seven games.

But true Iowa fans could forgive him for that. Instead, they remembered the seventeen consecutive nonwinning seasons before he got to Iowa City. They remembered his three Rose Bowl appearances. They remembered his 143–89–6 record, his three Big Ten titles, and fourteen bowl games. They remembered his character—and him *being* a character.

In many ways, I owed my career to him. That was a man you'd run through *two* walls for.

Then, almost immediately after Coach Fry's announcement, my name was mentioned in the media for the job. I understood why, but I hated it.

I'd always thought there was a vulture-ish quality to fans and reporters who treated firings and hirings like some sort of sport. I had seen another view of it. I had seen good friends and good coaches who had their lives and their family's lives turned upside down by those firings. I understand the public interest, but I never understood — and still don't — how rumors can somehow pass for facts or even educated guesses.

Coach Fry hadn't been fired, but I'm sure he would have preferred to leave under different circumstances. Anybody who watched him pause to compose himself that day, or who heard his voice crack as he talked about his time at Iowa, knew the human investment in these jobs.

I never commented about other positions, especially if there wasn't an official opening. I had made it clear to reporters that I wanted to be a head coach and that I felt prepared for the next step in my career. But I didn't lobby, publicly or privately, for jobs.

Because of my connection to Iowa, and because I had gained some momentum as an assistant coach, reporters often asked me about the Hawkeyes job. I would always say the same thing: that I'd forever have a soft spot in my heart for the place and that whenever Coach Fry left, there would be no shortage of people who wanted to run that program.

Now the rumor machine roared to life again. I stayed away from the moving parts.

Meanwhile, Florida tumbled to number eight in the polls after our regular season-ending loss to FSU. We moved up to number seven after the November 28 games. But here's the crazy part: if we just could have beaten FSU, we would have been in perfect position for the two-peat.

Why? December 5, 1998, that's why.

On that day, unranked Miami beat number-three UCLA, and Texas A&M beat Kansas State, which was number two in the *AP* poll. Our jaws dropped in Gainesville.

Had we beaten FSU, we would have been ranked no worse than number four and in no danger of losing again, because our regular season schedule was complete. We would have sat back and watched in amazement — like the rest of the country did — as the upsets took place on December 5.

I felt bad for us. If we had taken care of business, it would have been us in the national title game.

I felt bad for Kansas State and Snyder. I still knew players and coaches on that staff, including my brother Mike, who was the defensive coordinator at the time. I knew how much it would have meant to that community and university to play for number one.

Tennessee would go on to beat Florida State in the Fiesta Bowl for the national championship. I didn't care. I don't even know if I watched the game.

I had more important things to do.

I had a new job. I was a head coach.

Chapter Seven

Ready

The sleeping giant called me.

So did Mama.

Oklahoma was the giant, the program I had followed since my high school days.

"Mama"—that's how Bear Bryant described his alma mater when he left Texas A&M to return to Alabama—was Iowa, *my* alma mater.

It all happened because of back-to-back blockbuster announcements.

On November 22, 1998, Oklahoma fired head coach John Blake.

On November 23, Coach Fry resigned at Iowa.

Both programs obviously had great professional and personal appeal to me. And I was thrilled when representatives from each school asked if I would interview for their respective openings.

The first would be with the Oklahoma contingent. We were scheduled to meet at the Dallas–Fort Worth International Airport. The next day, I'd fly to Atlanta to meet with the Iowa people.

The day before I was supposed to fly to Dallas, I was with Carol and our daughter, Mackie, at our condo in Crescent Beach. Coach Spurrier and his family were there, too.

We were sitting at the pool with our families, just relaxing in the sun, and Coach Spurrier said, "Bobby, I'm just thinking this through. I'm sure you got a really good chance at Iowa. I bet Oklahoma will try to hire an established head coach."

I nodded, but as Coach Spurrier was talking, I suddenly realized that I didn't have a coat and tie with me. I had left them back in Gainesville. I had to jump in the car, go to a Belk's department store, and buy some dress clothes for the job interview Coach Spurrier *didn't* think would result in an offer.

As usual, word leaked out that I was on the list of OU's candidates. Instead of flying out of Gainesville, where I was worried about being recognized by fans or spotted by the media, I drove to the larger Jacksonville airport to catch my November 28 flight.

As I was trying to low-key it in the terminal, Jamie Speronis and his wife, Kristy, were in the same airport catching a flight to North Carolina. "Dude, what's up?" asked Speronis.

"Shhh," I said. "I'm trying to get out of here without anybody noticing."

Speronis moved along, but he later told me he'd seen a television cameraman prowling the area. The cameraman said he worked for a TV station in Oklahoma and had heard I was interviewing for the OU job.

Joe Castiglione was the newish athletic director at OU. He only had been there since late April 1998, having come from Missouri. Jim Leavitt, a former Mizzou player, had introduced me to Joe years earlier. It was a quick handshake, a few minutes of small talk. Now we were meeting a second time under much different circumstances.

Joe had inherited a mess in Norman. The program once known for national excellence was now known for semi-irrelevancy, for failure. It was hard to believe.

Oklahoma had gone through three coaches in ten years. There had been a steady decline and a steady parade of supposed answers. Howard Schnellenberger had lasted one year. Blake had followed him and averaged four wins a season.

Beginning in 1993, our K-State teams beat OU three years in a row, and another two straight times after I left for Florida. I had seen Oklahoma's troubles firsthand.

When I stepped in here, this place was divided, completely divided. There were the Bud Wilkinson players, the former Barry Switzer players, and players of other eras. There were all these individual factions. All of them cared about Oklahoma, but it was a house divided.

There were several other programs in the hunt for a new head coach: South Carolina, Iowa, Auburn, Duke, Clemson. I had a list, and it included a mixture of sitting head coaches and some top assistants, offensive and defensive coordinators. But Bob Stoops was clearly the assistant I wanted to know more about.

I also had an awareness of other universities pursuing him in the past... They were in the Big Ten, they were in the SEC, but he hadn't left. I thought, "This is interesting. Perhaps he's waiting for a different type of situation and opportunity."

There was more than tacit pressure conveyed to me that we should hire a sitting head coach at Oklahoma, and I can understand why. The challenges were big. The program had lost its way. The natural thinking is to get someone with head coaching experience.

> — Joe Castiglione, University of Oklahoma vice-president for
> intercollegiate athletics programs and director of athletics,
> 1998–present

Oklahoma, man, it was a dumpster fire back then.

> — Jamie Speronis

My first game here, 1998, and its many hours before kickoff... the practice fields were near the stadium, and they had a high row of cedars around them, and there was a chain-link fence and barbed wire on it.

I happened to be out on those fields on the south end of the stadium, and the gates were open. People started to drive their cars onto the practice field. I ran over to the attendant and asked, "What in the world are you doing?"

He asked, "What are you talking about?"

I said, "Cars are driving onto the practice field. You can't have cars on the practice field."

He said, 'We've been doing this every year. This is the Touchdown Club, and they park their cars on the practice field."

And, sure enough, ninety minutes before the game, the place is packed with cars. People are tailgating where our team is supposed to conduct practice. I was in utter amazement.

I go out to the next practice, and there is food and trash on the field. It might seem like a crazy, silly, bizarre example, but it's just another indicator about where the priorities were.

I told somebody that day, that will be the last time that happens... some of the culture needed to be fixed.

—Joe Castiglione

We had been running in the red and had built up a large debt. Joe was already working things toward the right paths—working the budgets, starting to pay off part of the debt.

As I looked at it, you can only live on your reputation so long before it erodes away completely. The great football heritage was really on the ropes after four, five, six years of bad records, dissatisfied fans, and half-empty stadiums. I remember one time we brought a lot of underprivileged kids to the stadium and gave away free tickets so we'd have a decent crowd.

We were under tremendous pressure to rebuild this program, to rebuild it with the right person, and we didn't have any margin for error. If we waited too long... the heritage would be gone, the strength of the brand would be gone, and the following that OU football had would be impaired, perhaps permanently.

I even talked to [former OU all-conference back and legendary Texas coach] Darrell Royal. When I had to make a change with our coach, I called him and asked, "Coach, you ever watch the OU games?"

He said he watched the replays.

I said, "What do you think about the situation with our football team? What do you think of our football coach?"

He said, "I don't think you have a football coach."

—David Boren, University of Oklahoma president, 1994–2018

When I got on the plane to Dallas, I wasn't nervous. In a way, I was playing with house money.

As much as I was interested in the OU and Iowa jobs, I wasn't desperate to be a head coach. I didn't *have* to have it. If the worst thing that happened to me is that I remained at Florida for another season—or more—I was fine with that. There would be other head coaching opportunities.

Still, I was as ready as I could be.

I had played for two skilled and accomplished high school coaches: my dad and Don Bucci. They had instilled in me the values of preparation, respect, and toughness.

At Iowa, we had been at rock bottom. Coach Fry had rebuilt the program by the power of his personality, through his ability to identify and develop players and assistant coaches, and with his willingness to adapt.

At Kansas State, I had witnessed Coach Snyder build that program basically from scratch. He had almost willed the program to success.

Both Coach Fry and Snyder were like watchmakers, carefully and meticulously assembling their programs one tiny piece at a time. No detail was too small—from a day-to-day, week-to-week, month-to-month schedule to recruiting to helmet logos, to birthday cards to painting the visitor's locker room pink, to making sure everyone in the building knew, understood, and could execute the plan.

Coach Spurrier and Fry had taught me the importance of life/work balance, of taking chances, of swagger. They were good, they knew they were good, and if you followed their lead, you'd be good, too.

Coach Spurrier is the guy I most wanted to emulate. He embraced the expectations, the competition, the challenges. He was so sure of himself. I loved everything about his style, though I could never do the shirtless thing at practice like he would do later while coaching at South Carolina. That takes real confidence.

I know everybody refers to Coach Spurrier as the HBC: Head Ball Coach. But when he calls my cell phone, the initials *SOS* pop onto the screen. That stands for "Steve Orr Spurrier." He is my guy, my mentor. People ask if he's like a brother to me. He's more like an uncle—a really cool, fun, smart, talented, competitive uncle.

My time with him at Florida had prepared me to run an elite program. I had watched Coach Spurrier deal with the daily crush of duties. Everything at Florida was turned to a higher volume: the expectations, the goals, the facilities, the recruiting, the media, the staff size, the budgets. He handled and delegated. He gave you a job and trusted you to do it. I'm a big believer in the power of positivity, and he exuded it.

It might seem like a small thing, but Coach Spurrier had insisted that I meet with the media shortly after his weekly press sessions. At Kansas State, that would almost never have happened. Assistant coaches were off-limits to reporters during the week—Coach Snyder's orders.

By doing those weekly mini press conferences at Florida, I became more comfortable in front of cameras and notepads. I was getting media reps, just like a player gets practice reps with the first team.

Everybody was aware of the Stoops boys at Iowa. Coach Fry was putting out coaches at the time. There were a group of young guys at Kansas State with Bill Snyder, where you were going to work hard and have a very sound, fundamental base. I think Bob was very lucky to have mentored under him.

Then he went to Steve Spurrier, and Steve is one of the great offensive minds.

So two very different styles. Two very distinct personalities and philosophies. And I think that's good, if you could recommend a way to come up in the business. And then to have played for Hayden Fry, who was an innovator.

Bob was lucky to play for a dad who was a coach, too. And he had brothers who played and coached.

—Mack Brown, University of Texas head coach, 1998–2013; North Carolina head coach, 2019–present

I didn't go into those Oklahoma and Iowa interviews with a twenty-point plan or a PowerPoint presentation. I wasn't going to hand them a defensive playbook and pretend I was some sort of schematic genius.

What I had to offer was five years of squeezing the most out of my physical abilities as a player at Iowa. It was another five years learning from one of the best head coaches and staffs ever assembled. It was helping resurrect an Iowa program.

It was seven years of painstaking work at Kansas State, where they not only had forgotten how to win but, until we got there, had barely won at all.

It was three years with the charismatic and otherworldly gifted Coach Spurrier. It was a place where we had already won one national title, where anything less than an SEC Championship or a national championship was considered a disappointment.

President Boren was on the American Airlines board of directors at the time, so he arranged for the November 29 interview at a conference room in the Admiral's Club at DFW. He would tell me later that it was the same conference room where Joe had been interviewed by OU earlier that April.

There were about ten representatives from OU there: President Boren, Joe, three members of the board of regents (any more than three and it would have been a quorum, which means it would have had to be a public meeting), and a handful of advisers and consultants.

Joe and I had talked repeatedly on the phone throughout the week. In fact, I even had met with Joe at DFW on Wednesday, November 25. He had walked me through the entire situation at Oklahoma, the good and the bad. He was honest about it. He said he was "unpacking the entire suitcase" of OU's troubles. It was a very large piece of luggage.

We discussed the program's culture, scheduling philosophy, conditioning programs, sports medicine, facilities, and the hiring of assistant coaches and staff. If it related to OU football, we talked about it.

Joe had done his homework on me. He had spoken with Coach Snyder, Jeremy Foley, and Coach Spurrier. He had talked with folks in the Iowa program. He had spoken with a prominent Florida high school coach about my recruiting methods, and the same coach mentioned the time his team had arrived early at a Gainesville stadium for their state championship game, only to find themselves locked out—and that I had helped make sure they had gotten into the stadium and settled properly.

Once Joe called, well, that was the type of place made for Bobby Stoops. Incredible resources and history.

It was the perfect job. This will be the perfect job for him.

—Jeremy Foley

I arrived at DFW under the assumption that there were other candidates for the job. I didn't know who they were, and I didn't care. Joe would later tell reporters that several "very notable" college head coaches had reached out to him about the job. A couple of NFL coaches also had contacted him.

Makes sense. Even though the OU program was covered in mediocrity at the time, it was still Oklahoma.

We whittled it down to two, and a backup if I needed to go there. To this day, I've never told anyone who the other coaches were.

—Joe Castiglione

When we got down to the end, Bob Stoops was one of the three. [Then–TCU coach Dennis] Franchione was also on the short list.

—David Boren

The interview began at 11:00 a.m. that Sunday. I was the first guy to be interviewed. I was straightforward in my assessment of the OU program. In our earlier phone conversations, Joe had briefed me on all the internal challenges facing the program, so I addressed those head-on, too.

It would not be an easy fix, but Iowa hadn't been easy, Kansas State hadn't been easy. Oklahoma wouldn't have been looking for another head coach if it were easy. But I knew it could be fixed, and I felt confident that I knew how to fix it.

The school reps in the room took turns asking me questions. I didn't hard-sell myself. That's not me. I simply outlined my philosophies and my understanding of OU, and I let my record as an assistant coach speak for itself.

Seven hours later, the interview ended. When I was done, Joe asked me to wait in a separate room.

When he finished, I turned to the group. "I know what I think, but I'd be curious to know what the rest of you think. You still want to speak with anyone else?"

—David Boren

Everybody in the room thought he was the right person to hire. We told the other candidate we weren't going to interview him at that time.

Someone in the room asked, "So who's going to give up his seat on the university plane so we can take Stoops back to Norman?"

—Joe Castiglione

Joe brought me back into the room, and I was offered the job, just like that. "You're going to be the next great coach at Oklahoma," he said.

Soon they put a contract in front of me and wanted me to sign it on the spot. That wasn't going to happen. "I don't feel comfortable signing something right now," I told Joe. "I'm not an attorney; I'm a football coach. I want to make sure it's what it needs to be. Surely you want a smart coach, don't you? You don't want one who's just going to sign something."

It seemed like Joe was a little bit upset about that. He wanted to close the deal. As much as I wanted the job, I wasn't going to sign a document without my lawyer and agent looking at it.

President Boren was standing nearby, and he sort of chuckled. He understood.

Nobody chuckled, however, when I told them that Iowa wanted to meet with me the next morning.

"It's my alma mater," I said. "I gave them my word that I would meet them face-to-face."

I felt I owed it to myself, to Iowa, and to Coach Fry, who had been so good to me, to honor that commitment. But I also knew I was risking the Oklahoma job. What if they gave me an ultimatum: choose now, or they're moving on to candidate number two? If they did, I was going to have to tell them that a promise was a promise—and I had promised the Iowa people I would meet with them in person.

Joe pulled me aside. "One of the things that makes you very attractive to the University of Oklahoma is your character," he said. "You're telling me you gave your word, and you're following through on it."

Joe didn't want me to go—he also made that clear. But he understood the connection between me and Iowa. So did President Boren. Before I left that day, he asked if he could speak privately with me.

President Boren said he knew this was a difficult decision, not so much because of the Iowa factor but because I had one chance to make the right decision for the right head coaching job.

And then he said something that meant a lot to me. He said, "We will not be fickle. We will stand by you and give you every opportunity to succeed. We will give you time to rebuild this program, and we will not interfere with the decisions you make. I just have a deep feeling that this is the right fit and that we share the same basic values. We hope you'll say yes to this."

I shook everyone's hand and told them how grateful I was for their time, their offer, and their understanding as it related to my Iowa visit. Then I had to catch a flight to Atlanta.

I had some delays and didn't get to my Atlanta hotel until late that night. I think I slept fine that Sunday night, but I know Joe didn't. He later told reporters that he was worried about the emotional pull of Iowa, that it would be hard for me to say no to my alma mater...to Mama.

I believe in the randomness of life. Things come to you for different reasons, and your faith and spirituality help you find meaning and purpose in those developments. Sometimes, things are just meant to be.

Going into those interviews with Oklahoma and Iowa, I prayed and asked God to give me some type of signal, to show me what was best for my life, for my family, to guide me down the right path.

I felt that Oklahoma was the stronger job overall. But Iowa was special to me for all the obvious reasons. I began preparing myself for the possibility of having to choose between the two.

My Monday, November 30, interview with the Iowa officials began later than scheduled. Bob Bowlsby was the Iowa athletic director, and he was there with a larger contingent than Oklahoma's.

I had promised to call Joe as soon as we were done with the interview, which I originally thought would be finished by late morning.

I can remember him calling me when he had a break during his Iowa interview. Oklahoma was putting pressure on him. He called and said Oklahoma needed an answer.

I told him, "Don't wait another second. Oklahoma is the better job. Take that job right now."

They had won national championships there. They had access to more players in driving distance. With Oklahoma and Texas, you don't have to leave that area for recruiting. They had great tradition. They had money, and they were hungry. It was the right time to go in there, because there was a little buffer, because they had had a few coaches who had stumbled.

—Barry Alvarez

Ten o'clock, eleven o'clock, twelve o'clock comes and goes. Joe was in my office. It was considerably later than when we'd expected a call.

—David Boren

Remember what I said about asking God to direct me to the right path? During the interview with the Iowa officials, it became clear that I wasn't going to get the job — at least not that day, I wasn't.

They told me they had an interview scheduled the next day with another candidate. I knew him: Kirk Ferentz.

Kirk is a good man, and I have great respect for him. He joined Coach Fry's staff as the offensive line coach when I was a junior at Iowa. I later got to know him better as a graduate assistant and volunteer coach there.

He had gone on to become a head coach at Maine and then coached for Bill Belichick at the Cleveland Browns. He had then followed the team to Baltimore when it became the Ravens. He had serious credentials. And he understood the football DNA of Iowa.

But I couldn't wait another day for Iowa to decide. It wouldn't have been fair to Oklahoma. And anyway, my path had been identified.

As I walked out of the Iowa interview without an offer, it hit me: *that was the sign . . . no offer!* OU wanted me . . . Iowa wasn't sure yet.

I thought, *Thanks, Lord. I get it now. But did you have to slap me in the face to make me understand?*

Carol and I talked about the decision. Iowa meant a lot to us. She had been born and raised in the state, had gone to school at Iowa. I had played there, worked there, developed friends for life there. But to everything, there is a season.

The phone rings. My secretary comes in and says, "It's Coach Stoops on the line."

—David Boren

I think President Boren and Joe were both on the line. I told them I had just finished talking with the Iowa folks. And then — and I didn't do it on purpose — I paused, probably too long for Joe's liking, and said, "I would just like to ask, when do you want me there?"

There were congratulations on their part, thank-yous on my part.

Joe said he was going to arrange for a booster's plane to bring Carol and me to Norman to sign the contract. He said he would carefully coordinate the announcement strategy and make sure all the details were in place before it became public.

By the time Joe had returned to his office from Evans Hall, the news was out. President Boren apparently had told a few people, who had told a few people, who had told a few people after that.

The next day, Iowa hired Kirk.

In retrospect, I probably should have accepted the Oklahoma job when it was first offered. If I had to do it over again, that's what I would have done. But I had given my word to Iowa, so I felt an obligation.

I'm not a fan of hypotheticals, but had Iowa also offered me its head coaching job, I think I still would have chosen Oklahoma. My emotional ties were—and still are—strong with Iowa. But I was ready for a new challenge in a new place.

Norman, Oklahoma, was it.

Chapter Eight

Lonely

Watch the video.

If you want to know exactly how it feels the moment your life changes in ways you can't yet calculate, watch the video of me being formally introduced as Oklahoma's twenty-first head football coach on December 1, 1998, at the university's Evans Hall.

I stepped up to the microphones. I grabbed the sides of the podium like they were the shoulder pads of a tight end I was trying to steer out of bounds. I took a big breath, as if was going to try to swim underwater across nearby Lake Thunderbird. You could see the reality of it all on my face: *Oh, shit, here we go.*

If you've ever taken a ride on the Slingshot at the State Fair of Texas, then you know what I mean. One moment, your life is orderly, safe, almost predictable. The next moment, you're flung into the upper reaches. You control nothing, yet you're supposed to control everything. The velocity of events stuns you—and you thought you were prepared. Hah. Nothing fully prepares you for the moment you become a head coach.

I relied on two words. I used them that day and every day after that for the next eighteen seasons.

No excuses.

That was my two-word mantra when I had interviewed with the selection group. That was my mantra when I stepped up to that podium, my heart trying to escape from my chest.

You can't rebuild a program if you make excuses. You can't earn trust if you make excuses. You can't overcome adversity if you make excuses.

128

Behind me and to my left at Evans Hall was Barry Switzer. Joe had called him the night before and asked if he would attend the announcement.

Coach Switzer was one of the first people to shake my hand before I addressed the crowd of OU supporters. He had never met me. He had barely heard of me. But he had made the effort to show up that day, to try to bridge the divide between the OU factions, to show support for the thirty-eight-year-old new coach. It was symbolic, but his gesture meant a lot to me.

Twenty-five years earlier, Oklahoma had hired a thirty-five-year-old first-time head coach. I know this because he was standing behind me and to my left that day. Even today, that photo of Coach Switzer on those steps remains one of my favorites. I even like that he once referred to the event as my "swearing in," as if I were an elected official.

I live on campus, about a mile or two from where the event occurred. I was there with [Oklahoma icon] Lee Allan Smith. I wanted to see the new coach.

I was in the crowd, and President Boren asked us to join them on stage. First time I'd met Bob Stoops. I didn't know he was on the [Iowa] squad with Hayden Fry.

I thought it was good he was an assistant coach. Oklahoma had always hired assistant coaches for the most part. I was glad he was coming up through the ranks. He was a defensive-minded guy. I liked that. The first thing you got to do is play good defense.

—Barry Switzer, Oklahoma head coach, 1973–1988

I think at the time when Coach came here, there was a hunger for a new vision, a new spirit, a confidence. When I look back on it, Coach walked onto this campus with confidence. Bob was never arrogant. He was sincere, confident.

Then he backed it up day by day, week by week, year by year.

It gave us all a lift.

—Sherri Coale, Oklahoma women's basketball head
coach, 1996–present

I was on the OU campus for the first time since 1994, when our Kansas State team beat the Sooners, 37–20. I had accepted the Oklahoma job without coming to Norman during the interview process.

In the morning, I introduced myself to the team. They sized me up, probably a thousand thoughts going through their minds. Would they get a fair shake with the new coach? Could he win? Should they transfer?

I had my own questions. OU was coming off a 5–6 season, and it hadn't been to a bowl game since 1994. My question wasn't, "Can we win?" We were going to win. I wanted to know how many players in that room were committed to winning.

I knew the players had been through a lot of turmoil. For fifth-year seniors at OU, I'd be their third head coach. Coaching changes are hard on a program. Instability creates doubt.

It was obvious that the previous regime or two hadn't had any true plans or strategies for success—or if they had, maybe nobody had believed in them. The program was in complete disarray. Those previous coaching staffs had been grasping at straws rather than trying to build something with a foundation.

The defense had played well for the most part. Rex Ryan, the defensive coordinator in 1998, had done a strong job. The offense, though, had struggled.

When I addressed the players that day, I wanted the message to be short and direct: I told them that I empathized with their situation (I had had two different head coaches during my first two years at Iowa), that I wanted their OU experience to be a good one. But there would be no excuses, and this would be no rebuilding year.

I told them that there were no preconceived notions about any players in that room. We were going to embrace them as if we had recruited all of them. They were our guys, and we were going to win or lose with them. We were very clear on how we were going to conduct the program. We were going to play hard, play smart, and be tough. Doing those things does not depend on talent.

I don't doubt that some of those guys were used to setting their own pace, setting their own tempo. Those days were over. We were going to do it our way, based on what we had done at Florida.

Coach Spurrier was my main template. I had seen how his inner confidence and presence could impact an entire team. I wanted to project that same attitude. We were also going to use his practice schedule, his month-by-month program schedule, his team pregame warm-up schedule... everything. Why wouldn't we? It had been so successful for Coach.

I also called Coach Holtz for advice. After all, he had a long history of rebuilding programs. "Bobby," he said, "there are three ways to get a team better: Recruit. Develop. Eliminate. You recruit the best talent, develop the best you got there, and eliminate."

"Eliminate?" I asked.

"Yeah. There are people pulling you down, not doing what needs to be done," Coach Holtz said. "You eliminate those. You tell 'em, 'Don't be one of those guys who needs to be eliminated.'"

I never watched football. I was just a kid from Union City, California, who liked to play tackle football. I didn't know coaches from other schools.

Everybody knew FSU because of their helmet. You knew Notre Dame because of the gold helmet. But I didn't know anything about Coach Stoops.

I came here in 1998. It's not bad. Only thing—I had seen that Twister *movie, so every time I saw a cloud, I thought it was a tornado.*

When they fired Coach Blake and before Coach Bob got there, we actually had a players' meeting—who's staying, who's leaving. When you get brought in by a different coach and then someone else takes over, there's going to be some rocky years.

Coach Bob was a young, energetic, hungry coach who wanted to win. I remember that first meeting. He laid down the gauntlet on us. We were sitting in the meeting room, and he introduced us to whatever staff he had at the time. He said his most important staff member was Jerry Schmidt. He said, "Don't come talk to me, talk to him."

"Him" was Jerry Schmidt. That was a man not to be messed with.

—Roy Williams, Oklahoma safety, 1998–2001

I was a junior at Fort Gibson [Oklahoma] High School. My dad said, "OU hired the defensive coordinator from Florida. Supposed to be an up-and-coming coach."

I knew nothing about him. We just didn't watch football that often. We didn't even have cable at my house until I was maybe a sophomore in high school.

No one from my school had ever had a scholarship to play Division I football. My grandma is from Kansas, but her family has roots in Nebraska. I was so embarrassed when I was in high school—my grandmother wrote a letter to Bobby Bowden about me. Her brother told Nebraska they should recruit me.

I never got a letter from anyone. No calls. No one did anything. The previous [OU] staff didn't recruit me at all.

But no, I knew nothing about him.

— Teddy Lehman, Oklahoma linebacker, 2000–2003

During that same morning, Joe gave me a tour of the facilities. Our offices were in trailers. Construction on the new football offices was about 85 percent complete, so we were in double-wides for the time being. I didn't care. I would have worked out of a booth at Waffle House.

As we were walking through the locker room, which hadn't been remodeled, Joe pointed to a dilapidated sign on the wall. The sign had split in two and was pointed downward. If you tilted your head just so, you could make out the words. One part of the sign read, "Sooner"; the other read, "Magic."

"Sooner Magic" was a Switzer phrase. I was sixteen when it was born on November 26, 1976. That's the day Oklahoma overcame a ten-point, fourth-quarter Nebraska lead in Lincoln—and did it late in the game with a fifty-yard halfback pass, then a hook-and-ladder play, then the game-winning three-yard TD run with thirty seconds left.

By the time Coach Switzer was done at Oklahoma, he had gone 12–5 against Nebraska.

Now Sooner Magic was gone. OU hadn't beaten Nebraska since 1991. The last two times they had played, 1996 and 1997, the Cornhuskers had won, 73–21 and 69–7. It also didn't help that the athletics department, thanks to the dismal state of the football program, was in hock millions and millions of dollars.

"Bob," said Joe, "is that not more than a physical sign, but an indication of what is broken here?"

He was right. OU needed its magic back.

The very first thing I did after I was formally introduced at OU was to get on my just-issued school cell phone and call one of the top players in the state, Jason White. White was a senior quarterback from nearby Tuttle, Oklahoma, and for reasons I'll never understand, OU hadn't made any effort to recruit him.

He was big (six foot three and 215 pounds at the time), athletic, strong, and a pro-style passer. I knew I wanted to throw the football, and I knew he could do it. So did the University of Miami: that's where he had verbally committed to play.

I remember coming home from school that day. My mom said the new coach from OU had called. She said she had never heard of this guy. I called him back.

He asked, "How long does it take to get to Tuttle?" I said about forty-five minutes. "Well, I'll be there in about forty-five minutes," he said.

I had made up my mind I was going to Miami. That's where I had made my first official recruiting trip. It was beautiful. I was wearing the Miami hat, Miami shirts. Everybody knew that's where I was going—until Coach Stoops came to the house.

—Jason White, Oklahoma quarterback 1999–2004

I hadn't packed anything. I had one suit. I thought I was going to have a chance to go back to Gainesville after the announcement, but I didn't have time. Everything came at me so fast. You think you're ready, but until you're exposed to the full scope of the job, you have no idea. In those first few days, it was like a giant wave swept over me, and I tried not to get pulled under. So I walked into the Whites' house, and the first thing I did was apologize for wearing the same clothes.

It was me, my mom and dad, and Coach Stoops. He said he was going to bring OU back to the national spotlight, and he said it with enough confidence that you believed him. Yeah, he's going to do it!

I loved OU. I remember growing up as a kid watching OU games with my dad on Saturdays. I was in OU's backyard, but Coach Blake never recruited me. It was devastating—they never even called.

At the very end of the conversation, he said, "All I'm asking is, at least come over to OU and see what we're about. Come see the guys. See how you'd fit in."

That's all he had to do, was to get me over there.

—Jason White

When I left Jason's house that night, I knew I had a chance. He was an Oklahoma kid. He knew I had a background of success and that I wanted to throw the football. That's how Coach Spurrier had won at Florida: throwing the football.

Not long after that, I went over to OU, and I kept telling myself, "Have an open mind. Put South Beach aside—and all the beautiful sites."

I'm walking through the halls at OU, and I see all the players on the wall that I had grown up watching.

I got home Sunday from my recruiting trip. I had basketball practice, got home from practice, and then took a nap. When I woke up, it hit me right there: I wanted to change my mind.

My mom and dad were on the front porch, and I said, "I'm going to go to OU." They sat there with their mouths wide open, because they knew how much I had wanted to go to Miami.

I called Coach Stoops. I said, "I changed my mind. I want to be part of this when you bring OU back to the national spotlight."

There was a long pause. Finally, he said, "I think I landed my first recruit."

—Jason White

Jason was a statement recruit for us. He was a good player, a dang good athlete in high school, and I knew we had to get him to get things started for us. The other recruits saw that. They saw the best player in Oklahoma was coming with us.

We were recruiting by the seat of our pants. I didn't have a coaching staff yet. It was like a mom-and-pop operation.

At the end of our first day at OU, after the press conference, the meetings, the tours, the interviews, the quick recruiting visit to Tuttle, Carol and I finally left campus for our room at a local bed-and-breakfast. We were overwhelmed by the day's events.

On our way back to the B and B, we stopped and ordered a pizza and then sat in the car until it was ready to go. When we got to our room, Carol closed all the drapes, and for the first time that day, we felt a sense of control and privacy. We could exhale. We weren't on display anymore.

As we sat at the kitchen table and finished our pizza, I asked Carol to start writing down the names of the assistants I wanted to hire. Joe Castiglione had given me a salary pool for coaches, so the trick was to stay within budget.

When we were done, Carol added up the salaries, and we were *way* over budget. So we started over, and little by little, we adjusted our numbers. You paid by experience, position, and title. It was a puzzle of sorts, and we couldn't make all the pieces fit. In the end, I had to ask Joe for an increase in the pool.

Carol was exhausted. "I'm so tired. I think I'm pregnant," she said.

I told her it was probably just the cumulative effect of the recent events: the OU interview, the Iowa interview, the OU hiring, the hurried flight to Norman, the introductory day. It was enough to knock anyone off their feet.

"Nope," she said. "It's pregnant tired."

The next day, she flew home and took a pregnancy test, and sure enough, it showed up positive.

My first hire to arrive at OU was Bobby Jack Wright. He had coached at Texas for twelve years and knew the state like I knew Youngstown. He never had to pull out a map; he knew where every high school in Texas was located by memory. He'd been to just about every one of them.

The second guy to arrive on campus was Jerry Schmidt. I had first met him during my interview at Notre Dame and then saw the work he had done at Florida as strength-and-conditioning coordinator.

Schmidty *looked* like a strength-and-conditioning guy. His muscles had muscles. His crew cut could beat you up. He became a cornerstone of the program, one of the best and most important hires I've ever made. And one of the most dependable friends I could ever have.

In those first few weeks after I got the job, me and Bobby Jack were either on the road recruiting or with Schmidty in our trailer office on the south side of Memorial Stadium. Our football operations guy during those initial weeks was Merv Johnson, who had coached with Switzer and others over the years. Merv was an OU institution. He would sometimes stop by the trailers, and we'd brainstorm about recruiting.

Most major programs have a recruiting coordinator. There's a recruiting war room, a detailed list of recruits, travel schedules for coaches, contacts, databases, recruiting services, real-time updates of where a program stands with a certain recruit, which other schools are recruiting a player, a list of official and unofficial visits, and so on.

We had nothing. The previous staff had left us high and dry. Whatever computer files there were, were empty. The recruiting files also were gone or destroyed.

So to compile intel on high school and junior college players in our recruiting radius, we bought all the newspapers we could. From Oklahoma City. From Dallas, Austin, San Antonio, Tulsa, Houston. We dug through *Dave Campbell's Texas Football* magazine.

Dallas was our main target. We started making phone calls to coaches and writers. Who were the better players in their areas? Were there any hidden jewels we should know about? We slowly put together a master list by area and positions. We determined levels of interest—on our part and theirs.

Our trailer would shudder when the cold December and January winds and ice storms blew through. The lighting was terrible; the heater had a mind of its own. We had a table, folding chairs, and a grease board.

Schmidty, armed with a black marker, was our stenographer. "Hey, Schmidty, write this name down," we'd tell him.

We evaluated game film. We targeted the prospects we needed to see in person.

Bobby Jack arranged a recruiting trip to Houston. He was going to pick me up when I landed there. I got off the plane that afternoon, walked outside the terminal, and called Bobby Jack to tell him to swing around and get me. My head was spinning.

"Bob, there's no way you can already be there," he said.

"I'm here," I said.

But I actually was at Love Field in Dallas. I'd forgotten I was supposed to connect in Dallas to Houston.

December was a blur. It was terribly lonely. I lived in a hotel, and at day's end, there it was—just me and HBO. Coach Spurrier was my security blanket: the guy who had seen it all, done it all. But I couldn't call him *every* day for advice.

Everything and almost every face I saw was new to me. Boy, talk about not knowing who's for you and who's not.

One day, a longtime friend from K-State named Debbie Key stopped by my office to say hello. Her husband, Jack, had worked in the K-State athletic department business office when I was there, and now they were in Norman at OU's athletic department. It was a courtesy visit on Debbie's part.

I don't know what came over me, but I hugged her like she was my wife. I was just so happy to see a familiar face. Here was an actual friend, someone I'd known in simpler times.

Debbie must have thought I was nuts, but I made her go to lunch with me. I just needed to talk to someone with a connection to my past. It surprised me that I reacted that way, but that was the depth of my loneliness.

I finally sneaked back to Florida in time for Christmas. A friend of mine, Rick Rundle, picked me up at the Jacksonville airport on December 23.

I must have looked exhausted, because as we were driving back to Gainesville, Rick asked, "Dude, you all right?"

"Rick," I said, "I think I just ruined my life. Swear to God, I think I ruined my life taking this job."

I had left a near-perfect situation at Florida. Now I was overwhelmed by the instant responsibilities that had come with the OU job. I was trying to hire a staff. I was desperately trying to make up for the lost recruiting time between Blake's firing and my hiring. My office was a trailer. I missed my family. I missed the clothes in my closet. I missed Napolatanos. I missed Coach Spurrier and the team.

I felt bad about not being able to help the Florida coaches get ready for their Orange Bowl game against Syracuse. The best I could do was check in with the defensive staff when I got back to Gainesville that day. They had already put together a game plan.

From there, I drove to the obstetrician's office to meet Carol. Carol knew she was pregnant, but we hadn't done an ultrasound yet.

We had Mackie, but I had always wanted more kids. Carol loved kids. too, but Mackie had been a tough pregnancy. I certainly couldn't blame Carol for being conflicted about the possibility of another challenging one. Already she was so sick that her sister had come to help take care of her. The sonogram had been arranged to help determine why Carol was feeling so ill.

As the nurse glided the transducer across Carol's abdomen, I looked at the screen and then at Carol. The screen...Carol.

Then the images appeared. I could see one gummy bear–sized shape here and then another gummy bear there.

The nurse blurted out, "Oh, my gosh! There's two!"

"What do you mean, 'two'?" asked Carol, who was frightened by the nurse's reaction.

"You're going to have twins!" said the nurse.

Carol looked at me and said, half crying, "You *always* get your way."

As if that wasn't enough, two hours later, we had a For Sale by Owner sign in our front yard. Two women saw the sign, knocked on the door, and asked if they could see the house. After they took a tour, they made me an offer on their way out. I countered, and four hours later, we had a deal. That's when you know it's meant to be. Another slap in the face from God, saying, "You belong in Oklahoma. You'll be OK."

Another omen that all would be well: Florida beat Syracuse in the Orange Bowl. So that made me feel less guilty about things. And at last, my coaching staff was coming together.

Hiring a staff is like building a car from scratch. Even though I was scrambling to catch up to the other schools in the Big 12 (the expanded conference began play in 1996), I refused to speed up the assembly line.

I needed coaches who understood what we were up against. I needed coaches who could recruit, who could collaborate, who could develop players, who could be nimble enough to adjust to my defensive and offensive philosophies. I needed all these things—and then I needed to keep all the hires within my salary pool for assistants.

When I'd first began researching the Oklahoma job, I'd been torn about which direction I wanted to go on offense. At first, I thought an option attack might work best. I didn't want to run the wishbone—Coach Switzer ran that offense to perfection—but I was leaning toward a Nebraska/Turner Gill–type option.

I had played against Gill when I was at Iowa. He was incredibly gifted, and when I was hired at Oklahoma, he was the quarterbacks coach at Nebraska. In fact, I had tried to hire him. It didn't work out.

I also had extensive talks with Syracuse offensive coordinator Kevin Rogers, who ran a run/pass option–style attack. It was hard not to be impressed with his work with quarterbacks Donovan McNabb and Marvin Graves.

Next, I called Hal Mumme, who was the head coach at Kentucky. Mumme's offense had always caused me problems when I was at Florida. We beat him, but they put up points with an innovative passing attack. In 1998, they were second nationally in passing offense, third in total offense, and eighth in scoring offense. I think even Coach Spurrier was impressed. I was.

If they were doing that at Kentucky, why couldn't we do that at Oklahoma? We'd build our offense around the pass, and then sometime down the road, after we had recruited enough linemen and running backs, we'd transition to a more balanced system.

I knew I couldn't get Mumme, but maybe I could get the mini-Mumme on that Kentucky staff.

I called Hal. Hal called the plays at UK, but he had an offensive coordinator named Mike Leach. "Hal, can Mike call the plays here?" I asked. "Can he do what you do?"

"Yes. Absolutely," he said. "He has leadership skills."

Then I called Leach. I didn't know him very well; we'd seen each other before games and offered a "hi" here or there.

"With this kind of offense, we're going to be able to attract quarterbacks," I told Mike. "We're thin at the position right now, but we're working on it. If you come here and we do things well, I bet you'll have a chance at some head coaching jobs."

Leach accepted the position. He pushed for me to hire a guy he had worked with at Valdosta State with Mumme, someone named Dana Holgorsen. I told Leach that I wanted my first staff to be my own hires. Plus, if Leach eventually left for a head coaching job, I didn't want him taking his own guy with him. Then I'd have lost two assistants.

> *It wasn't anything against me. Bob was going to bring his own staff in there, and that's obviously what he did.*
>
> *I grew up in Iowa. I went to Kinnick Stadium, watching the Hayden Fry days. I just knew the Stoops name and their storied past. I was in junior high, I guess, and Bob and Mike were just really good players that I watched. I just followed wherever they were. I just always had my eye on them.*
>
> —Dana Holgorsen, University of Houston head coach,
>
> 2019–present

I did with Leach what Coach Spurrier did with me: I gave him the freedom to do what I had hired him to do. His job was to create a state-of-the-art passing attack for us. His offense, my defense. But I kept in mind a piece of advice that Coach Spurrier had given me about the key to successful offenses: always make sure you can run the ball.

Leach wanted a junior college quarterback who could come in immediately and be our starter. He found one in Utah: Josh Heupel.

Not everyone on our staff was sold on Heupel. Some of the coaches were concerned that we were the only major program recruiting Josh. But Leach believed in him, and I believed in Leach—so Josh joined the team early in January 1999.

In February, Jason White signed his national letter of intent to come to OU.

That summer, Nate Hybl transferred to OU after he was redshirted during his freshman season at Georgia. Hybl's father had known Leach for years.

Suddenly we were looking pretty good at quarterback.

When I look back at it, I can see that Leach is the one who started it all here. He was one of my best and biggest hires. I didn't know what a gem I was getting until I saw him work firsthand.

I was excited about the idea of putting the two of us together, Bob and me.

When we first got there, they had just moved into their new offices. There wasn't any furniture, and the place had that sort of resiny, nylon-glue carpet smell.

We needed to get a quarterback. We needed Josh Heupel. Given where we started, getting him was huge.

Bob very solidly had my back. I make the offensive decisions. He gave the team and the coaches clarity and confidence. What's important about that is, even if there are some imperfections, at least there's direction to it.

—Mike Leach, Oklahoma offensive coordinator, 1998

Leach was a piece of work, but in a good way. He had an unconventional mind, and I liked that about him.

He had a law degree from Pepperdine. He had a fascination with all things Geronimo, the great Apache warrior. Geronimo died and was buried about ninety minutes southwest of Norman in Fort Sill, Oklahoma. Just ask Leach; he's been there to see the gravesite. He even had a huge photo of Geronimo in his office.

You may have heard Leach go stream-of-consciousness on any number of topics. That's how he was at Oklahoma, too. I'd walk by his office, and he'd stop me and start telling one of those long, involved stories about who knows what: Geronimo, lunar rocks, the latest movie, a case to be heard in front of the Supreme Court. Sometimes we'd actually talk about football.

Luckily, I had the luxury as head coach to be able to cut the conversation short and walk away if need be. But more times than not, I stood there and listened to his takes on life.

Of course, the Oklahoma football community didn't entirely embrace my take—and Leach's—of building our offense around the pass. The program's history had been a testament to the run.

At the time, OU had three Heisman Trophy winners—Vessels, Owens, and Sims—and they were all running backs. Coach Switzer was a wishbone offense guy. More than a few times, I heard fans and reporters politely ask (and sometimes not so politely), why were we going all in on the pass? They said the Oklahoma winds and harsh weather weren't conducive to the passing game.

I appreciated their interest, but I didn't make decisions based on fan sentiment. We were going to throw because we didn't have the personnel to run the ball just yet, because I had hired one of the brightest offensive minds in the game, and because we had just signed a juco quarterback who would quickly become a team leader...and much more.

There would be no debate about this. This was going to be our offense. Even after I hired the rest of the staff, including Mark Mangino as assistant head coach/offensive line coach/running game coordinator, we weren't going to "blend" offenses. I wanted it clear to everyone—players and coaches—that we were going to run Leach's offense. It was going to be our offensive identity.

I was pretty excited about the job, but I had a family dilemma. My daughter was in the middle of her junior year at Manhattan High School in Kansas. And my son was in eighth grade. What was I going to do? Take the kids out of school? I eventually took the job. My family stayed back in Manhattan for eighteen months, until my daughter got out of high school.

The first five months I was there, I slept on a couch in the football office. A student secretary was throwing out an old, terrible-looking couch, but I got it and slept on it.

Then I got an apartment. All I had was a mattress, a few plates, forks, and a little TV. It was so small, I needed binoculars to see the screen.

I went to school at Youngstown State. I'm from Newcastle, Pennsylvania, which isn't far from there. Yeah, I'm a Youngstown guy. I knew Bob's dad before I knew Bob.

When I got to OU, it was in worse shape that it looked from the outside. But Bob, he doesn't let anything beat him down. If I was having a bad day, he'd say, "Don't let them get you twice." That was his favorite saying. In other words, deal with a problem once and then move on.

—Mark Mangino, Oklahoma assistant coach, 1999–2001

My brother Mike, Brent Venables, and Bear (our nickname for Mangino) all joined the staff not long after Kansas State played Purdue in the Alamo Bowl. (A supposedly undersized quarterback named Drew Brees beat K-State in the bowl game.)

Mike was the associate head coach/co-defensive coordinator. Venables was the co-defensive coordinator/linebackers coach. I had recruited Venables at K-State and later asked Snyder to hire him, which he did—first as a graduate assistant and later as a linebackers coach.

I felt really confident about what we were going to do on defense. Mike and Brent would be using the same schemes and philosophies I first used at Kansas State and then at Florida. They were experts on those schemes.

I hired former OU quarterback Cale Gundy as my running backs coach. I loved his OU background. When I was an assistant at K-State, I'd loved competing against him.

Jonathan Hayes, a former teammate at Iowa who went on to a dozen-year NFL career, was my tight ends coach. When I called him about the job, he was participating in a rodeo. He was cutting horses.

It was this simple.

Me: "You want to be an assistant coach?"

Him: "You know what? That's a hell of an idea."

Jackie Shipp, another former OU star, was my defensive line coach. I liked guys who knew the ins and outs of a school.

I had been considering a candidate for the final position on the coaching staff. We flew him in, put him up in a hotel. I called that night to check in with him, confirm our meeting the next morning, and help make arrangements to get him back home.

That's when he mentioned that he wouldn't be going home immediately after our interview. "That's OK, Coach," he said. "I'm heading to Stillwater to interview there, too."

"Oh, are you? That's fine," I said when he told me about his appointment with our in-state rival Oklahoma State just eighty-two miles away.

I called him back an hour later. "Hey, why don't you just head on directly to Stillwater," I said. "I'm going in another direction."

Maybe that was a petty thing to do. Maybe I was wrong to react that way. But it just didn't sit right with me at the time.

I ended up hiring Steve Spurrier Jr., who joined the staff as the wide receivers coach after working five years on the Florida staff. He did a great job for us.

Our very first recruiting class was a miracle of sorts. We signed twenty-one players (about the average class size in our conference that year), thanks to that grease board, Bobby Jack, and a little luck. Included in that class were Heupel, White, safety Brandon Everage, cornerback Derrick Strait, defensive back Michael Thompson, wide receiver Antwone Savage, running back Quentin Griffin, linebacker Torrance Marshall, safety Matt McCoy, and defensive tackle Kory Klein. Sixteen of the twenty-one signees came from the states of Texas and Oklahoma.

The recruiting services didn't think much of the class. But the recruiting services weren't always right. If you ranked the top-ten recruiting classes in the history of Oklahoma football, the 1999 group would be in the team photo. Point being, we hit the jackpot that year, even though we started from scratch. There are guys on that list, not many of them highly recruited, who I wouldn't have traded for anybody.

Most of those players wouldn't arrive on campus until summer. They were the lucky ones. The holdovers from the 1998 roster had to deal with Schmidty and his winter conditioning drills.

I had been fortunate to hire Schmidty from Florida. His family was from Nebraska, and his wife's family was from Texas. So I had geography working for me. A huge break. Your strength-and-conditioning coach is with your team more than any other staff member. Few people know the heart and soul of a team more than the strength coach.

We weren't into slogans, but Schmidty issued "No Excuses" T-shirts to our players. We put those words up in the weight room, along with a single goal: win the Big 12.

Our weight room was fine, but our indoor facility was a mess. The artificial turf was decaying. There was junk everywhere.

Schmidty's dad came to visit. He took one look at our facilities and asked Jerry, "What have you gotten yourself into?"

I knew the feeling. Everyone did.

I get there, and I can't believe the facilities and the attitude of the players. The place was in shambles; it really was. Awful. That sign going into the showers—Sooner Magic—half the sign was gone. That reflected their self-worth. They played to that level, almost.

Growing up, watching OU, you never think of them that way. But you get there, peel it back a little bit, and—holy smokes.

Over time, it got better. We replaced the lockers, updated the signs. We painted.

I do remember we had a cricket infestation. We had billions of crickets. Bob was outside the locker room and at the entrance of the facility with one of those leaf-suckers, just vacuuming up those crickets. Players are coming to the meetings and practice, and there he is.

How many head coaches would have done that? He's never backed away from doing things that need to get done.

—Matt McMillen, Oklahoma assistant athletics director for football operation, 1999–2017

Our locker room seats were wooden two-by-fours. I'd get splinters in my butt. I'd have to put a towel over my seat.

—Roy Williams

We can all laugh about it now, but our first-ever team workout might have been the worst in college football history. It took place in February at the indoor field.

Those players had gone home for Christmas break, then sat on their tails, didn't do anything—had turkey and dressing and then had come strolling back to school. None of them were in shape. It was pretty comical. They found out about Schmidty really quick. That first workout was a doozy.

It was our first full-on coaching with them. The workouts started at 5:00 a.m.—well, the warm-ups did—and then the real thing went from 5:30 a.m. to 6:30. Schmidty didn't even work them that hard.

—Bobby Jack Wright

We're warming up, and guys are falling down everywhere. With that turf, you'd catch your foot on the seams all the time. Guys are throwing up everywhere.

We'd just come from Florida. There were studs there. Now we're at OU, and these guys are falling down during warm-ups.

We're done with the warm-ups, and I say, "Let's start the real thing."
Once we got going, guys started dropping like they were shot by snipers. Bob
looked at me—gave me that look, like, "Wow, we got some work to do."

—Jerry Schmidt

People were tapping out, quitting.
Then we started the real workout.

—Roy Williams

It was bad. Schmidty had just stretched them out and warmed them up a little, and we had four, five guys already in the trash cans throwing up. Guys couldn't even do the most basic things. They looked awful. The workout was raggedy. It was depressing.

I had no idea how poorly conditioned they were. It was obvious that my new staff members were in shock over what they had seen during the workout. Afterward, we had a coaches' meeting.

"I know that didn't look like much," I said, "but don't any of you guys leave here looking for a new job. We'll be better in a week or two.

"We got what we got. Let's believe in them. We'll get 'em in shape."

Why did my body change? It's called "Jerry Schmidt."

Every year, we did baseline testing. In 1999, when they first got there, we
were doing baseline bench press. Keep in mind, when I was in high school, I
didn't like lifting weights.

When it was my turn, I tried to wait until everyone's attention was on
someone else. I only had 185 pounds on the bar. I lifted up the bar, and it
was like, "Goddamn, this is heavy."

I bring it down to my chest, and everyone is going, "Go, Roy! Go, Roy!" I
push it back up. I mean, this was an accomplishment.

Then I hear Coach Schmidt.

"One," he says.

By the time I left OU, I did 225 pounds nineteen or twenty-one times at
the [NFL] Combine. I went from a snotty-nosed little boy, pear shaped and
pudgy, to Bronko Nagurski. I came out of my cocoon, so to speak.

—Roy Williams

We did get better. Nobody on my staff defected, but there were a few players who transferred or quit.

Part of my plan was to go back to the future. During team meetings, I showed videos of former great Oklahoma players and coaches. I showed those championship teams. "This is what we're supposed to be," I said. "This is our heritage. We need to start identifying with these players and with this past. We need to make it our present and our future."

I asked my team to embrace our history, and I did it, too. So many of our former players and coaches had felt alienated and forgotten as the program had begun to falter and splinter. I invited them back to OU. I *wanted* them around.

Those players and coaches were legends. We were standing on their shoulders, only building on their accomplishments. I wanted to celebrate that, and I wanted to celebrate the men whose trophies filled the glass cases and whose faces stared down from those framed photos on the walls.

They gave me a locker in the coaches' locker room. I traveled with the team. A lot of coaches wouldn't have allowed an old guy from the heyday with the Sooners to do that.

He embraced Coach Switzer. He was confident enough in himself to embrace the history of Oklahoma. Bob's not afraid to ask anyone for help or for advice.

—Joe Washington, Oklahoma running back, 1972–1975

As soon as those former players and coaches saw improvement in the program and saw that we were sincere about bringing them back, the more they came around to OU. We had photos on the walls of former Oklahoma assistants. We wanted them, as well as the former players, to know this was still their place, whether they had played or worked for Bud Wilkinson or Coach Switzer, Gary Gibbs, Howard Schnellenberger, or John Blake. It was their school and their program.

My respect for the past wasn't limited to Oklahoma's. Not long after I became OU's coach, I wrote a letter to Tom Osborne, who had retired in January 1998 as Nebraska's head coach after a twenty-five-year career and three national championships.

In the letter, I thanked him for the quality of play of his Nebraska teams through the years and explained how his program had challenged me as a coach. Jim Leavitt and I were constantly trying to figure out a way to stop Nebraska. If you could stop an Osborne-coached team, you could stop anybody. I wanted him to know that he had as much to do with my development as a coach as Coach Fry, Coach Snyder, and Coach Spurrier.

I've always held Bob in high regard.

So many guys, when they take over a program, somehow want to put their own stamp on it. Bob embraced the past at Oklahoma, which I thought was very smart. Oklahoma had a great history, and he put his own spin on it. I think by embracing the past, he made the transition for himself much easier.

—Tom Osborne, Nebraska head coach, 1973–1997

Of course, our program needed some help. We fixed the sign in the locker room, and Joe found some money to get the place repainted. But during my first year there, I found chicken bones and bottle caps on the practice field—relics of the car-parking and tailgating days.

My players were supposed to practice on a place used as a Saturday party site and dumping ground? Are you kidding me? What does that tell your players?

We were trying to change the culture, the facilities, the perception of the program. But there was one thing I was never going to change: our helmet logo.

Coach Fry had changed Iowa's. Coach Snyder had changed Kansas State's. But no way was I going to tinker with perfection.

The interlocking OU is iconic. You see that helmet, and you know it's Oklahoma—the same way you instantly know Michigan's helmet, USC's helmet, Alabama's helmet.

You don't monkey with those uniforms. In 1999, I slightly widened the stripe on the pants, and it became big news. You would have thought I'd put sequins on the whole uniform.

Years later, we'd have one game a year where we'd change up the uniforms because the recruits liked it and the players liked it. But just one game.

Whenever I needed a perspective check, an affirmation that we were on track, I'd glance at an unframed, unlaminated, creased and crinkled sheet of paper on my desk. If you didn't know any better, you'd think it had been pulled from the trash. It was straight Youngstown, baby. It was a copy of Rudyard Kipling's poem "If."

I can't remember how I got it, but it became a fixture on my desk only a few days after I got the OU job. And it stayed on my desk during the entirety of my Oklahoma career. In fact, I still have that worn piece of paper.

So much of the poem resonated with me. I even highlighted in yellow marker the lines that I tried to apply to my own life:

If you can keep your head when all about you
Are losing theirs and blaming it on you,
If you can trust yourself when all men doubt you,
But make allowance for their doubting too;

And later:

If you can dream — and not make dreams your master;
If you can think — and not make thoughts your aim;
If you can meet with Triumph and Disaster
And treat those two impostors just the same;

I'm not the first person to find comfort in the poem. But it was — and still is — a valuable reminder of the need for balance in life.

There were times when I had difficulty keeping it together, when I needed to tell myself to trust the plan, to trust my instincts. If others questioned me, I needed to understand why they were doing so and not dismiss it with arrogance.

As a football coach, or anyone in a position to lead, the concept of treating Triumph and Disaster — wins and losses — with the same outlook has meaning to me. I didn't want to be defined by either extreme. I think humility is the equal to success; that tenacity, toughness, and dignity are worthy opponents to failure.

The media. The fans. The opponents. Your own inner pressures and expectations. If you have the will to endure through those long seasons, to not give in to the doubt, to not let something beat you twice, then you'll be OK.

All I know is, that poem got me through more than a few tough days in my career. So did coming home to Carol and a family that had grown to include three kids. Our twins, Isaac and Drake, had arrived in June, born about seven weeks early. They were so tiny—one three and a half pounds, the other four and a half—that I could hold one in the palm of each hand.

Once again, it had been a trying pregnancy for Carol, beginning with mandatory bed rest not long after she had returned to Norman with Mackie. Then she had been in and out of the hospital and spent the final two weeks there leading up to the delivery of the twins. We were blessed that everyone was OK.

As the 1999 season unfolded, I realized how right Mike Leach had been about his handpicked quarterback Josh Heupel. Heupel was a leader, he could spin the ball, and he fit well into our new offense—all the things that Leach had said he would be.

Meanwhile, there was resistance from some of the older players on the defensive side of the ball. Some of the players didn't understand why we were altering the successful schemes used under Rex Ryan.

They didn't fall in love with us, and we didn't fall in love with them. We were fighting buying into the system. And we didn't know how to win when Coach Bob came in. We lost some games we should have won.

—Roy Williams

We led in every game that year in 1999. Led at Notre Dame. Led in the Texas game. We just couldn't hang on.

—Bobby Jack Wright

We were 3–2 going into our homecoming game against Texas A&M. If every season has a defining game, this was ours.

A&M had a four-game win streak against Oklahoma, and the previous two games hadn't been close: 29–0, 51–7. The Aggies were ranked thirteenth in the *AP* poll. We had been ranked number twenty-three after a 3–0 start, but that didn't last long after we blew an eighteen-point lead to Notre Dame and a seventeen-point lead to Texas.

I'd had it with OU being A&M's soccer ball. I didn't want this program to be kicked around. "This ain't happening anymore," I told our players. "We're going to be aggressive, take chances. But I'd better not see anyone even crack a smile if we get ahead early."

On our first possession, we were stopped on third down. So I did as promised: I took chances.

I called a fake field goal, but somehow, we relayed the information to everyone but our kicker. He was supposed to go through his kicking motion, find a seam through the line, and get open in the middle of the field for a pass from our holder, Patrick Fletcher, a little tough-ass who also was our backup quarterback.

The ball was snapped and our tight ends ran routes in the flat and the corner, leaving the middle of the field wide open for our kicker. But since he had never gotten the signal, he had no clue he was supposed to run a pass route.

My man Fletcher instantly recognized what had happened and bolted eight yards for a first down. He barely made it. We scored three plays later.

"You saved my rear," I told Fletcher later.

We called a fake punt. Our blocking back in the formation—future North Texas State head coach Seth Littrell—ran for forty-one yards on that one. He also recovered a fumble later.

We ran the hook-and-lateral. We ran shovel passes. We used a formation with three receivers on each side and just three offensive linemen. We threw it forty times in the first half. We finished with thirty first downs compared to the five first downs a season earlier against the Aggies. We scored on our first six possessions. Leach and Heupel were a machine.

It doesn't get talked about enough, but that win against A&M helped us turn the corner on learning *how* to win. Before, it was as if our players were surprised to have a lead. Now they knew they could take the lead and hold it—and that I had a willingness to do whatever was necessary (fake punts, field goals, whatever it took) to win those games.

We finished 7–5 that season.

We went to the Independence Bowl. It felt like we were going to the Rose Bowl.

That first team at OU, they were all special. Those were guys who laid it on the line. Rocky Calmus, Littrell—I could go on—but they knew what OU stood for. They were hungry. They wanted to be great. They didn't want to be dogs.

—Jerry Schmidt

Remember my preseason prediction to Leach? It came true, though faster than anyone thought. He became the head coach at Texas Tech at season's end.

As for our first recruiting class, ranked an unimpressive forty-second or something by one of the recruiting services, well, Marshall was named the Big 12 Defensive Newcomer of the Year, Heupel the Big 12 Offensive Newcomer of the Year, and Savage the Big 12 Freshman of the Year. We had our foundation. Heupel, Savage, Derrick Strait, and Jason White would go on to become first-team All-Americans, with Jason winning the Heisman Trophy in 2003.

Leach—and that recruiting class, and the players who had stuck with us from the previous team—helped us take the first step back to being OU. The second step would be one for the ages.

Chapter Nine

The Trophy

During two-a-day practices, which is about as fun as it sounds, I tried to change the mood and lighten the load. Those guys were working hard in that late-summer Oklahoma heat, so when we got done with our second session, I took them over to the OU swimming pool, and everybody jumped in.

Another time, we took the players to the softball field for batting practice. This wasn't beer league slo-pitch; this was fast-pitch against Patty Gasso's OU softball team, which had just won the Women's College World Series several months earlier. (Patty has won three more national championships since then.)

We had a home run hitting contest—our guys against the national champs.

> *I said, "Coach, you got to take a swing of the bat."*
> *He was reluctant, but he did it.*
> —Patty Gasso, Oklahoma softball head coach, 1995–present

The players were goading me on, giving me a hard time. But I walked up there with a plan. I told myself that it was just like golf: stay behind it, don't try to swing too hard.

The mound, by the way, felt like it was right on top of me. Patty was close.

She threw the pitch, I swung...and knocked it over the centerfield fence. I did a bat flip and said, "I'm done."

The players went crazy. They couldn't believe their head coach had done that. You know players—they think anyone older than twenty-five qualifies for Medicare.

He hit a bomb. He just dropped the bat and walked away.

But I loved that he brought his team over. He was sharing his culture with ours. That's what sets him apart.

Over the years, he's been out to the World Series to see us play. He's come out and supported us. He has a very strong feeling toward women's athletics. He was really outstanding about allowing us to bring recruits to meet him. Very engaging and very humble at the same time.

With my recruits, he would never talk about himself. He'd always ask about them. I've dealt with others here before him who were quite different. But when I brought recruits and their parents to a football game, Coach Stoops would chat them up and shake their hands during the pregame warm-ups on the sidelines—and the fathers would just melt.

He's the ultimate of cool.

—Patty Gasso

He knew my players, knew their names, knew our schedule, who we'd beaten, where we factored in on the national landscape.

When things weren't going great, he'd walk into practice, come down the tunnel at Lloyd Noble Center, give me a hug, and ask, "How you doing?" Bob would stay in the background when you were doing great, and he'd show up when things weren't going great.

And Bob—I've seen him shoot a little bit. I think I'd rather have him set a screen and roll, or maybe have him guard somebody.

But he has a shot. A little bit. A little bit.

—Sherri Coale

The season is too long not to have some fun. I was the same way with my staff. I learned that from Coach Spurrier: you can have fun and still win at the highest level.

I would tell our coaches, when you come to work, work—and when you're done with your work, get out of here. We didn't have time clocks.

Nobody punched in. The last thing I wanted was coaches who sat in their offices and doodled smoke coming out of a chimney. Point being, if you get to where you're just sitting there drawing something like that, then it's time to go home. Yes, I was serious as hell about winning football games. But they don't give you championship rings for "Most Hours Worked."

During the season, we usually met at 8:30 a.m. every day. A lot of our coaches had young kids, including me. I wanted them to be able to spend some time with their families, help their wives with breakfast, drive the kids to school.

I didn't want tired guys. You make mistakes when you're tired. I'd shoo guys out of there by 9:00 p.m. on most nights. On Sundays after a game, we'd maybe stay until 10:00 p.m., but that's only because I gave everybody Sunday mornings off. I wanted them to spend that time with their families.

We began the 2000 season ranked nineteenth in the *AP* poll. The top five were Nebraska, Florida State, Alabama, Wisconsin, and Miami. We were an afterthought, a team to fill out the back end of the voters' top twenty-five.

We won our three nonconference games and moved up to fourteenth. We beat Kansas and moved up to tenth in the polls.

Then came what people called Red October—a brutal three-game stretch in a month where we beat number-eleven Texas, 63–14; number-one Kansas State at Manhattan, 41–31; and, two weeks later, number-two Nebraska.

It could have gone sideways against Nebraska. We were down 14–0 after their first two possessions. They already had gained 169 yards on us.

An Oklahoma team hadn't beaten Nebraska in the last seven tries. During that span, OU had been outscored 265–61, so I'm sure there were lots of people in the stands covering their eyes.

They house two runs, and it's, "Oh, here we go again."

[Bob] pulls his headset down his neck, gathers the defense, and says, real calm, "You guys are fine. Settle down and relax. You're just overpursuing everything. You'll be fine."

They were waiting for him to flip out, but that's the way he handled it.

That was the turning point in our program, that Nebraska game. Most coaches would have freaked out: "Oh, we're going to get our ass kicked now." Not him.

—Jerry Schmidt

We held them scoreless for the remaining fifty-three minutes of the game. We scored thirty-one straight points and won 31–14. Our fans, who had been waiting to beat Nebraska for years, tossed oranges on the field (the national championship was going to be played at the Orange Bowl that season) and tore down the goalpost.

In the postgame press conference, a reporter told me that this was the first time a team had beaten the number-one- and number-two-ranked teams in consecutive weeks since 1988, and before that, 1964.

So what? At some point, you either start beating teams that matter, or you don't. We were starting to beat them.

When we beat Nebraska at home, the party went on until the next morning, and Lindsey Street, which runs right through campus, was like a parade route. People were honking their horns, celebrating until 6:00 a.m., 7:00 a.m.

The whole season was insanity.

—Teddy Lehman

When did we win the coaches over? Red October in 2000. That's when we won them over.

—Roy Williams

From then on, if we told our guys we had to practice at 3:00 a.m., they couldn't wait. They totally bought in.

—Bobby Jack Wright

We moved to number one in the polls after the Nebraska win and stayed there—though we had to work for it. But with each win, our belief in ourselves grew stronger—to the point where we simply didn't think we'd ever lose.

Perfect example: on November 11, we were down by fourteen points in the third quarter and ten points in the fourth quarter at number twenty-three Texas A&M. An Oklahoma team hadn't won at A&M since 1903. And at the time, we were playing in front of the largest crowd (81,188) ever to see a football game in the state of Texas.

If we lost, our number-one ranking was gone, and our chances of playing for a national championship were in huge trouble.

All week long, we had been telling linebacker Torrance Marshall that A&M loved to run play-action and then throw to its tight end over the middle. And all week long, Marshall kept getting fooled. He just couldn't cover it.

With 7:18 left in the game (we had narrowed the score to 31–28 by then), A&M ran its bread-and-butter play-action pass to the tight end. Oh, no.

But this time, Marshall recognized the action, dropped back perfectly, intercepted Mark Farris's pass, and then returned it forty-one yards for what ended up being the winning touchdown. After he scored, I got on the headphones with my coaches and said, "You know what, guys, we can't lose."

I also loved what Marshall said after the game, when describing his interception and scoring run: "That's what it was. It was Sooner Magic."

The sign in our locker room had been fixed. Now the real Sooner Magic had been repaired, too.

Leach and his Texas Tech team came to Norman the following week. They left with a loss.

We squeezed past Oklahoma State in Bedlam and then faced Snyder and K-State again in the Big 12 Championship.

It is difficult to beat a Bill Snyder–coached team once during a season. Now we had to face K-State a second time, knowing the Wildcats would love to end our perfect season, end our national championship title hopes, and avenge the October loss when they had been ranked number one.

Each week on a grease board in our team meeting room, I'd underline the name of the most recent opponent we had beaten. There were eleven underlined names.

I told our players about Hernán Cortés, the sixteenth-century Spanish explorer who, when faced with the possibility of his sailors fleeing an impending battle, ordered that his ships be scuttled. There would be no retreat.

I erased all the names on the grease board, erased our 11–0 record, erased our number-one ranking. "We have nothing right now," I said to the team. "We've got nothing to lose. It's all or nothing."

It was a chilly, dreary, wet night at Arrowhead Stadium. We didn't play well during a lot of the game, but we played well when we had to. The difference makers: an option pitch on fourth-and-inches at the beginning of the fourth quarter; a quick-count quarterback sneak up the middle on third-and-a half yard with 2:37 remaining; and later, another clever call by Mangino on second-and-four with 1:59 left—an option play to the outside, when K-State expected something up the middle. Tim Duncan kicked a field goal, and we held off Kansas State at the end, 27–24.

Afterward, Heupel hugged his father, a football coach...just like my dad. Brian Bosworth, one of those OU alums we wanted back in the program, worked his way through the dressing room.

Carol waited outside. She told a reporter, "Bobby and I are such positive people. We'd never say something couldn't be done."

We were 12–0 and headed to the Orange Bowl. Our opponent would be Florida State, a team ranked number three in the polls but number two in the rankings that mattered: the Bowl Championship Series computer results. The BCS formula had determined that FSU, not number-two Miami, which had defeated the Seminoles in October, deserved the second berth in the national championship game.

We didn't care.

We were going to the Orange Bowl, and everyone was unbelievably excited. It had been an early winter in Oklahoma. They'd even had to plow the snow off our field.

On the day we flew to Miami, the weather was so bad that a lot of our guys had a hard time getting to the plane. They deiced the plane, we took off, and we were headed to Miami! The Orange Bowl. Warmth.

We get off the airplane, and the buses are all lined up on the tarmac. We're smiling. It's a nice temperature. We're in Miami. We figure we're going to the hotel.

The families and support people get on one bus, and they leave. We get on another bus, and we take a different route. We're looking at each other: "Where are we going?"

We go straight to the practice field and get dressed, and they run us like dogs. Tongues hanging out. The coaches didn't say much. I think Bob was telling us, "We're here to work, not to play on South Beach."

We had full scrimmages, tackling to the ground. They set the tone right away.

—Teddy Lehman

Even though Florida State was the defending national champion and playing in its third consecutive national title game, we weren't intimidated. We had been tested more than FSU had. They hadn't beaten a higher-ranked team that season, but we had beaten number-two Kansas State and number-one Nebraska.

During the almost-daily sessions with the media that week, I intentionally kept mentioning that Oklahoma had a history of beating Florida State. I said the same thing to my team. I wanted my players to know an OU victory wasn't unprecedented.

Coach Switzer had beaten the Seminoles in the 1981 Orange Bowl, in the 1980 Orange Bowl, and during the 1976 regular season. Why, I said to my players, wouldn't we expect to win?

One reporter started to list all of the reasons why FSU was favored. They had quarterback Chris Weinke, who had just won the Heisman Trophy; they had this guy and that guy. I cut him off. "Hey, we have some athletes too, you know," I said.

I was aware of FSU's accomplishments during the 1990s: a record of 109–13–1 and fifty-seven wins in its previous sixty-two games.

But guess what? OU had more national championship trophies, more All-Americans, more Heisman Trophy winners...more everything.

Even when Coach Bowden and I had joint media appearances, I didn't back down. Bowden would look at us like, "Do they really think they can beat us?" He didn't know whether we were crazy or if we knew something he didn't. They were so used to teams obsessing about them—and then those teams wouldn't play well.

Don't get me wrong; FSU was a fabulous team. The Seminoles had the number-one total offense, the number-one passing offense, the number-six total defense, and the number-two scoring defense.

But we were pretty sure of ourselves. too. Schmidty and I had been part of the Florida staff that had beaten Florida State for the national title in 1996. We felt like we knew its makeup and attitude—and how to attack it.

You couldn't back down to FSU. If you did, it would bury you. We gave their guys our ultimate respect, but our attitude that week was blunt: we're not taking any of their shit.

We were the number-one-ranked team in the country, but we were double-digit underdogs? All of a sudden, people think we can't play? Nuh-uh—we were going to do this. We were going to beat these guys.

When we played him for the national championship, he really surprised me. I noticed every time we had a gathering of both teams, he was so confident when we were called up to speak.

There was a big banquet, maybe a thousand people there. I made some remarks; he made some. I couldn't believe how confident he was. I couldn't understand his overconfidence. He didn't hide it. He came there to win. It seemed real. It didn't seem fake.

I wasn't quite as confident. I was more of a scaredy-cat.

—Bobby Bowden

We thought we matched up pretty good with them. That's what we sold our players on all week long.

They had Weinke, but they didn't do much that was too complicated. We had faced offenses a little bit harder to prepare for. And we had two weeks to practice and get ready.

—Bobby Jack Wright

We were going to play the game at what was then called Pro Player Stadium. It wasn't actually in Miami but closer to the Dade and Broward county line. It was a nice enough stadium, but it wasn't the original Miami Orange Bowl, the one that had opened in 1937 and been the site of some of the greatest college and pro games of all time: Doug Flutie's Miracle in

Miami, Joe Namath's guaranteed win against the Baltimore Colts, Miami's victory against Nebraska for a national title. The list was amazing.

I'm a stadium junkie of sorts and had always wanted to play there. Since we couldn't, we did the next best thing: we practiced there one day. It was a thrill.

I was the host chair for Oklahoma that year.

They were practicing at Barry College almost every day, and Matt McMillen asked if we could help set up a dinner at the practice field. It was a late-afternoon practice, and Bob wanted the players to be able to finish, then eat, then have free time that night.

I helped them get a caterer. Steak dinners.

The players ate, and the majority of them got on the bus for the ride back to the team hotel. A few of them were still finishing up with dinner.

The dining area where they ate looked like a pigsty when they were done.

Bob saw it, and he pulled everybody off the bus. He brought them back into the dining tents. He said, "Look, you treat this like it's your own home and living room. We don't eat like this."

And every player cleaned that place up. He made sure it was left spotless. It was an eye-opening experience and a story that illustrates Bob's character.

—Barry Kates, Orange Bowl committee member, 1996–present

I didn't have a bunch of team rules. We had a standard, and we expected our players to live up to it.

Even if we came back from a road game at 2:00 a.m., I'd make sure we had trash bags at the charter bus door, and all the players would dump whatever garbage they had into those bags. We'd tie up the bags and help the driver put them in the storage area for removal.

I'd walk through our locker room and make a point of picking up towels off the floor after a game. I wanted the players to see what I had seen when I was younger: my dad mopping the locker room floor after a game, or washing a load of jerseys as the last guys were leaving the room. I picked up those towels in my dad's honor. I wanted everyone to know I wasn't above cleaning up the place.

One time during another season, there was a dinner for the players at the east-side stadium suites. When they were done, it looked like there had been a gigantic food fight. Plates left on the tables...food on the floor...a mess.

I began cleaning it up. The people who had served dinner started to come out to help me, but I told them it wasn't their responsibility.

Then a few of the players who were still there got up to help. I told them to sit back down.

Word spread: *Coach is cleaning up the whole damn room!*

Point being, I was trying to teach some respect to those players at the stadium suites that night—and at our Orange Bowl function years earlier. The person who serves you and the person who has to clean up your mess is somebody's mom, sister, dad, brother.

The sort of privileged behavior I saw in some players irked me to no end. It didn't happen often, but if it did, the punishment was swift.

During that Orange Bowl week, there was some injury drama leading up to the game. Heupel had banged his hand on a helmet during practice. In the pregame warm-ups, his passes to our receivers were wobbling. "What the heck is going on?" I asked Chuck Long, our quarterbacks coach. "We going to be OK?"

"Well, his hand is bothering him," he said. "What are we gonna do? We're here, and we're not going with anyone else."

Heupel was a gamer. His hand wasn't 100 percent, but he gutted through it. He was our guy. He wasn't going to miss the final game of his college career or miss a chance to play against the guy that beat him out for a Heisman (Heupel had finished second in the voting).

I remember walking by Florida State's locker room before the game, and they were kind of snickering at us like we were no-names, like they'd run us out of the stadium.

You could kind of feel it, like there was no respect.

—Jerry Schmidt

I always tried to stay on an even keel before and during a game. I wanted to project intensity but also calm to my team and staff. If I was bug-eyed before the game, they might be. too.

That game was different. I was wound up. I was so wound up that I forgot to give instructions to our game captains for the coin flip. They were out in the middle of the field, and I began yelling at Seth Littrell, trying to get his attention.

Meanwhile, Marshall started talking smack to Weinke, who had won the Heisman earlier in December. Our team wasn't happy about the voting results.

> *They came out for the coin toss, and one of their guys says, "You got my boy's f—ing trophy."*
>
> *I say, "What?"*
>
> *"You got my boy's trophy, and I'm coming to get it," he says.*
>
> *I say, "No, you aren't."*
>
> *"We'll see," he says.*
>
> *It was crazy.*
>
> —Chris Weinke, Florida State quarterback, 1997–2000

Our team was a bunch of scrappers. I wanted to set an example for them, so Schmidty and me started pumping our arms and trying to rev up our defense. We wanted them to feed off our energy and confidence.

Early in the game, Weinke threw a swing pass to Anquan Boldin. Our strong safety, Ontei Jones, came up and planted Boldin. Schmidty and me could hardly contain ourselves.

Jones was a senior from Homestead, Florida, whose family had lost everything when Hurricane Andrew struck South Florida in 1992. Their house had been destroyed. One of the very few things his mom could salvage was their birth certificates.

Blake had signed him, and Jones had stuck it out with us. That night, he set the tone for the game with that hit. It was like, "Yeah, that's how we're going to play. This is us *all* day."

It was a defensive masterpiece. We won, 13–2, and shut out one of the most prolific offenses in major college history. We held FSU to forty-two points below its season scoring average. The Seminoles rushed for only twenty-seven yards, and for the first time all season, Weinke didn't throw a touchdown pass, though he did throw two interceptions and fumbled once.

Mike called a great game. In fact, our whole defensive staff—Mike, Brent, Jackie, and Bobby Jack—was outstanding.

Heck, we gave them their only points. Late in the game, we snapped the ball over the head of our punter, who recovered the ball and did what he was coached to do: run into the end zone for a safety. Otherwise, zilch.

Marshall, another kid from the Miami area, intercepted a Weinke pass, had eleven tackles, and was named the game's MVP.

Roy Williams, the guy who could barely bench-press 185 pounds when we got to OU, recovered a fumble and had an interception.

Quentin Griffin scored the only touchdown of the game on 30–Base. OU still runs that play today.

Griffin was the kid we signed out of Houston in 1999 that nobody else wanted. Bobby Jack had gotten a call from Griffin's high school coach and went down there to look at his film, then called me to say we should give him a scholarship. Griffin was five foot seven, and the only other school offering him was I-AA Sam Houston State, I think.

In Bobby Jack I trust, right?

One thing that distracted us: our offensive coordinator, Mark Richt, had been named the new coach at the University of Georgia. It kind of took away some of his time. He was trying to do both things.

Chris Weinke had won the Heisman, and he had missed some time. That scared me a little bit going into it.

But that's not why we lost. I really felt like Bob outschemed us. They played with an edge. But the thing I remember most about that game is how much Bob Stoops confused us with that style of defense.

—Bobby Bowden

I watched the national championship game.

The whole time, just because we'd put together that offense and that group of players and they had elevated and grown and grown, we thought it would be successful.

I wanted both. I wanted to be the head coach at Tech and the offensive coordinator at Oklahoma.

THE TROPHY

I don't know if they would have let me do that.

—Mike Leach

Someone dumped Gatorade on the back of my shirt and sweater vest, and as the game ended, I walked down the sideline and found my brother Mike and gave him a hug. We'd come a long way since Detroit Avenue.

Coach Bowden and I met somewhere in the madness to shake hands. He was his usual gracious self. "Boy," he said, "you just whipped our tail."

After the presentation of the crystal football trophy, ABC's Lynn Swann (now the USC athletic director) referenced the low-scoring ballgame and the fact that we had been double-digit underdogs.

I couldn't help myself.

With Carol at my side, I said on national television, "To be honest with you, we fully expected to play that way, and as a team, we fully expected to win. And it's easy to say that Oklahoma's back!"

I tell people all the time that I don't think it will ever be like that again. Right now, everyone is tapping a foot, waiting for another national championship. But back then, they had been through such a down period in the nineties.

—Teddy Lehman

Our players playfully stormed the ESPN set (part of it actually gave way) and started giving Lee Corso a good-natured hard time for predicting that Florida State (his alma mater) would beat us. We got our photo taken up there.

We went back to the Fontainebleau Hotel in Miami Beach, and, man, did we have a party. Barry Kates helped arrange it in the hospitality suite.

He brought in a deejay. There were cans of Silly String that we sprayed at anyone who moved. Barry ordered a hundred pizzas. My whole family was there. We stayed up the whole night, and then some.

I just wanted to enjoy it and share it with the people I loved, with the people who had believed in me. I had this jet stream of thoughts going through my mind that night. I celebrated. I reflected.

It was so much fun to see my mom laughing. I missed my dad, but I knew, in some way, he was there, too.

All of Youngstown was there. We danced the entire night. Nobody went to bed, including my mother.

Bob danced. Oh, yeah, he was out there. It's the happiest I've seen him and Mike together...it was fun watching the two of them achieve it together.

—Reenie Stoops Farragher

My dad would be beside himself with pride.

—Kathy Stoops Kohowski

We always felt like we have this angel.
His dad is still talked about.

—Carol Stoops

The party was still going in the morning when Barry said, "Look, we've got to get you going. You've got a 10:00 a.m. media conference. You've got to change your shirt and go."

It was nine o'clock. I went back to my hotel room, closed my eyes for maybe thirty minutes, showered, changed, and talked to the press. But now that the excitement of the game had worn off and our celebration had ended, I experienced a letdown—an empty feeling similar to the one I had after the 1996 national championship at Florida. The chase was finished, and I lived for the chase.

You don't think a three-and-a-half-hour game can change your life. But that game did. It changed everything.

And I wasn't ready for it.

Chapter Ten

Identity

Now what?

I was forty years old, and our program had just won a national championship.

I was comfortable with success, but I was much more comfortable with the pursuit of success. Here I was, in only my second year as a head coach, and the success I had chased was already caught—I wasn't prepared for it.

We spend our entire coaching careers preparing for practice, for a game, for workouts, for the off-season, for spring camp, for fall camp, for recruiting—but I wasn't prepared for the aftermath of winning a national championship. How about that?

In an instant, people started treating me differently. I hadn't changed, but the circumstances around me had. I went from being Bob Stoops to being National-Championship-Head-Coach-Bob-Stoops. That was my new name.

I liked the sound of it. I just didn't like the stuff that came with it.

This isn't a complaint. That victory against Florida State will be in the first or second paragraph of my obituary. It will be in the first or second obituary paragraphs of most of the players and coaches on that 2000 team. It was an achievement in which we take great pride and joy.

I also realize how many great college head coaches have never won a national championship. I worked for and with several of them: Coach Alvarez, Coach Snyder, and Coach Fry. I've coached against them: Gary Patterson, Fisher DeBerry, Chris Petersen, Mark Dantonio. I've watched some of them: Bo Schembechler, Earle Bruce, Frank Beamer, and John

Cooper, among others. I have respect for them all and mention their names only to show how tiny the margin of error can be. One game, one play, might have been the difference.

One of the reasons I love football is that it's the ultimate team game. Before that national championship, I was the face of the OU football program, but it was always a shared experience.

Now I felt like too much of the attention was on me, which wasn't fair to my players, my assistant coaches, or my staff. I understood my responsibilities regarding the media, fans, boosters, appearances, speeches, and everything else associated with the job. But I didn't necessarily like doing it all. I didn't want to be the center of attention. I'm an introverted extrovert, or an extroverted introvert—something like that.

I felt this sudden weight to "be" Bob Stoops, the Football Coach. Does that make sense?

I went home to Youngstown shortly after the national championship. That's the place where I was always just Bobby Stoops. I was Ron Sr.'s kid from Mooney.

But this time, I went home and I got treated like a celebrity. My hometown was proud of me, to be sure, and I appreciated it. But this was different. It was almost uncomfortable. All this because of winning a *game*? I didn't think that way. I couldn't process it.

I struggled with it, I really did.

I met my buddy Snake when I got into town. We were supposed to meet family and friends at the MVR Club on North Walnut, one of my favorite Italian restaurant hangouts. But before we drove over there, I said, "Snake, let's you and I head up to the Coconut Grove. Let's go do that before I have to be 'Bob Stoops' tonight." The Coconut Grove was a dive bar not far from where I'd grown up.

So we did, just him and me. We smoked cigars, shot the breeze, had a couple of beers, relaxed for an hour. And then we made our way to the MVR.

An OU fraternity had a scavenger hunt going on, and one of the items on the list was a Bob Stoops signature. People knocked on our door, looking for me to sign something. Carol told them I wasn't home. (My own mom—and I'd do anything for her—once asked me to sign a game program. That was surreal to me.)

After our win, there was more attention, and there were more demands. Again, I'm not complaining about it. That's what happens when you win. What I'm saying is that I had to deal with that, and I didn't deal with it very well, or as well as others have.

The outside world suddenly wanted more out of me. There were so many speaking invitations, appearance requests, media requests. I told Carol that I turned down 90 percent of what crossed my desk. She said, "But you have no idea how much that ten percent has grown."

I wanted to accommodate people when I could. To a certain extent, I wanted to use the win to our program's advantage. The added exposure certainly would help us in recruiting.

But I didn't know how to handle a national championship in only my second year as a head coach. I fought it, and I fought it for a long time.

It also didn't help that my name had been associated with other job openings beginning as early in the 2000 season as November. Some people might like that kind of attention. To me, it was a pain in the ass.

Only a few days after we had beaten Nebraska, Alabama announced that Mike DuBose wouldn't return as its head coach in 2001. A year earlier, DuBose had been the SEC Coach of the Year. That's how fast it can turn.

About the same time as the Alabama announcement, Joe approached me and my agent about increasing my salary and extending my contract. We agreed to the extension, and that was that. A win-win for OU and for me.

I don't think the Bama announcement and OU's extension offer were connected—not that I would have left Oklahoma for Bama at that time. And I don't use job openings as a bargaining tool. Never have, never will.

Then, the day before we played for the national title, Ohio State fired John Cooper. True, he had struggled to beat Michigan, and his bowl record was poor. But he had won a lot of games for Ohio State over the years. Now he was out of a job.

Given my Youngstown and Big Ten background, my name was immediately connected with the opening. Reporters asked Joe if OU would grant Ohio State permission to speak with me—and they asked him this not long before kickoff of the national championship game. Probably not the best time for that question.

And about a week after we beat FSU, the Cleveland Browns fired Chris Palmer. And my name came up.

Let me set the record straight:

I wasn't going to leave Oklahoma for Ohio State.

Ohio State is a Mt. Rushmore program, but I felt an incredible sense of loyalty to President Boren, Joe, and Oklahoma. I had been at OU for only two seasons. To me, Oklahoma wasn't a stepping-stone program; it was a destination. It belonged on the same mountain face as Ohio State—or any other program of that caliber.

Yes, Ohio State asked for permission to talk to me, as well as my brother Mike. I know Joe told reporters that he would deny Ohio State permission to speak with me about the job, but if I had really wanted to discuss the opening with Buckeyes officials, I would have. But I didn't.

I did get a couple of back-channel phone calls from Ohio State people trying to gauge my interest. But I just knew there was no way I could go down that road.

At that point in my career, if I was going to coach a college program, Oklahoma is where I wanted to be. Period. If anything, I was hoping Mike would get the job.

Ohio State did hire a Youngstown guy of sorts. It went with longtime Youngstown State coach Jim Tressel, who had won four I-AA national titles there.

About a month later, Carol and I were at the ESPN ESPY Awards at the MGM Grand in Las Vegas. OU was the College Team of the Year winner.

Just by chance, we walked into the after-party with Jack and Barbara Nicklaus. The Golden Bear had attended Ohio State, and the Jack Nicklaus Museum is located next to the Buckeyes' football facility on Olentangy River Road. He was, and still is, a huge OSU fan. He once even dotted the *i* in Script Ohio.

We started talking, and he said, "I thought we were going to get you to be our coach."

We laughed. But, no, that wasn't going to happen.

I was, however, intrigued by the Browns opening.

I didn't hide my interest in talking to the Browns. I told the Tulsa *World*, on the record (none of this back-channel, don't-use-my-name stuff), that the NFL had always intrigued me and that I'd be happy to talk to them. Nothing came of it.

I made it clear—and it's a stance I've taken throughout my head coaching career—that I wasn't going to audition for the job, because I already had a great job. Either you want to offer me the position, or you don't.

Carmen Policy, a Youngstown guy who had attended Ursuline High, was the president of the Browns at the time. He reached out to me and my agent, Neil Cornrich. The Browns said they were serious about trying to hire me, but again, there was no official offer. I thought about it, but I was enjoying OU too much to make that jump.

Plus, I didn't want to go through a long interview process. And in those situations, word would have leaked to the media and affected our recruiting at Oklahoma. Other schools would have told recruits, "He's trying to go to the NFL. Sign with us instead."

The day after the Tulsa *World* story appeared, I was back in Norman and attended the Kansas-OU basketball game. Our team was honored at halftime, and I used the occasion to clarify things: "Regardless of what you may have heard, I plan on being at Oklahoma for a long, long time," I told the crowd.

I think I kept my word.

With the Cleveland Browns, you had to think of the financial security of your family. That offer, for example, was probably three times the salary that we were paying him at that time. He got some very attractive offers. I never felt like I had to talk him out of it. I think he always felt like he had to ponder those offers.

Leverage? Never, never, never. He just wanted my advice and counsel and confirmation that he should stay here. It was never about money. I was very impressed that, unlike some coaches who use opportunities and offers from elsewhere to try to get better deals—play one university off another— he would never do that. I think he felt very firmly committed to this place. He became part of this university, part of the fabric of this university.

—David Boren

With Heupel gone, we had to choose a new starting quarterback. We had Nate Hybl, who had transferred in from Georgia, and Jason White, who had been the first recruit to commit to me and OU. White had played in two games in 1999, hurt his back while working out, and received a medical redshirt.

We didn't make a final decision until fall camp. We chose Hybl.

Obviously, I didn't agree with the decision.

We were in two-a-days. Between the first practice and the second practice, I made calls to other coaches. I talked to [Virginia Tech's] Frank Beamer, and I had a call in to Larry Coker, who was at Miami, my original school pick.

When I came back for that day's second practice, Coach Long was standing outside, waiting for me. "Hey, I heard you're looking to transfer," he said.

"I made a couple of calls. I was going to talk to you guys after practice about me leaving OU."

Coach Stoops talked to me about it. At that time, I was so mad, so upset about not being the starter. Instead of putting my head down and working my ass off, I got angry. Now, when I look back—what the hell was I thinking?

—Jason White

I knew Jason would be disappointed with the decision. Both me and Chuck Long met with Jason. "Look, nothing is final about naming a quarterback," I told him. "A lot's going to happen this year. Keep training. Keep pushing. You're going to have your opportunity. Be ready for it."

He nodded his head. You could tell he wasn't sold on the idea, but he stayed.

Of course, whatever issues I was dealing with after the national championship and our quarterback competition paled in comparison to what happened late that summer.

Carol and I had noticed that Mackie, our five-year-old daughter, didn't have the stamina to play as long and hard as the other kids. Her neck hurt often, and she sometimes complained of headaches.

I was in the middle of two-a-day practices when Carol took all three of our kids for their annual checkups. Our pediatrician in Norman, Dr. James Fields, decided to test them for scoliosis, which is a sideways curvature of the spine. He detected it in Mackie and ordered an MRI immediately.

When the images came back, I saw the concern in the face of the specialist as he examined them. There were dark marks, splotches of sorts, up and down Mackie's spine. They told us they could be fluid, tumors, or something else.

Talk about your heart in your stomach. Here was our five-year-old daughter, and something was obviously wrong. We were beside ourselves in fear. We were scared of the unknown and scared for our baby girl.

About that same time, Matt McMillen called me with a question related to something in our football office. He had no idea about what was going on with Mackie, but he could instantly sense in my voice that there was a serious problem. Shortly after the call, Matt's wife, Gina, walked into the doctor's office, looking for us. She worked across the street at another Oklahoma City medical building. She said that when Matt heard how shaken I was, he had asked her to go find us . . . that something was terribly wrong. It was a gesture we've never forgotten.

The MRI results were sent to more doctors. For hours—it seemed much longer—we waited for a diagnosis. That's a long time to hold your breath.

Eventually, they told us the dark marks weren't tumors but fluid on the spine. They said the scoliosis was the result of another condition called Chiari malformation, which, in Mackie's case, meant that brain tissue had extended into her spinal canal and was acting as a sink plug of sorts, blocking the flow of cerebrospinal fluid—it couldn't circulate properly.

So now we knew what it was. Next, we had to fix it.

Dr. Brock Schnebel, who led our medical team, did a nationwide search for the best pediatric neurosurgeon for this type of procedure. He whittled the list to five, but one name kept coming to the top: Dr. Arnold Menezes, who just happened to work out of the University of Iowa Hospitals and Clinics system in Iowa City.

Carol and I looked at each other and couldn't believe it. We instantly knew where we were taking Mackie. There was such a comfort level in going back to Iowa. It was home.

After studying the MRI and other information, Dr. Menezes explained that Mackie would require surgery at the base of the brain. He warned us that it was a very delicate procedure, and there were no guarantees of success. As parents, for us to hear those words was terrifying.

There are some dates you never forget. I'll never forget Monday, August 20, the day Mackie went in for surgery.

We were opening our season at home against North Carolina that Saturday—like I cared. A few days before I left for Iowa City to be there with Carol and Mackie for the surgery, I called our players together. I told them about Mackie's condition, and as I did, I broke down in tears. I couldn't help it, nor did I try to fight it. At that moment, I wasn't a coach. I was a father, and my baby girl was sick.

I told them I was going to be in Iowa and that I didn't know exactly when I'd be back. So much would depend on the operation.

The players were quiet at first. But then, one by one, they told me not to worry about football, or them. Take care of your family, they said. We'll be praying for Mackie.

I had walked into that meeting room to reassure my players. I walked out with them having comforted me.

The media would notice my absence, so we said that Mackie was having "a corrective procedure." We wanted to keep it as quiet as we could. But the fact that we were leaving the state for the surgery—and that I was leaving the team—made it clear that this wasn't any normal corrective procedure.

The surgery took place at the University of Iowa Stead Family Children's Hospital. That's the same hospital now famous for the Iowa Wave, where the entire Kinnick Stadium crowd, including players on both sides, turns and waves to the patients who are looking down from the windows adjacent to the stadium. There are a lot of great college football traditions, but the Iowa Wave is as good as it gets.

Carol's sister and her family drove from their home in Minnesota to be with us. And the kindness and support we received from Kirk Ferentz and his entire staff in the nearby Iowa football offices was overwhelming. He was wonderful, as was the hospital staff at the Children's Hospital. And there was a steady flow of people who came by the hospital to offer their prayers and support.

The surgery lasted about six hours. As a football coach, you're used to being in control. You control the daily schedule, the play calling, the practices...everything within that football world.

But there isn't a more helpless and horrible feeling than having no control over the fate of your own daughter.

Carol is the one who explained the situation to Mackie. She said that the procedure had to be done, that it might be painful, but that it was the only way to get better. It's amazing how children instinctively know how to be courageous in those kinds of circumstances. Mackie was only five, but she understood.

When the surgery was completed, Dr. Menezes told us he felt good about it, but he wouldn't know for sure until Mackie was awake and he knew she could function, that she could talk.

More waiting. More praying. More hoping.

When Mackie woke up, she began vomiting every hour for the next twenty-four hours. And for weeks, we were worried that the surgery had affected her personality. But little by little, she improved. She was going to be Mackie again.

I stayed in Iowa City until Thursday and then flew back to Oklahoma. Our season started on Saturday, but my mind was 672 miles away. "I'm not going to have much energy and intensity for this game," I told my assistants. "Make sure you cover for me and ramp up your players."

We beat North Carolina, 41–27. That win goes on my record, but it really belongs to those assistant coaches and players. I did my best to help, but I was mostly a zombie that week.

Happiest I've seen Bob? When he knew Mackie was going to be OK after surgery. Probably as happy as I've ever seen him.

— Matt McMillen

To this day, I still have a connection with the Children's Hospital at Iowa. Carol and I donate to a foundation related directly to Dr. Menezes's work and research. Anything that helps further the cause, that helps ease or cure the suffering of a child, I'm all in.

You want to know why I'm a regular visitor and contributor to the

Children's Hospital of OU? Mackie is why. Those brave, tough kids in that hospital are why. The parents of those kids are why.

I would have given Dr. Menezes ten years of my salary for what he did for Mackie, who still has a scar that runs from the back of her lower neck to her skull, the result of fifty surgical staples.

I always laugh when I hear TV announcers say something like, "What a courageous throw that was." Or, "That took some courage to make that downhill putt."

Please. Courage is those kids battling their illnesses. You want perspective? Go visit those folks. You lose a football game? Big deal. Nah, wake up—it pales in comparison with what those kids are handling.

For about ten years after her surgery, Mackie went back every six months for a checkup. Then it was once a year, then once every two years—and now, not at all.

In that win against North Carolina, we started a true freshman defensive tackle named Tommie Harris. Harris was a top-thirty-five national recruit from Texas, and on his very first college play, he recorded a tackle. It wouldn't be his last.

We had won the 2000 national championship with twenty-three freshmen and sophomores on our two-deep roster. Now we were adding more talent and depth.

If Harris was a top recruit, then freshman defensive tackle Dusty Dvoracek was on the other end of the spectrum. He might have been the fiftieth- or sixtieth-ranked high school defensive tackle in the country. He wasn't without his share of scholarship offers, but there were questions about his size.

Mike and I had watched him on tape and loved his motor. We weren't going to obsess over his size; he was big enough. And we didn't care that his Dallas-area high school had never had a player get a Division-I scholarship.

Dvoracek was on a recruiting visit at OU in 2000 when we beat Nebraska. He had been on the field and was waiting in the weight room near our locker room when I saw him. "Why wouldn't you want to be at OU and be part of this?" I asked.

"I do," he said.

"I'm going to hold you to that."

My girlfriend wanted me to go to Texas A&M. So even though I had ver-bally committed to Oklahoma, I went to A&M on a recruiting visit on the same Saturday they played OU in 2000.

I had great seats, and everybody was nice and kind to me. But then Mar-shall returned the interception late in the game, and I jumped up and started cheering. OU won.

Needless to say, I didn't stay long with my girlfriend. My girlfriend was crying when I said I was going to OU. Sorry, Aggies.

— Dusty Dvoracek, Oklahoma defensive tackle, 2001–2005

We were 4–0 with Hybl as our starter and ranked number three in the *AP* poll going into the Red River game against number-five Texas. Hybl got hurt in the first quarter, and White went in. What had we told him about unexpected opportunities?

White was so nervous in the huddle that our tight end Trent Smith had to call the first play for him. Then he got sacked on the play.

White calmed down and led us to a touchdown on that drive—and to a 14–3 win. He remained our starter in wins at Kansas and then against Baylor, when we climbed to number two in the rankings. His season ended the fol-lowing week at number-three Nebraska when he tore the ACL in his left knee.

Any chance of possibly playing for a second consecutive national cham-pionship ended November 24, when we lost at Oklahoma State.

We beat Arkansas in the Cotton Bowl to finish 11–2.

A few days later, a bombshell exploded in college football: Coach Spur-rier resigned at Florida. He was fifty-six, had been at Florida since the 1990 season, and was ready to pursue a job in the NFL. And earlier in Decem-ber, Notre Dame had fired Bob Davie.

Once again, my name popped up as a leading candidate. This happened at the same time that Roy Williams was deciding about his playing future.

After the Cotton Bowl, I all but pushed Roy out of our program. He had another year of eligibility remaining, but there was no possible reason for him to stay at OU. There were times during our season when I thought he was almost bored in a way. He was that much better than everyone else. He never got tired. He never got hurt. He was always prepared. He was as strong and durable as titanium. I don't think he ever missed a practice. The former pear-shaped kid was ready for the next step.

Roy called me not long after the game and said he was thinking about skipping his last year to enter the NFL draft.

"Roy, you've got my blessings," I said. "I believe you're a top-ten pick."

He said, "Coach, you come back, and I'll come back." He was laughing when he said that, but I think part of him really meant it.

"If I do, I do," I told him. "But I feel good about you going to the NFL. It's the right thing for you."

I made a run at Bob when Steve left. By then, he'd been there two years. I called him, and he was surprised about Steve.

—Jeremy Foley

Unlike Roy, however, Coach Spurrier hadn't given me a heads-up about his decision, so it was a surprise but not a shock. I knew how he felt. He always said that everything had its own lifetime. In this case, his lifetime of coaching at Florida had reached its end. It was time for something new.

Jeremy called and asked if he could come to Norman and meet with me.

"Jeremy, you don't have to come here," I said. "I know what Florida is all about. I know what you're all about. You sure you want to do this?"

"Bobby, I have to do this for myself and for the fan base at Florida. I have to come there so I can speak with you in person. We have to have that conversation."

I felt such an allegiance to Jeremy that I couldn't tell him no.

When he landed, reporters and TV cameras were waiting for him at the local FBO. They had tracked Jeremy's flight by an online service that monitors the tail numbers of private planes. So much for the secret meeting.

However, he did manage to get to my house without anyone following him.

This will tell you about Bobby Stoops:
After we met, he said, "I want to talk to Carol. I think this is what I want to do, to come to Florida."

I called him back later, and he said, "I don't think I can do it. They gave me my first chance here."

It was exactly the decision he should have made. I wished him well.

That's the kind of guy he is. He did the right thing. He didn't play the game.

—Jeremy Foley

I almost took the Florida job. Of all the times I've been approached about working at another school, that was the closest I came to leaving OU.

I had a great relationship with Jeremy. I loved The Swamp. You knew you could keep it going at Florida. It wasn't very far from my beach place. And Carol and I had had such a good time there when I was the defensive coordinator. So much about the offer made sense.

I really believe that some things might fit you, but the timing isn't right. The timing wasn't right with Florida. I just couldn't do it. Again, it came down to loyalty and what we had built at Oklahoma. I believed in Oklahoma, and the people at OU believed in me.

As for the Notre Dame opening, there was nothing more than a couple of phone calls to me and Neil asking if I'd be interested in talking. We took a respectful pass.

By the way, three months later, the Dallas Cowboys selected Roy with a number-eight overall pick of the draft.

He left, but I came back. No regrets.

Chapter Eleven

Adversity

Oh, no, it couldn't have happened again, could it? *Not that football is fair... but please tell me it didn't happen again.*

That's what I was thinking when I saw Jason White crumpled on the ground, grasping his right knee in agony, our home crowd suddenly quiet.

We were playing Alabama in our 2002 home opener. Brent Musburger and Gary Danielson were there for ABC. At the time, there were thirteen national championships between the two programs.

We were ranked number two in the *AP* poll, were big favorites against the unranked Tide, and were facing the coach (Dennis Franchione) who had been on the short list for the OU job in 1998.

It was a simple option play. Jason could keep it himself or pitch it to Quentin Griffin, who was flared out to Jason's right.

There was 1:15 left in the first quarter when he took the snap, and 1:08 when his right knee buckled and he fell to the artificial turf. Nobody had hit him. It was eerily and horribly similar to what had happened to him a season earlier against Nebraska: a rollout to the right (that time a pass play), his left knee planted as he threw, no contact, a torn ACL.

I ran out to where Jason lay on the ground, our trainers kneeling next to him. What do you say? How do you comfort someone who knows that his career might have been altered, maybe ended, by what had happened during the previous seven seconds?

If you've ever torn your ACL, you know. There's usually a sound, a pop, a burning feeling, and then the realization that something is terribly wrong.

I didn't have time to do much. I hoped for the best—maybe he had just sprained the knee—but somewhere in my mind, I knew better. We had to get Hybl in the game, get ready for the next play. Football is impatient that way.

Two of our trainers helped Jason off the field and into our stadium locker room. Of course, the eventual diagnosis was as everyone feared: a torn right ACL. Another surgery. Another season lost. Would he come back? Could he come back? If he did, could he play? And what would happen to our season if he didn't?

But those were questions for another day. We had to beat Alabama first, which we did, but it wasn't a victory we would celebrate. We had lost Jason, and we had done everything we could to keep Bama in the game—and we had succeeded.

Then we did something else: we got better. By the week of November 3, we were number one in the *AP* poll. We were in a position to do what all coaches hope for: to control our own postseason destiny.

Instead, we lost at Texas A&M. And three weeks later, Oklahoma State ended our national championship hopes.

But we still could win the Big 12 Championship, and if things broke the right way, we even could end up in the Rose Bowl.

Colorado was our Big 12 title game opponent. We had beaten CU earlier in the season but then had to hear its postgame predictions about a rematch. One of CU's freshmen defensive backs had even guaranteed a win against us if we met in the conference championship.

If, if, if.

I said it then, and I'll say it now: football isn't golf. It ain't like walking up to the local country club and you get a mulligan on the first tee box. Gary Barnett, the Colorado coach, wanted a mulligan. Hey, we were set to play that first time, and we had won.

Anyway, Colorado got its rematch. It also got beat again, this time worse than the first. I didn't hear any more talk about rematches and guaranteed victories.

In 2002, there was no playoff system in major college football. Back then, it was the BCS—the Bowl Championship Series. With our win against CU, we were guaranteed a spot in one of the big BCS bowl games:

Sugar, Rose, or Orange. Miami and Ohio State were going to play for the national championship in the Fiesta Bowl.

We ended up in the Rose Bowl against Washington State, which somehow offended the purists—and some of the Rose Bowl officials themselves—who wanted co–Big Ten champion Iowa in the game instead of us. That would have kept the usual Pac-10 (that's what it was then) versus Big Ten arrangement.

We weren't going to apologize for the Rose Bowl invitation. It's not like we were going out to Pasadena on a load of wood. We weren't driving there in a turnip truck. We had some football pedigree: those seven national championships, Heisman Trophy winners, tradition. Instead of grousing about who wasn't there, maybe some of those folks should have been glad *we* were there.

I know I was happy about it. This was the first-ever Rose Bowl for OU. I hadn't been back to the Granddaddy of Them All since the 1985 season, when I was a graduate assistant at Iowa. I had played in the game during the 1981 season.

It was my favorite place to play or coach—and still is. I love the venue, the history, the San Gabriel Mountains in the distance, the lushness of the field, the tradition. When we were there with Iowa, the great Jim Murray of the *Los Angeles Times* would write about the game. It was all part of the experience.

We did our part. We beat Washington State by twenty. Hybl was the Rose Bowl MVP.

I've never understood why some of our local media and some of our fans didn't give Nate the recognition and appreciation he deserved. Or maybe they did, but I've never felt he was appreciated enough.

He came in as a transfer, sat out a year, won the starting job, led us to a Cotton Bowl win, lost the starting job, never complained, and then led us to a Rose Bowl win. His name is forever etched on the wall as a Rose Bowl MVP. I was just happy and proud of him for doing that.

Since our first season in 1999, we had won a national championship, the Cotton Bowl, and the Rose Bowl. But we wanted more. We wanted a chance to add to our national championship total.

During the 2003 and 2004 seasons, we got our wish.

Jason, who was granted another medical redshirt year, returned to the practice field with two surgically reconstructed knees. But could he play? Could his knees hold up? Of course, we were rooting for him. We were rooting for us, too. A healthy (relatively speaking) Jason White improved our chances to win.

In late summer, we announced that White had won the starting job. It was a remarkable rehab effort on his part.

We began the season ranked number one, and we stayed there from August 30 through November 22, when we beat Texas Tech to complete an undefeated regular season, our second in four years.

We were 12–0, and White wasn't just having a comeback season, he was having a Heisman-quality season. Going into the Big 12 Championship against Coach Snyder's K-State team, the media was speculating about us in historic terms — as in, were we one of the best teams ever?

I cringed when I heard that. Yes, White was the Heisman favorite (we had outscored our opponents by a 35.1-point margin while playing the fourteenth-toughest schedule in the country), our defense was very good (ranked number one in total defense), and we had trailed our opponents a grand total of less than six minutes the entire season. We had won twelve games and had a big lead in the BCS rankings, but we hadn't earned anything yet — not the Big 12 Championship, and not a place in the national title game.

Leading up to the Kansas State contest, Mike was named the new head coach at Arizona. It was a great moment for him and the entire Stoops family. We congratulated him and were happy for him, and then everyone returned their focus to the Big 12 Championship.

The game couldn't have started any better for us: we stopped K-State on its first possession and then drove sixty-five yards in just eighty seconds to take a 7–0 lead.

It would be our only touchdown of the game. We lost, 35–7.

Afterward, I told the media, "They outplayed us in every part of the game. They outcoached us. They took it to us in every part of the game. They made the plays that mattered."

Up to that point, it was the most lopsided defeat in my five seasons at

OU. With the loss, there was the possibility we could slide to number three in the BCS rankings.

We flat-out overlooked them.

After the game, several people said that loss cost me the Heisman. At that time, I was more concerned about us playing for the national championship.

—Jason White

The BCS rankings were released the next day. We had survived. We were still number one and would play Nick Saban's number-two-ranked LSU team in the Sugar Bowl. Meanwhile, once-beaten USC, which was number one in the *AP* and Coaches polls, would play Michigan in the Rose Bowl. I understood the controversy—and understood why USC was upset with the system—but I also believed we were deserving of a spot in the BCS Championship. We had carried the weight of being ranked number one from preseason to the Big 12 Championship, and carried it well. Even with the loss to K-State, we hadn't dropped to number two or three in the BCS. I wasn't going to apologize for a thing. We had earned our place.

A few days after that, we learned that Jason was one of four finalists for the Heisman, along with Pittsburgh's Larry Fitzgerald, Michigan's Chris Perry, and Ole Miss's Eli Manning.

If anybody deserved a trip to New York, it was Jason, who led the nation in pass efficiency, had thrown forty touchdowns and nearly twenty completions of forty yards or more. The people who said he was a "system" quarterback didn't know what they were talking about.

When Jason's name was announced as the winner in a close vote over Fitzgerald, there was a huge sense of pride, mostly for Jason himself, who had overcome so much. His story was one of perseverance, toughness, and excellence.

I wanted Jason to soak in the evening, but I told him, "Hey, enjoy this, but let's get ready for the big game we've got. We've got one more."

Around that same time, a headhunter type representing the Atlanta Falcons contacted me. The Falcons, owned by Home Depot cofounder Arthur

A Stoops family portrait, early 1970s. Top row: My dad, Ron Sr.; me; Kathy; my mom, Evelyn; Ron Jr. Bottom row: Mike, Mark, and Maureen.
(Courtesy of Stoops family)

Our middle school basketball team in Youngstown. That's me, back row, fifth from the left. Future boxing world champion Ray Mancini is in the front row, fourth from left.
(Courtesy of Stoops family)

Dad coaching us up at Cardinal Mooney. *(Courtesy of Stoops family)*

Look closely at my Cardinal Mooney uniform, and you'll notice I'm wearing my Joe Washington OU cleats. *(Courtesy of Stoops family)*

See the back of my jersey? At Iowa, I was Bobby, not Bob.
(Courtesy of University of Iowa Library)

My parents often made the drive from Youngstown to Iowa City. This time
they brought Mark along to visit Mike (No. 2) and me.
(Courtesy of Stoops family)

Mike and me holding our favorite flowers after beating Michigan State to earn the Big Ten's berth in the 1982 Rose Bowl. It was Iowa's first appearance in the game since 1959.
(Courtesy of Stoops family)

From wanting to transfer during my redshirt freshman season to being named a team captain for my senior season. What a journey. From left to right: Brett Miller, Mark Bortz, Mike Hufford, me, and Norm Granger.
(Courtesy of University of Iowa)

A proud moment: Coach Fry presents me with the 1982 team MVP award. *(Courtesy of Stoops family)*

Coach Fry had a rule: always hire assistants who aspire to be head coaches. Our 1983 Iowa staff (I was a graduate assistant) had its share of head-coaches-to-be. Back row, from left: Bill Snyder, Del Miller, Kirk Ferentz, Coach Fry, Carl Jackson, Don Patterson, and Bill Dervrich. Front row, from left: Bernie Wyatt, Barry Alvarez, Bill Brashier, Dan McCarney, and me. *(Courtesy of University of Iowa)*

My parents with the groom.
(Courtesy of Stoops family)

I couldn't have asked for a better best friend than Jimmy "Snake" Braydich.
He was there the day Carol and I got married.
(Courtesy of Stoops family)

The adventure begins. Carol and I leave Iowa for Kent State and my first full-
time assistant coaching job.
(Courtesy of Stoops family)

The 1990 Kansas State coaching staff (head coach Bill Snyder back row middle, me to his right, my brother Mike second from the right). One of the fondest memories of my entire coaching career came in 1989—Coach Snyder's first at K-State—when our team ended a thirty-game winless streak. *(Courtesy of Kansas State University)*

Notice the perfect shooting form during a driveway hoops game with our
Kansas State defensive backs.
(Courtesy of Stoops family)

Mackie and me at the Swamp.
(Courtesy of Stoops family)

I loved my three seasons as defensive coordinator at Florida.
(Courtesy of University of Florida Athletic Department)

Me, Carol, Jerri Spurrier, and the Head Ball Coach at the 2018 Heisman Trophy ceremony. My first experience against Coach Spurrier's offense didn't go well.
(Courtesy of Stoops family)

I loved when Carol brought the kids to practice. That's Jason White (No. 18) talking to Chuck Long. Mike and I are chatting up another player.
(Courtesy of Stoops family)

Mike has a victory cigar during our 2000 National Championship
celebration party.
(Courtesy of Stoops family)

Celebrating with Jason White and our staff after he won the 2003 Heisman
Trophy. Jason was the first player to sign with OU after I got the job.
(Courtesy of Stoops family)

Nothing better than a family photo after a win against Texas.
(Courtesy of Stoops family)

We weren't the only ones not to offer Baker Mayfield a scholarship out of high school. But I made sure he got one after he walked on at OU. That's me, Carol, and Baker after the 2017 Big 12 Championship game. *(Courtesy of Stoops family)*

After winning the 2016 Big 12 title on our home field (a first in my eighteen seasons at OU), we pulled the kids out of the locker room for a family photo. Except for Carol, nobody knew that I had just coached my final game at Memorial Stadium. *(Courtesy of Blake Kuenzi)*

Two Youngstown guys from the neighborhood: Boom and me.
(Courtesy of Stoops family)

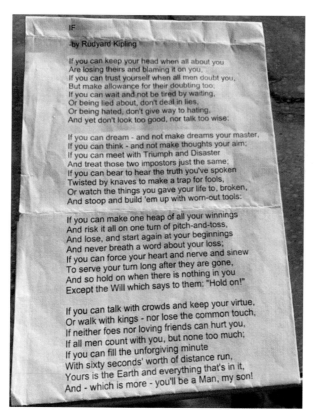

This Kipling poem has gotten me through some tough times. I kept a worn copy of it on my OU desk—and took that folded sheet of paper with me when I left.
(Courtesy of Stoops family)

My family doesn't know what to make of a larger-than-life me. I feel the same way. It's an honor to have a statue at OU, but also a surreal experience. *(Courtesy of Stoops family)*

Blank, were looking for a new head coach after firing Dan Reeves and replacing him with what amounted to a late-season interim coach: Wade Phillips.

The Falcons had quarterback Michael Vick and were in the process of hiring Rich McKay as general manager. Blank certainly was an owner of substance and accomplishment.

I told the representative, "I'm talking to the owner, or I'm not doing this."

I didn't need to practice interviewing for a job. I had a job, and a damn good one. In my opinion, if you were at Oklahoma, you shouldn't have to interview for a job.

Plus, if I was going to discuss a position with an NFL team, then I wanted to do that with the person who actually owned it. I had heard a handful of stories involving college coaches who had been romanced by NFL franchises—and who had thought the job was theirs—only to be dumped for someone else at the last minute. I wasn't going to be one of those guys.

After we hung up, I figured that was the end of that.

A few nights later, I was driving home after finishing up some recruiting calls. My cell phone rang. I didn't recognize the area code, but I answered anyway.

"I understand that you don't want to talk to anybody but the owner."

It was Arthur Blank.

We had a nice, brief chat about the job. But there was nothing close to an offer. He was just kicking the tires on me.

I thanked him for the call. The Falcons later hired San Francisco 49ers defensive coordinator Jim Mora Jr.

Going into the game against LSU, we thought we had the better team. Maybe, but LSU had the better night. They beat us, 21–14.

There were some OU fans who said LSU had an unfair advantage, what with the Sugar Bowl amounting to a home game for the Tigers. Some thought Mike's departure to Arizona might have had an effect. (He didn't coach in the national championship; Brent Venables assumed all the defensive coordinator duties.) Sorry, no excuses. We didn't do enough to win. Saban and his team were just a little bit better.

I would miss Mike because of all the great work he had done for our program, and because we were family. But I had a lot of confidence in Brent and our defensive philosophies.

Meanwhile, a man-child from Palestine, Texas, would soon arrive in Norman.

His name was Adrian Peterson.

Only a handful of players came to Oklahoma during my watch whom I knew, barring catastrophic injury, were destined for greatness. Adrian Peterson was one of those few. He was six foot two and about 216 pounds, but he ran like a sprinter and ran right over would-be tacklers like a Peterbilt semi. I'm actually surprised anybody could tackle him in high school.

The 1981 Iowa version of Bobby Stoops might have relished coming up in run support and throwing my 180-something pounds at him. But I don't think it would have turned out too well for me.

Every major program in the country wanted him. He was a five-star recruit, the number-one-ranked player in the country, if you believed the recruiting services. And in this case, we did.

On the Sunday before that 2003 Big 12 Championship game against Kansas State, Cale Gundy and I had gone to visit Adrian's father, Nelson, in the Federal Correctional Institution in Texarkana. It was the same facility where former Heisman Trophy winner Billy Cannon of LSU had served three years for making counterfeit money.

Nelson was serving a ten-year sentence for money laundering from drug proceeds. Adrian was only in seventh grade when Nelson was convicted in 1999.

For me, it was an important reminder that we weren't recruiting a jersey number and football statistics. We were dealing with young men with human frailties, with families who do their best to battle life's challenges with dignity and grace.

Yet there was no way I could personally relate to the situation. Nor could I know what it must have been like for an eight-year-old Adrian when his nine-year-old brother was killed by a drunken driver only a few feet away from where he stood. Later, he had to deal with whatever emotions had come over the divorce of his parents and his mother's subsequent remarriage.

ADVERSITY

Adrian's mom, Bonita Jackson, had been a high school track star, and Nelson a former college basketball player. They both wanted the best for their son.

We had spoken with Adrian on the phone in the past, and he had visited the campus. But it was important that we had a family visit, even if that meant going through metal detectors.

Adrian had been to the correctional facility before to see his dad. For this visit, though, we had had to get special permission from the warden. It had taken nearly six months to arrange the meeting.

For several hours, we all sat around an outside table—me, Cale, Nelson, Bonita, Adrian, and several other family members—and talked about Oklahoma and why it might be the right place for Adrian.

I told them we ran a tough, hard-nosed program. I said I wanted to offer Adrian a scholarship, but I couldn't offer him a starting job at running back. He would have to earn that on his own. I would give him every opportunity as a true freshman to do that, but there would be no guarantees. If he needed one, then he should probably go to another school.

We discussed academics, quality of life, support systems, and geography (Adrian's family would be a four-and-a-half-hour drive from Norman).

Nelson was wonderful, as was the whole family. We had a great visit, and Cale and I left there thinking that we had made a strong case for OU.

Another development helped us: after our meeting, the warden decided he couldn't accommodate all the other recruiting visit requests from other coaches. We were the only ones who got to sit down with Nelson.

Still, Adrian had lots of good college choices. He eventually whittled it down to OU and Pete Carroll's USC program.

I read later in an ESPN story that during the recruiting process, Adrian had visited Nelson in Texarkana, and they each had written down their school preferences on pieces of paper and then folded them up. Adrian showed his first.

He had chosen OU.

Adrian then had asked his dad for his choice. Nelson gave him the paper, and when Adrian unfolded it, it read, "Whatever decision you make, I'll be happy."

And that, if you're a parent, is how you're supposed to do it. It's your kid's decision, not yours.

Some recruitments are an ordeal. The parents are overbearing. The players are spoiled with entitlement. But recruiting Adrian was the best. He publicly committed to OU during the January 3, 2004, All-American Bowl in San Antonio. The next night, we lost to LSU.

Even after he verbally committed to us, we still called to check in. I guess it was habit, because some recruits actually keep track of which coaches and schools call the most. After one of our calls, Adrian finally said, "Coach, don't worry about calling me all the time." He didn't need reassurance. In fact, he preferred that we not call at all. He had made up his mind, and now he wanted a break.

We respected his wishes, but there was a tiny bit of apprehension as National Signing Day approached. We didn't doubt Adrian, but there have been more than a few eleventh-hour changes of mind in the recruiting world. According to the Tulsa *World*, someone had taken out a full-page ad in his local newspaper all but begging Adrian not to leave the state of Texas to play football.

True to his word, though, he signed with OU.

Cale deserves the credit for developing a true trust with Adrian and his family. And maybe we owe that warden a thanks, too.

When Adrian got to campus (we called him AD—short for what Nelson called him: "All Day"), I took him over to the indoor facility to meet with Schmidty. NCAA rules didn't allow me to watch Adrian in those early workouts. I told Schmidty not to push AD too hard, that he had tweaked a hamstring or something in a recent track meet. And then I left, figuring we'd get Adrian's baseline workout numbers at a later date.

Later, Schmidty told me, "You can't believe this guy. He is a beast. He wins every race, every conditioning contest."

He ran a 4.43 and a 4.42 forty-yard dash that day. And he wasn't even wearing real workout gear. I think he had on high-tops when I dropped him off.

He did a ten-foot-seven broad jump and a thirty-nine-inch vertical. What?

He just walked into our program as a physical freak. He was going to win everything. Not one time during a practice did I ever see him get beat in a conditioning drill.

We had an experienced team that year. Our players had seen highly recruited and touted freshmen come into the program and then wither at that level.

Adrian wasn't one of those freshmen. He rushed for 1,925 yards, with 1,365 of them coming *after* contact. If he couldn't run around you or past you, then he'd run through you.

Dan Cody was our senior All-American defensive end. He wasn't easily impressed by anyone. But he had faced Adrian in scrimmages and practices and had seen him make fools of quality defenders on other teams. So when a reporter asked him how good Adrian really was, Cody said, "When the guy's foot hits the ground, the earth moves in the opposite direction."

Quentin Griffin had been a great back for us. His OU career doesn't get the recognition it deserves. He is top ten in OU rushing yards and rushing attempts for a season and a career. He is number one in rushing touchdowns in a game, number one in one-hundred-yard games in a season, and top ten in career rushing touchdowns and career one-hundred-yard games.

Adrian, though, elevated us to a different level. Jason put up big numbers again, and our defense was playing outstandingly at the back end of our schedule.

A game that sticks with me was our early-November win at Texas A&M. We had beaten them 77–0 at our place a season earlier, the worst loss in their program's history. I knew they'd be motivated, but Jason threw five touchdowns in a comeback win, and he did it with a heavy heart.

My favorite game of my career would be the Texas A&M game in 2004. I had had a really rough week. My grandfather had passed away in St. Louis. We had practice on Tuesday, and I had a flight to Missouri late Tuesday night. The funeral was going to be on Wednesday.

As soon as I got the news, Coach Stoops was always there for me. "Hey, you OK?" he'd say. "What can I do?" He was always checking up on me.

My flight got canceled Tuesday night, so me and my sister rented a car and drove all night to St. Louis. It took eight hours to get there. We went to the funeral and then flew home.

Against A&M, we were down, 14–0, in the first quarter, but if you looked at Coach Stoops, you'd never know we were behind. You'd think we were winning the game.

We ended up winning that game.

—Jason White

Once again, we finished the regular season undefeated and beat Colorado, 42–3, in the Big 12 Championship. Brent kept the pressure on them with blitzes, and CU gained just forty-six total yards, was 0-for-12 on third downs, didn't cross midfield until the second half, and had only three first downs (two by penalty). Their quarterback—Joel Klatt—has since gone on to a successful TV career, but that day, we held him to just fifty-two passing yards and eight completions.

The victory earned us a spot in the national championship against USC in the Orange Bowl. Jason and Adrian were Heisman finalists. (Adrian finished second, Jason third in the voting behind USC quarterback Matt Leinart.)

USC and OU had been ranked number one and two during the entire season. It seemed only right that we met in the title game.

Our whole team mantra in 2004 was one word: "Finish."

In 2003, we had a great team, certainly talented enough to win a national championship. But we didn't finish. We ended our season by losing to K-State and then to LSU in the Sugar Bowl.

Our 2004 season was going to be different. And through twelve games, it was. And then I made the biggest mistake of my career. I'm not sure there's even a second place. It still haunts me.

We took a 7–0 lead, and then USC beat us like a drum the rest of the game. We lost, 55–19. Leinart, LenDale White, Reggie Bush...they whipped us. We had four turnovers. Adrian was held to eighty-two yards. Their defense shut us down. We were a better team than we played that night, but the score is the score.

As I was leaving the locker room late that night, I saw one of our players, a senior, slide into the back seat of a limousine. When I got back to the team hotel, I saw six, seven, eight of our players talking with agents. My heart sank.

I want to make this clear: USC whipped us. But you can't have players who say they're all in, who say they want to finish strong, and yet they have one foot out the door. If you're going into a game thinking, *I can't wait to get back to the hotel, sign with an agent, and get my money*, then you can't be all in. Either you're totally invested, or you're not.

You think back to things that happened that week: do you really think they really checked out? I don't know. I know there were some guys that didn't ride the bus with us after the game. Only way that happens is if you talked to someone before the game.

—Jason White

I'm not saying our players did it maliciously or that they didn't care. But subconsciously, it had to affect them. They probably don't think they did anything wrong. The game was done; they could see all the agents they wanted.

It was my job, and my job alone, to make sure they understood the commitment required for that game. For whatever reason, I didn't reach the players that week. I didn't get them to finish through the national championship. That's on me.

I was in charge of the players' mental preparation and toughness. How did I not see that coming? To have all those talks with your team but not recognize whatever undercurrent there was regarding agents? That's entirely my fault.

In the following years, I talked to my players before every bowl game about the importance of being all in. I told them about the 2004 team. I asked them to simply wait until they got home *after* the bowl game to make their business decisions. Don't commit to anything until you're home, when you have time to deal with it and make a smart decision.

I can't remember the exact year—it was a season or two after we had won the 2000 national championship—but I was at a Christmas party at Toby Keith's house in Moore, Oklahoma, which is just down the road from Norman. Toby is a longtime OU fan and has become a close friend.

We were sitting around the bar with Coach Switzer, who was talking about the different teams he had faced in national championship games.

His OU teams had won three national titles (1974, 1975, 1985), but he said he had lost out on three others.

We had won ours in my second year. Maybe that's why Coach Switzer had looked at me and said, "You young shit, you think you're going to win every one of 'em."

Maybe I did. Isn't that the way you're supposed to think?

Turns out, he jinxed me.

Chapter Twelve

Statue of Liberty

One day in 2005, I got home unexpectedly early from a weeklong recruiting trip. I didn't have a key to the front door, so I rang the doorbell. It was dinnertime, so I knew Carol and the kids were probably eating supper at the kitchen table.

A few moments later, the door swung open. My son Isaac, who was five or six at the time, was wearing a Cardinal Mooney cap on backwards and didn't bother saying hello. Instead, he turned and yelled to Carol, Mackie, and Drake, "Hey, everybody, Bob Stoops is here!"

Later, he asked if I could sign his hat. That one made me laugh. "Why do you want me to sign your hat?" I asked.

"Because I see you sign everyone else's hat."

Celebrity was a concept he didn't fully grasp at that age. But, then again, neither did I. "Is it OK if I just write 'Dad'?"

He nodded. I signed his hat. It was a little strange doing that.

It also was strange being called "Big-Game Bob." The media had given me the nickname, and it was meant as a compliment. But the first time I saw it, I rolled my eyes. Seriously? Because when your nickname is "Big-Game Bob," that means you're expected to win every big game for the rest of your life. And that's not going to happen.

Over the course of my eighteen seasons at Oklahoma, our record against top twenty-five ranked teams was the best in the nation. Against our two main rivals, Texas and Oklahoma State, we were a combined 25–11.

But I wasn't crazy about the nickname, much like Coach Switzer wasn't crazy about being called "The King." It's like going to Vegas and thinking you're going to stay on a hot streak for eighteen years. It isn't possible. The same thing goes for college football. There are peaks and valleys.

Relatively speaking, we had a valley in 2005. It's the only season I ever lost three of my first five games as OU's head coach.

Paul Thompson had started the season as our quarterback, but we made a change after our season-opening loss against TCU. Redshirt freshman Rhett Bomar, who had signed in the same 2004 recruiting class as AD, replaced Paul for the rest of the season.

We were thin at some of our positions. Ten of our players from the Sugar Bowl team had been drafted by the NFL earlier in 2005, so we had some holes to fill. I knew it was going to be a challenging year. AD made it a little more challenging.

We had a class attendance policy for our players. We got tired of chasing them to class, so our athletic department instituted a penalty system. If you missed three classes, you were suspended from practice for two days and not allowed to start in the next game. If you missed another class, you were suspended for the next game.

I was fine with that. I would have felt like a hypocrite had I played guys who didn't bother going to class.

Going into our third game of the season—a road trip to UCLA—I learned that AD had missed three classes. We held him out of practice, per the rules. "Coach, I'm not going to start?" he asked. It was killing him.

"Sorry, AD," I said.

He was devastated. Then I got a call from his dad, who was still in the correctional institution. "I just wanted to be sure that AD was doing what he needed to do," he said.

"Nelson, I didn't choose not to start AD. He chose it when he didn't go to class."

"Hey, Coach, I wouldn't start him, either."

Like I said, Nelson got it, and so did AD. I don't think he ever missed another practice or game because of academics.

After our shaky start, we won six of our last seven games, including a win against number-six-ranked Oregon in the Holiday Bowl. We were unranked at the time.

I went through a divorce during my early years at OU. I fought to keep that marriage together, and it cost me a lot of money in attorney fees, et cetera. I had very little money left in my account.

Bob had asked me to emcee our annual football banquet. I had done it for several years. When we were flying out to San Diego for the Holiday Bowl, Matt McMillen walked down the aisle, stopped at my seat, dropped an envelope in my lap, and said, "Merry Christmas."

There was a big check in it. I turned around and looked at Matt. I got pretty emotional. It's a moment I'll never forget.

I assumed Bob had something to do with that. I said something to Bob about it, but he just blew it off.

To have that arrive during the holidays was doubly helpful. I have a hard time telling that story even today without getting choked up about it.

—Kenny Mossman

That second-half burst of success in 2005 was a nice launching point to the 2006 off-season, but the fact remained that we had ended the year unranked, had lost to Texas, and didn't play for a Big 12 title. Let's face it, in our world at OU, if you weren't the Big 12 champ or contending for a national championship, it was a down year. Everybody, including my own staff and players, had gotten used to seeing our names in the top twenty-five and in a BCS bowl.

Then, as we prepared for the start of our 2006 training camp, OU officials informed me that three of our players allegedly had violated NCAA rules by accepting payment for work they hadn't performed in off-season employment.

The players were offensive guard J. D. Quinn, walk-on Jermaine Hardison, and our starting quarterback, Bomar. According to the OU investigation, the players had worked only minimal hours at a local car dealership while submitting bogus time sheets for full weeks. The dealership, which was a supporter of OU football and aware of the players' scam, had paid them based on the doctored time sheets.

This had happened months earlier. Basically, they'd clock in, come back to OU, go to classes, work out, go to meetings, take part in practice, and then return to the dealership and clock out at the end of the day.

We had had a small issue involving the same dealership and AD's purchase of a car there, but in that case, it had been determined there was no wrongdoing.

This was different.

Throughout my career, one of my steadfast rules was this: I'd lose before I would cheat. I told my assistant coaches that I'd fire them in a heartbeat if they intentionally cheated or bent the rules. I told opposing coaches in my conference that if I caught them cheating, I'd turn them in, and I wouldn't tell them I was doing it. And I told them that if they discovered we were doing something wrong, they should turn us in.

I had seen too many honest coaches lose their jobs because they had lost games to dishonest coaches. I hadn't been raised that way. And I hadn't been part of staffs that operated that way. Coaches Fry, Crum, Snyder, and Spurrier were above reproach. As far as I'm concerned, there are no gray areas on the subject—the earth is round; the sun rises and sets; and if you cheat, I don't want to be associated with you. Those are absolutes.

I called Bomar into my office the day before fall practices began. I had the investigative report. We also had the class attendance records of the players. Point being, we knew that the three players had been paid thousands of dollars for work they had never performed—and that the dealership had been complicit in the scheme.

"Did you do this?" I asked. "Our people are telling me they've done a thorough investigation."

"Yeah, I did," said Bomar.

"Well, then you're gone. I'll see you."

"Like, for the year, and then I'll play again?" he asked.

"No. For good. You need to find somewhere else to go play. We're finished here."

It was a decision I wish I had never had to impose on Bomar and the two other players. But it wasn't a difficult decision. They had knowingly, intentionally, and methodically broken the rules. It was premeditated cheating, and by doing so, they had put their team in total jeopardy.

They had gamed the system, and it was clear they had been more concerned about making a fast buck than being part of a team. No player or coach, myself included, was bigger than the team or the program.

Their actions, and the actions of the booster, eventually resulted in the NCAA ordering Oklahoma to vacate our eight wins in 2005, to forfeit two scholarships for two years, and to be placed on two years of probation. That was in addition to OU's self-imposed penalties and whatever damage had been done to our program's reputation.

Many of those penalties, including the vacating of the wins, were reversed eventually by the NCAA Infractions Appeals Committee.

There were those who thought I had known about the pay-for-no-work scheme from the very beginning, that I *had* to have known about it. I didn't.

C'mon, do you think that if I had helped set up this scheme that I also could kick them off the team when it was discovered? And that they and the booster would go quietly away?

Anyway, it gave us a black eye and made it seem like we were a renegade program linked to some of OU's more inglorious moments. That simply wasn't the case. We constantly talked to the players about NCAA rules. We also talked about the repercussions of violating them.

I could have kicked Bomar off the team for a year. It certainly would have been the convenient football thing to do. After all, he had set an OU freshman passing record in 2005, had helped us win a bowl, and now had some valuable playing experience.

But I just thought his actions were so knowingly wrong and done for such a long period that he hadn't given me any other choice but dismissal. I didn't want a quarterback—the leader of our team—who so blatantly didn't care about his teammates.

Bomar's departure meant we needed a starting quarterback, and we needed one immediately.

Paul Thompson had been our backup in 2002 and 2003, been a starter for one game in 2004, and then, without complaint, moved to wide receiver. Not once during any of those seasons had I heard from his parents asking why he had lost out to Bomar or any threats to transfer or go public with any dissatisfaction. Paul and his parents were beautiful people.

Paul's chances at an NFL career probably were greater as a wide receiver than a quarterback. This was going to be his final season at OU. But when

I spoke with him, I said, "Paul, the only chance we're gonna have this season is if you switch back to quarterback. If you come back as a quarterback, it might not be the best thing for you, but it's going to be the best thing for this team. You need to decide, but I will understand if you want to stay at receiver.

"Go home; call your parents. I don't want you to say yes because you think I'm putting pressure on you. I'm not. But if we're going to have any kind of team this year, you're the guy who's going to do it."

If that sounded like a strong-arm tactic, it wasn't. I just told him exactly what the situation was. I could live with whatever decision he made, and with no hard feelings. If we had to get another quarterback ready, we'd do our best.

Paul found me the next day. "Coach, I'm your guy. I'll be the quarterback. I'll be all in."

We went 11–3 that season and won the Big 12 Championship. That was a cold December night in Kansas City, but Paul made it a lot warmer with an eleven-play, ninety-nine-yard touchdown drive in the third quarter that gave us the deciding fourteen-point cushion.

We won that game without AD. In fact, we won seven in a row without Adrian in the lineup.

In our October 14 win against Dan McCarney's Iowa State team, AD broke loose for a fifty-three-yard touchdown run with less than seven minutes remaining in the game. He fell hard in the end zone, and when he got up, you could tell something was wrong.

By the time the game ended, we got the news: AD had broken his collarbone.

It was an unfortunate ending to a day when AD had rushed for 183 yards and scored two touchdowns—and done it all in front of his father, Nelson, who had just been released from an Oklahoma City halfway house about nine days earlier. Nelson had seen AD play on TV numerous times, but his prison sentence had prevented him from watching his son in person during Adrian's high school career and for the first thirty games of his OU career.

According to the doctors, AD might be able to play if we reached a bowl game. Given the circumstances—AD was a junior and eligible at season's end to enter the NFL draft—there was a very good chance he had played his last down for the Sooners.

By winning the Big 12 Championship, we were invited to the Fiesta Bowl. It was the right place, just the wrong week. The national championship was going to be played there on January 8, 2007. Our game against Boise State would take place a week earlier.

AD practiced leading into that game, but I knew he was thinking about the NFL draft. He had another year of eligibility left, but he was ready for the pros.

"AD, you don't need to play in this game," I told him. "If you're going in the draft, you don't have to play. I'm OK with that."

I know how AD thinks. I wanted him to know that I was good with him skipping the game. All of us were good with it. We had a great kid behind him in Allen Patrick, and with all due respect to the good people of the Fiesta Bowl, my priority was AD's future. He really didn't *need* to play in that game.

AD looked me dead in the eye. "Coach, if they tell me I'm good to play, I'm going to play."

That's how he is. And there was no stopping him from running out on that field.

We were ranked number seven, and Boise was number nine—and if you were a Boise State fan or just a fan of college football, it was an unforgettable game to watch. But at Oklahoma, Boise State still is treated as if it were Lord Voldemort in Harry Potter: he who must not be named.

Boise State? I'm not going to talk about it.

— Bobby Jack Wright

Boise State won the game. See how I didn't melt when I wrote that? It wasn't the end of the world.

Everybody at OU acts as if the loss to Boise was so tragic. You know what? If we had lost, 43–42, in overtime *in the national championship game*, then I'd say, yeah, that one would leave a permanent bruise.

We had trailed by eighteen points midway through the third period but then fought back to tie the game with 1:26 remaining to play. And to do that, we had to convert a two-point conversion from the seven-yard line.

On Boise's next drive, Marcus Walker intercepted a pass and returned it thirty-four yards for a touchdown to give us a 35–28 lead.

Here's the thing: if Marcus had run out of bounds at the one-yard line instead of scoring, this game would have become a nice footnote in OU history. We would have run the clock down (Boise State only had two timeouts left) and, in all likelihood, kicked a short field goal and won the game.

But in the heat of the moment, he saw the open field, the end zone, and he scored. I certainly couldn't blame him for that.

I remember the rest of it, of course. We were in a prevent defense. They had fourth-and-eighteen with eighteen seconds left in the game. They scored on a fifty-yard hook-and-lateral to tie it.

You had to respect the audacity of the play, but it was a one-in-five-thousand chance. They just hit it right with the timing. You couldn't help but admire the execution.

In overtime, we took the 42–35 lead on what would become the final carry and touchdown of AD's Oklahoma career.

They scored, and rather than go for the tie, they ran what would become one of the most memorable Statue of Liberty plays in college football history. Ian Johnson scored on the two-point conversion for the win.

We had expected a trick play and had called a blitz that would have put our safety in position to make the tackle on Johnson. But there was a miscommunication, and it never happened. So I guess we'll never know.

Johnson proposed to his girlfriend on the field, and everybody lived happily ever after.

I told Carol later, "You know, we're going to see that play forever."

It was a great play by Boise and a great call by Chris Petersen, who is a fabulous coach. And it was a great win for their undefeated program. Had we won, it would have been expected. We might have finished fourth or fifth in the polls as opposed to the number eleven that we ended up at. Was it really that big of a deal?

What was a much bigger deal to me was the health status of AD. He had rushed for seventy-seven yards and scored in overtime, but he reinjured his collarbone during the game. It was a serious injury—but luckily, he was able to fully recover in time for the NFL Draft.

The loss hurt, but certainly not as much as a loss in a Big 12 Championship or national championship defeat. That fact allowed me to accept the outcome a little quicker.

Boise State had an experienced and talented team. But it was almost as if we couldn't overcome the energy of everyone wanting Boise to win that game. My own mother-in-law said she would have rooted for Boise if not for Carol and me.

I was over the loss fairly quick. If you had told me back in July that we would lose our starting quarterback to dismissal and lose one of the best players in the country to injury for seven games, but we'd win the Big 12—and eleven games—I would have taken it. To me, the story of that season was Paul Thompson.

About three or four years after that loss to Boise State, Chris Petersen called me and asked if he could swing by and watch one of our practices. He was coming through Norman on spring break and was bringing his young son, Sam, with him.

I told him no, he wasn't welcome.

Just kidding.

Of course, we invited him and Sam to spend the day with us. Sam was about eight or nine, near the same age as my twins. During our practice, Sam, Isaac, and Drake started playing a little game of touch football.

At one point, they were trying to decide on a play to call. "How 'bout the Statue of Liberty?" Sam said.

"Hey, that ain't funny," said Drake.

We got a kick out of that one. And a few years later, I went out to Boise to watch one of their practices.

In 2007, it was basically the same result as 2006: another Big 12 title (we never got tired of those; we beat number-one Missouri, 38–17), another eleven victories, and another Fiesta Bowl loss—this time to West Virginia.

We beat Texas that year, beat Missouri twice (once when they were ranked number one), but the bowl game is what people tend to remember.

West Virginia was a win away from playing in the BCS Championship. They were twenty-eight-point favorites against Pitt in their final regular season game but struggled after quarterback Pat White dislocated his thumb in the second quarter. By the time we played them, Rich Rodriguez had taken the Michigan job, assistant coach Bill Stewart had stepped in, White had returned to the lineup, and we were dealing with the loss of several key starters.

Stewart did a great job of unifying his team and convincing the players they had something to prove. They beat us by twenty.

But I had a good feeling about what was possible in 2008, mostly because of our recruiting class of 2006.

That was the class that included quarterback Sam Bradford, defensive tackle Gerald McCoy, running back DeMarco Murray, tight end Jermaine Gresham, running back Chris Brown, offensive tackle Trent Williams, and offensive guard Brandon Walker.

We had played Gresham, Brown, Williams, and Walker in 2006 but redshirted Bradford, McCoy, and Murray.

In 2007, Sam burst onto the scene by throwing for thirty-five touchdowns and more than three thousand yards. He led the nation in pass efficiency. Gerald was named the Big 12 Defensive Freshman of the Year. DeMarco scored five touchdowns in his first game that season and fifteen for the year (tying AD's freshman record), but he missed our final three games after dislocating his kneecap. The *Oklahoman* called Sam and DeMarco the "Backfield of Dreams."

Meanwhile, Brown, Walker, Williams, and Gresham were making their own impact.

We were headed in the right direction. But in 2008, I wanted it to be in the general direction of Fort Lauderdale, Florida—site of the national championship game.

Chapter Thirteen

Subjectivity

Recruiting is an art and an inexact science. It's luck. It's intuition. It's trust. Sometimes it's a leap of faith, and you hit it big. And sometimes you splat.

Everyone with a pair of eyes knew Adrian Peterson was going to be a star. My mom could have done the scouting for us on AD.

But Sam Bradford? He was a three-star quarterback from Oklahoma City and a second-team all-state selection by the local paper. One of the national recruiting services had him as their 340th-best prospect. C'mon. Compare that to Matthew Stafford, who was rated number six that year. Tim Tebow was number twenty-one. (We did try to reach out to Tim but never got very far in the recruitment process.)

Other recruiting services had Sam listed higher, but generally speaking, he wasn't considered an elite quarterback prospect. He had offers—good ones—but the world wasn't knocking down his door.

We had him in our camp, and I really liked what I saw. So did Chuck Long, who was very high on him. Sam's dad, Kent, had been a lineman at OU in the late 1970s. It was a family of Sooners.

Despite the three-star ratings, I was absolutely convinced Sam was going to be a great quarterback when I saw him play...basketball?

I learned a lot about a prospect if he played basketball, especially when it came to skill players. Yes, you assessed them on the football field, at camps, and on film. But it was on a basketball court that I really could see their level of athleticism.

I had played basketball in high school. I always thought it was an indicator sport. It was a game whose athleticism could translate to football.

One day I watched Sam play at basketball practice. There was a jumble of bodies battling for a ball that had rolled off the rim. Suddenly I saw someone hammer back the miss with a ferocious dunk.

It was Sam.

He had me at slam.

Sam could have played college basketball. He was on the same AAU team as Blake Griffin, who played at OU. Sam was an accomplished golfer. He had hockey skills. He even played the cello. I like kids who don't limit themselves. Do different things. Play different sports. Find what you love.

My DeMarco Murray basketball moment came during a 2003 visit to Bishop Gorman High School in Las Vegas. I was there recruiting Ryan Reynolds, a linebacker who would later sign and play for us and eventually become a graduate assistant on the staff.

I was walking with the head football coach at the time, David White, and we had to cross the basketball court to get to a meeting room. DeMarco was on the court.

"DeMarco, can you show Coach Stoops some dunks?" asked White.

DeMarco, only a sophomore at the time, was hesitant. But White insisted.

DeMarco ran from the top of the key, threw the ball against the cement wall behind the basket, let it bounce once in the lane, and then, from the top of the key, he reached up with one hand and tomahawked it through the hoop. Had he been at the NBA All-Star Game dunk contest, he would have scored perfect tens.

"You have to be kidding me!" I said. I turned to White. "Well, Coach, I'm not allowed to talk to DeMarco [according to NCAA rules], but you tell him he has a scholarship at Oklahoma and he can play whatever position he wants."

I was serious. With that sort of athletic ability, he could have played at almost any skill position. It's safe to say, given how his career turned out, that he found the right spot.

Basketball told me a lot about a player's athletic chops. I watched cornerback Derrick Strait play basketball for only five minutes when I turned to Bobby Jack Wright and said, "I want this guy."

Derrick was five-ten but was dunking like he was six-ten. He became a four-year starter and an All-American who won the Nagurski and Thorpe awards. Most of the great DBs I've had through the years were great basketball players.

By the way, we got Derrick out of Austin, Texas.

When I watched a prospect on film or in person, I kept it simple. Either they're influencing the game or they're not. They're having success or they're not. They're helping their team win or they're not.

To me, productivity was the key. I didn't care about how many recruiting stars anyone had next to their names. And while I was interested in the measurables—size, weight, speed, and so on—productivity on the field was what mattered most.

Character and a commitment to academics were equally important to me. You weren't getting in our program unless you had those qualities. Did we occasionally misjudge some guys? You bet. There is no 100 percent success rate in recruiting.

If we felt pressed to choose talent over character, more times than not, we would fold our hand. We just weren't going to go in that direction. I don't want to work with bad people. I don't care what the talent level is, it's just not worth it.

Context and perspective are always important. We recruited players who had had issues as freshmen or sophomores in high school but showed signs of growing out of it. If we believed a kid could continue to make progress, we'd take a chance. But with a really high-risk-character kid, most of the time, we stepped away. We hated that for the individual—we wanted to give everyone an opportunity—but there were limits on how far I'd take a chance.

We miscalculated more than a few times. We wanted Michael Crabtree, a great kid from Dallas (and a hellacious basketball player). Character wasn't an issue there; we loved him. But we were concerned about his academics.

Brent, who recruited the Dallas area, fought for him, and we should have trusted his faith in Crabtree.

What happened? Crabtree turned out fine on his academics, and we ended up having to deal with him for three years at Texas Tech with Leach.

He was an absolute wide receiver beast. That was a case where we blew it. Every time I saw him play, I got mad at myself.

Then there was Wes Welker, who made a career out of proving coaches wrong, including me. Welker was an Oklahoma City kid we passed on early in my career at OU. All he did was go on and have a fabulous career at Texas Tech and in the NFL.

I told him later, "I wish you would have played for us. I blew it by not recruiting you."

He said, "Nah, Coach, I had a great experience at Texas Tech. And let's face it—it's not like you've been shorthanded on receivers."

I am proud of some of the happy endings we had with recruiting. Offensive tackle Orlando Brown lost his father, and his high school grades suffered dramatically because of the tragedy.

I asked our academic committee to consider making an allowance for Orlando because of those circumstances. It did, and even though it was a challenge for him, Orlando recovered and flourished at OU. He did well academically, became an all-conference pick, and reached the NFL.

Brandon Everage was in our class of 1999, and he'll forever be one of my favorites. He was a wild-ass country kid out of east Texas who played safety with incredible energy. He was rough around the edges, but it was his goodness that helped convince us to sign him.

I would have to chase him to class, and there was hardly a week where he wasn't on the fringe of doing something wrong. He was high-maintenance, but he had such toughness and spirit that you just shook your head at his eccentricities.

In 2003, he was late getting to our facility to board the team bus to the airport. We were playing at Alabama that Saturday.

He finally pulled up in his beater Cadillac and got on the bus, and off we went. It wasn't until we arrived at our hotel at Bama that I learned why "Book"—that's what we called him (and it wasn't because he loved studying or reading)—was late.

Turns out he had run a stop sign and had been pulled over by the police. That's when they found a whiskey bottle under his seat. He ended up getting about eight tickets that day. When I asked him what happened, he said, "Coach, I wouldn't drink on the way to the bus. I didn't even know it was under there."

I wasn't happy about the situation. But this was typical Book. He never did anything intentionally wrong.

During a game in his senior year, he intercepted a pass, ran it back however far, and came off the field gasping for air and throwing up on my shoes. Right after that, we needed him on the kickoff coverage team. But he looked awful.

We were trying to find a replacement, but Book just grabbed his helmet, threw up again, spit out the rest, ran down on coverage, and was in the middle of the tackle. At our next team meeting, I showed the series of plays to our players. "If you're ever wondering why Coach puts up with Book, watch this sequence of plays. *This* is why."

Book drowned in 2011 while swimming in the Little River in Texas with friends. He was only thirty. I spoke at his funeral in his hometown of Granger, and the church was full of his family, friends, and former teammates. And I made sure to tell that story to everyone there.

Dan Cody was in our 2000 recruiting class. He was a two- to three-star guy who was six-five but only weighed 215. Nobody knew what to do with him. Where do you play him?

I told my staff, "He's an Oklahoma kid. I don't care; he'll play somewhere."

Cody ran like a deer, and I never had a problem taking a chance on an in-state kid if his talent level was in the vicinity of what we needed. All Dan did was become an All-American at defensive end.

Nowadays, there's so much more information available than there was when Schmidty, me, Merv, and Bobby Jack were in the trailer throwing darts at our recruiting board in late 1998. There are more camps, more video, more accurate measurables, more everything.

We would identify the players we were interested in and rank them by number, by position, by area. Did we have a real chance to recruit them? Would they take our call? You had to be realistic about it. You couldn't waste time on vanity recruiting: trying to get a kid just so you could say you did. For example, did we really have a chance at a kid in LA who had grown up watching USC or UCLA? Proximity matters to some recruits.

The whole thing is like trying to mix the perfect martini. If you do it right, you get a team that can make a championship run. That's what we had in 2008 with guys such as Sam, DeMarco, McCoy, Gresham, offensive tackle Phil Loadholt, wide receiver Juaquin Iglesias, and the rest of that roster.

Kevin Wilson was our offensive coordinator, and he had a history, beginning with his time as an assistant at Northwestern, of often using an up-tempo offense. We had Sam, the best quarterback in the country. We had DeMarco, a great all-purpose back. We had Jermaine, a great tight end. And we had a strong corps of wide receivers.

I told Kevin that we should consider running an up-tempo, no-huddle offense. If we could get Sam and our offense fifteen or twenty extra snaps a game, I liked our chances of outscoring anyone we played.

As a defensive coach, I knew what kind of stress a no-huddle offense put on a defense. Kevin implemented the new scheme, and we scored points in historic numbers. We scored ninety-nine touchdowns, which remains an FBS record. We scored 716 points, which is second in FBS history. We averaged fifty-one points per game.

We were ranked number one when number-five Texas beat us, 45–35. But we worked our way up the rankings again, partly because of that prolific offense and my big mouth.

On November 22, undefeated and second-ranked Texas Tech came to our place. We were number five. This was our season.

Earlier in the week, a reporter had asked me why my record at home was so strong. (At the time, I'd only lost two home games in nine-plus seasons.) I was feeling a little salty, so I said, "Well, it sure isn't because of our rowdy, raucous crowd."

Yeah, it was a dumb-ass thing to do, but I needed our fans invested that week. Leach had his spread offense at near perfection, what with quarterback Graham Harrell and my old buddy Michael Crabtree. I wanted our people volumed up. This wasn't the Masters; they could yell if they wanted to.

They had beaten us at their place the year before, ended our national championship chances. Sam and I had both got hurt in that game.

Everyone's saying, "Texas Tech, that's the new team running the Big 12."
We were like, "Hellllll, no."

We ran that conference. We considered ourselves the best team. Hey,
we're Oklahoma.

— DeMarco Murray

We rolled them. We beat them bad, 65–21, and it wasn't even that close.

Then we beat number-eleven Oklahoma State, 61–41. Sam played with torn ligaments in his nonthrowing hand, though you wouldn't have known it. He threw for 370 yards and four touchdowns.

We ended up going to the Big 12 Championship and beat Mizzou bad, 62–21. The only negative: DeMarco, who was having a spectacular season, suffered a partial rupture of his left hamstring on the opening kickoff. His recovery would take at least five months.

After the game, I did do something out of character. As far as I know, there's no video record of it, thank goodness. But it was something I had been practicing for, just in case…

Coach Stoops did his little dance. We got him to do some dance. He gave us a
little something.

— DeMarco Murray

I danced. This is true. I was celebrating another Big 12 title and the fact that we were going to play Florida in the national championship.

Then I celebrated with Sam in New York when he won the Heisman Trophy, just beating out Colt McCoy of Texas and Tebow of Florida. Sam broke all of OU's meaningful passing records and led the nation in passing.

Sam, who had had surgery to repair those ligaments after the Missouri win, wore—what else?—a red cast on his left hand during the ceremony. When Sam's name was announced, Billy Sims, who was on the stage with past Heisman winners, began shouting, "Boomer! Boomer!" It was Billy being Billy.

Not bad for a three-star, eh?

Sam won the Heisman, but Tebow and Urban Meyer's Gators won the national championship, 24–14. It was easily the fewest points we had scored all season.

We were stopped on third-and-goal from the one, fourth-and-goal from the one, and threw an interception on another first-and-goal. Another time, we were stopped on third-and-one and then had our field goal attempt blocked.

Would DeMarco have made a difference on those short-yardage situations? Of course. But injuries are part of the game. We had our chances and didn't convert in those situations.

It was our fifth straight loss in a BCS bowl game and our third national championship loss in six years. You could hear rumblings in the media and the fan base. There were the wisecracks about "Big-Game Bob" not being able to win the big game.

That's part of the business. Doesn't mean I liked it. Doesn't mean I agreed with it. Doesn't mean I listened to it very often.

There was part of me that wanted to remind folks how far OU football had come since our first season in 1999. But the public perception game is one that's hard to win. We had spoiled people. That's a by-product of success. I could live with that.

Right after the national championship game, a handful of our players had big decisions to make. Sam, Jermaine, Gerald, Trent, and several of our other guys were looking hard at their NFL Draft options.

At that time, there was much more fluctuation in what teams could pay their draftees in salaries and guaranteed bonuses. It isn't like now, when everything basically is slotted and predetermined.

I would always preach to my players to maximize their financial opportunities. Just do the math: compare the salary and bonus difference between being selected first and last in the first round. Same thing for the first and last pick of the second round. In 2018, it was about a $24 million difference between number one versus number thirty-two, and more than $3 million in the second round. The numbers are comparable in 2019.

I wanted a player to have all the information needed to make a smart decision. If he could maximize his earning power by leaving OU early, I was the first to shake his hand and wish him well.

I consulted with NFL guys about our players' potential draft status. I didn't try to talk anyone in or out of the draft. I gave them the information and let the numbers speak for themselves. I'd even bring them in, get in front of a blackboard, and start detailing the salary number and guaranteed money by draft rounds. I wanted to make sure they understood the differences.

There are plenty of kids who left Oklahoma who shouldn't have. They listened to the noise—"You'll be a first-round pick!"—instead of reading the numbers and considering the projections of NFL contacts and front office people.

It's just the facts: guys who go lower in the draft get cut first, have shorter careers, get less money and fewer guarantees, have a lesser chance of qualifying for the NFL pension, and often don't get those lucrative second contracts. That's just how it works. The NFL is a business. If those teams can find someone who does what you do at a cheaper salary, you're usually gone.

Of course, you can talk until you're blue in the face, and it won't matter to some kids. They think they're going to be the exception to the rule. Sometimes it happens, but not often.

Sam was projected as a first-rounder in the 2009 draft, but he decided to return to OU. (Tebow and McCoy returned too, by the way.) I think he liked the idea of betting on himself to go higher in the 2010 draft; plus he enjoyed living his own age. Too many players are in a rush to leave college for the pros. Sometimes it's OK just to be a college kid.

Sam wasn't the only one who stayed. Jermaine, Trent, and Gerald also announced they were returning. I was happy for them. I was happy for us.

Meanwhile, Carol was happy with me. After more than ten years of having my deflector shields up when it came to signing autographs, posing for photos, interacting with fans and boosters, and listening to the random Texas fan recite the Longhorns' two-deep depth chart on a flight, I gave in. For all those years, I had fought and protected myself from having to be "Bob Stoops."

Every Friday, my assistant, Julie Watson, and one of the team managers would bring in all the things people wanted me to autograph. There were usually at least fifty items.

On one of those Fridays, as I signed my name over and over, I asked Julie, "Who is Bob Stoops anyway?"

To me, it was just a name on a photo or a football or a pair of cleats. I didn't understand why anyone would value my autograph.

Carol used to tell me, "Bobby, it's not like you're going to wake up tomorrow and people are going to quit asking for a picture or an autograph." Yet I resisted, and Carol would have to circle back and do damage control with people in my grouchy wake.

The lesson I finally learned is that the sooner you accept the attention, the better. I didn't think I was special, but other people did, so why fight it? To the many people I'm sure I offended over the years, I apologize. I was trying to find myself, trying to figure it out.

During that same time, I was trying to figure how we could win another Big 12 title and compete for a national championship. With the talent and depth that we had, I thought we were going to be tough to beat in 2009. We had four new starters on the offensive line, but I really believed the only thing that could compromise our season was the same thing that can compromise any team's chances: injuries.

About a week before our first game, Jermaine hurt his right knee in practice. It was later diagnosed as a cartilage tear. It wasn't a major injury, but after surgery, there would be five months of recovery time. He was done for the season.

Then, in our opener against BYU, in the first college game played at the then–Cowboys Stadium, Sam sprained his throwing shoulder in the last few seconds of the first half. We lost Sam and the game.

He missed the next three games but returned and played well in a win against Baylor. The next week against Texas, Sam bootlegged into a blitz by their cornerback and landed hard on the same shoulder again. Like Jermaine, he was out for the year.

Freshman Landry Jones came in for Sam and did the best he could under the circumstances, but we were never the same that season.

We were 3–3 after our first six games but won five of our last seven, including a bowl win against Jim Harbaugh's Stanford team. I was proud of our team for hanging in there, but it was a struggle.

During the week of Bedlam, Trent Williams got a concussion during practice. It was one of those "you've got to be kidding me" moments. First Jermaine, then Sam, then Trent.

We didn't have another left offensive tackle who could play that week, so we put an emergency plan in place: Cory Brandon would move from right tackle to left, and reserve tight end Eric Mensik would move to Brandon's spot.

Eric hadn't seen much playing time the entire season, and we weren't in a hurry for him to see much action at tackle against Oklahoma State. He weighed only about 260 pounds. Trent weighed about 320.

We monitored Trent throughout the week, but he wasn't ready to play by Saturday. When Eric saw Trent go to the equipment room window and get a pair of sweats instead of a game uni, he just shrugged and said, "Well, I guess I'm playing tackle today."

Eric had never played offensive tackle in his career. He got coached-up a little bit during our short Friday practice, but I kept thinking, *How are we ever going to get through this game?*

His jersey number went from 88 to 69, and he played incredibly well. He knew all his blocks, didn't flinch on snap counts, and didn't make any major mistakes. The memory of it still puts a smile on my face. Those are the times when you love being a coach.

We were unranked, but we shut out number-eleven OSU. That rivalry win gave us a boost for the bowl game. Stanford did the opposite of us: they put tackles at the tight end position. They were huge, so we muscled up our defense to counteract their strong running game and won, 31–27.

Landry returned in 2010 with some important playing experience, and it showed. We ended Texas's two-game win streak against us, beat Nebraska in what would become the last Big 12 Championship game until it returned in 2017, and then soundly beat Connecticut in the Fiesta Bowl to finish 12–2. After losing Fiesta Bowls during the 2006 and 2007 seasons, it felt good to walk away from there with a win.

But it had been a bittersweet year, mostly because my lifelong friend Snake had died that fall.

Jimmy died of kidney cancer. He was diagnosed in March, was gone in October.

Jimmy had on an Oklahoma shirt in the casket. That's what he wore. That's what he was buried in.

No Excuses

You go to a funeral, and they always play funeral music. I told the funeral director we were going to play rock and roll. We played Bob Seger.

Bob spoke at the bereavement dinner. He was Jimmy's confidant. They had a special relationship. It was tough for Bob to come home and Jimmy's not here.

—Mark Braydich

It's weird, the things you remember. When I was a freshman at Iowa, I came home for my brother Ronnie's stag party and wedding. After the party, a bunch of us were headed out to a couple of other spots when somebody on the street threw something at our car.

In Youngstown, everybody was always looking for a reason to rumble. We all got out and started tussling. All of a sudden, the police came, and I got arrested and thrown into the cop car. They took me to a paddy wagon, loaded me up, and said we were headed downtown. On the way, though, the paddy wagon stopped, and the back doors flew open. The police had two more arrestees to load in.

It was Snake and another buddy—Billy Ritter, a.k.a. "Mama." (Snake gave out all the nicknames in our neighborhood.)

Our eyes were red from the mace. We spent the night in jail, and my cousin Tommy, who knew how to navigate the police station, bailed us out the next morning. Later, the arrest was removed from my record.

My dad found out about it. He walked up to our room, made sure we were OK, and just said, "You bunch of dumbasses."

Snake…he battled until the end.

In early December of 2010, Urban Meyer resigned at Florida. He had done the same thing after the 2009 season but returned after a day. This time, he didn't change his mind.

I thought about the Florida job. In hindsight, and from a coaching career standpoint, maybe I should have gone there in 2010. But from a family standpoint, I couldn't do it.

My kids had been raised in Norman. That's where they had gone to school their entire lives. That's where their friends were. In my business, it's almost unheard of for a head coach to keep his job that long.

There's a reason why Jimbo Fisher left for Texas A&M after eight years at Florida State, and it wasn't just the money. There's a reason that Nick jumped around before settling at Alabama. Urban, too.

In some cases, it's harder to stay at one place, because people want change for change's sake. They see the shiny new toy and think it's better than what they have.

Coach Spurrier stayed twelve years at Florida before moving on. It was his decision. I had been at Oklahoma for twelve years when Urban stepped down and the Florida job opened up. Perhaps I missed a professional opportunity then, but to me, it was worth the trade-off of not uprooting the kids.

We began the 2011 season by trying to honor one of our own. Earlier in May, starting linebacker Austin Box, who had been with our program since 2007, died from what medical examiners later determined was an accidental drug overdose related to prescription pain medication.

I remember the phone call. You always remember those kinds of calls.

I was overseas in Italy. At first, I was told that Austin had been found unconscious and had been taken to the hospital but that his condition was dire. Later, I got a call telling me they weren't able to save him. He was only twenty-two.

I was five thousand miles away. I thought about Austin and his family. I had this gut-wrenching, sinking, empty feeling in my soul. It was a feeling of helplessness. There had been no indication of a problem — to his family or to our trainers, doctors, or coaches.

Carol and I returned home and accompanied the entire team to Austin's funeral. We wanted to be there for his family.

Austin would have been a senior for that 2011 season. Our captains requested that we keep his locker as is and that each week, a different player could earn the right to wear his jersey number.

I thought it was a fitting tribute to Austin, who had been such a fun, easygoing guy. He had been a great student, and his teammates loved him. He had played so hard, and now they wanted to play hard in his memory.

Carol and I still keep in touch with Austin's mother, Gail. She is an incredible woman who was appointed to the board of the Oklahoma Department of Mental Health and Substance Abuse Services in 2019. Since Austin's death, she has been a strong and powerful advocate of opioid abuse prevention and education. Her mission, she says, is to turn Austin's tragic death into a vehicle for positive difference in the world. Austin was a leader in life, and, says Gail, through sharing her son's story with the public, he continues to lead, to make a difference. We think of her—and Austin—often.

Our team certainly thought of Austin as we began the season ranked number one and won our first six games, including a road win against number-five Florida State and a 55–17 win against Texas. We had it going, but later that October, we were upset at home against Texas Tech and then also lost at Baylor and Oklahoma State. Those hurt. We weren't used to losing to those programs. But we just weren't strong enough.

We beat Iowa in the Insight Bowl to finish 10–3, but it was a strange experience, sort of like beating your brother. Iowa was my alma mater, and Hawkeyes coach Kirk Ferentz was a really good friend. I'll take the win, but I wish it had come against another team and coach.

Speaking of brothers, Mike, whom Arizona had let go in 2011, returned to our staff in early 2012. The plan was for Mike and Brent to be co-defensive coordinators, with Brent making the calls. Mike would have input and, much like he had in the past, would be part of the discussion in game planning.

Instead, Brent accepted the defensive coordinator job at Clemson. It was a tough decision for Brent, and it was tough for us to lose him. But he had been at OU for thirteen years, and we understood his desire to make his mark at another quality program, to grow as a coach. For him, the timing was right to leave. As someone who had made those same decisions in the past, I could certainly relate to Brent's situation.

Some of our OU fans want to play the what-if game: What if Brent had stayed at Oklahoma? I'm not interested in doing that. It doesn't serve a purpose, and there's no way of knowing what would have happened.

Brent has done a great job at Clemson. I just tip my visor to him and wish him continued success.

In 2012, we beat our rivals Texas and Oklahoma State. We won the Big 12. Everything was fairly positive until we played Texas A&M and Johnny Manziel in the Cotton Bowl in Arlington.

Manziel was just a redshirt freshman quarterback who had never played a down for A&M when the season began. But by the time we played him, he was "Johnny Football." He was the Heisman winner. He was a problem.

He had helped lead the Aggies past Saban's number-one-ranked Bama team earlier in the season. It wasn't just his talent; it was his swagger. His team believed in him, and because of that, they believed in themselves.

He was as good as billed. He could scramble, run, and throw the ball well. Just a fabulous college player.

A&M beat us, 41–13. It was embarrassing. After that game, I had to get away. I just didn't want to go right back to Norman and hear the chatter about the loss.

This wasn't like the 2004 national championship blowout loss to USC, when I felt like I had misread my team. This was different. I just felt worn down by it all. I was beat up.

Carol and I headed to a resort out west where I could just decompress in peace. While we were there, I had a chance to do a lot of thinking. At one point I said to Carol, "I don't think I can do it anymore."

"I get it," she said.

When we got home, he was talking about going to the coaches' convention or recruiting. I literally thought he was going to be done with coaching. I said, "Bobby, are you going to finish recruiting and then be done?"

He looked at me like I was crazy, like it was an out-of-body experience. It was as if he had never said anything to me. But I truly thought he was done then.

—Carol Stoops

I guess I tried to follow the advice I had given others: "Don't get beat twice." I regrouped.

Nobody expected much out of us in 2013. If anything, people in the SEC were hoping we'd fall flat on our faces.

During the off-season at an OU Sooner Caravan stop in Tulsa, I had talked to several reporters before the event started. Someone asked me about the strength of the SEC and the "gap" between the SEC and the Big 12.

Alabama had won the national championship in January, giving the SEC seven straight national titles. The SEC had its own TV network with ESPN and had dominated the recent NFL Draft.

But I pointed out that there's more to a conference than the top two or three teams. Yeah, the gap between the SEC and everyone else was there when it came to winning consecutive national championships. You couldn't ignore seven in a row. It was an amazing accomplishment, and I made sure to say so.

But the gap between our conference as a whole and their conference as a whole? There wasn't much of a gap at all. They had two or three really good teams, a handful of programs that were decent, and a bottom six that struggled to beat anybody in the top half of their league. That's how it is in a lot of conferences.

I was tired of hearing about how great the SEC was. From top to top, yeah, impressive. From top to bottom, not so great.

I told the reporters that they were listening to a lot of propaganda. "You're more than smart enough to figure it out... what'd we have, eight of ten teams in bowl games this year?" I said.

I got ripped nationally, and especially by SEC fans and some media members, but I didn't care. I wasn't wrong. I stood by it then, and I'll stand by it now. Just because a team wins a national championship doesn't mean it belongs to the best league. There's a whole bunch of teams in the SEC that I would have loved to have played. But nobody wanted to hear that. They were too busy gulping down the SEC Kool-Aid.

The New England Patriots have won three of the last five Super Bowls, but nobody ever says the AFC East is the best division in the NFL. Florida State won the national championship in 2013, and Clemson won it in 2016 and 2018. You hear anybody saying the ACC is the best conference in the country?

The SEC has been riding Alabama's coattails for years. That's just fact. And that's the propaganda part I was talking about. Point being, those folks with SEC ties don't like people stepping up and talking shit to them. They're used to everyone throwing rose petals at their feet and saying how great they are.

Of course, I had more important things on my mind in 2013 than the SEC. We were ranked sixteenth to start the year and dropped as low as twenty-second in mid-November. Then we beat Iowa State to go to 8–2, then won at Kansas State and Oklahoma State to finish the regular season 10–2. We did it with a tag-team group of quarterbacks.

After the OSU game, Joe Castiglione pulled me aside. "I really think we've got a chance to be in a BCS bowl," he said.

"Seriously?" I asked.

"You know why?" he said. "Because we're Oklahoma."

"But we're not the Big 12 champions," I pointed out. Baylor had won the conference. "They'll still want us?"

"Probably."

I could never sleep late the morning after a game. On December 8, I got up at 5:30ish, made some coffee, and watched some game video of the Oklahoma State win. I had our TV on nearby. That's when I saw the ESPN ticker across the bottom of the screen.

It listed the BCS bowl matchups. When it got to the Sugar Bowl, it said, "No. 3 Alabama vs. No. 11 Oklahoma."

Joe had been right.

I waited until about 7:30 to go to our bedroom and see if Carol was awake. "What'd you find out about the bowl?" she asked.

"You want the good news or the bad news?"

"What's the good news?"

"The good news is that we're playing in the Sugar Bowl. The bad news is that we're playing Alabama."

Without missing a beat, Carol said, "Yeah? Well, over there, they're saying, 'We have to play Oklahoma.'" I loved her attitude.

Bama had been ranked number one the entire season until they'd lost to Auburn on the world-famous "Kick Six" play. Otherwise, they would have been in the national championship game against Florida State.

We were sixteen-point underdogs, and undoubtedly there were some writers in the Superdome press box who were counting the seconds until they could rip me if we lost to an SEC team.

Instead, we beat Bama, 45–31, and our redshirt freshman quarterback Trevor Knight had a game for the ages.

He had completed only forty-seven passes the entire season. Against Bama, he completed thirty-two of forty-four attempts for 348 yards and four touchdowns. He was named the Sugar Bowl MVP.

We had found ourselves a starting quarterback.

That sound you heard after the game? It was our team and fans cheering—and those reporters in the press box hitting the delete key on their laptops.

I didn't hear anything from those SEC fans, either.

When we got back to OU, there was a welcoming party waiting for us at the football facility. I said a few words to the crowd and then did a mic drop with, "So much for the big, bad wolf."

They knew what conference I was talking about.

As our staff turned its attention to recruiting and National Signing Day in February, I learned about a quarterback who had enrolled at Oklahoma and just wanted a chance to walk on.

His name: Baker Mayfield.

I don't know exactly how to describe the Baker football journey. It's a movie, a book, a TV show. Maybe it's all three. That's how incredible his story is. I couldn't make it up if I tried.

Baker had played at Lake Travis High School, which is about twenty miles west of Austin. Even though he'd been in the Texas Longhorns' backyard and went 25–2 as a starter, led his team to a state championship, threw for 6,255 yards and only eight interceptions during his high school career, UT didn't recruit him.

Guess what? We didn't offer him a scholarship in 2013, either. No other top major college program in the country did. That's right. The guy who would win a Heisman Trophy and become the number-one pick in the 2018 NFL Draft didn't get a single significant offer.

With OU, it wasn't really recruiting. My dad was good buddies with the whole Switzer staff back in the day. Through that, basically, they gave us tickets to a November 2011 game against A&M. We went up to the game, [co-offensive coordinator] Heupel sized me up—at the time, I was probably 5-[foot]-11—but I could tell the writing was on the wall essentially.

I never heard from them again.

—Baker Mayfield, OU quarterback, 2015–2017

Instead, we signed Cody Thomas, a four-star prospect from Colleyville, Texas. And, of course, we also had Trevor, who was considered the sixth-best dual-threat quarterback in the country when we signed him in 2012. Trevor's brother, Connor, played at OU at the same time.

Baker had decided to walk on at Texas Tech, where he became the opening-game starter for Kliff Kingsbury's Red Raiders. I remember taking a quick glance at that Tech-SMU box score. The Mayfield kid had completed forty-three passes, thrown for 413 yards and four TDs, and rushed for another one. Not bad for a true freshman walk-on playing in his first college game.

We had beaten Texas Tech in late October, but Baker hadn't played in that game. But he did start seven games that season and was named the Big 12 Offensive Freshman of the Year.

When I heard that Baker had enrolled at OU, I didn't know whether to be impressed or to question his logic. The stories I'd read said he had left Texas Tech because of a "miscommunication" with the staff. He was living in a student dorm at OU, but I hadn't met him.

It took some real nerve—and I mean that in a good way—to come to OU at that time. We had just beaten Alabama with a Sugar Bowl MVP quarterback who had three years of eligibility remaining. Baker didn't care. I didn't know it then, but Baker had always dreamed of playing at OU. When the time came to transfer, he'd told his friends, "I'm gonna go there."

There. OU.

I mean, who does that? Who has the stones to leave a Big 12 program where he might be the starter of the future and go to another program where he knows he's going to have to sit out a season because of the NCAA transfer rules? Who transfers to a program where Trevor Knight is already established as a starter?

As a way to begin the 2014 second semester, we had a "welcome back" team meeting and meal at the East Side suites at Memorial Stadium. Before the meeting began, the players were milling around, and a kid came up to me: sort of curly hair, little bit of a gap between his two front teeth... not a big guy—maybe six feet or so.

I was sitting with Knight, Cody, and Blake Bell, trying to get to know some of the guys. When Bob walked in, I got up and said, "I've got to go meet Coach real quick."

I told him, "I'm Baker Mayfield. I'd love to play quarterback for you."

To be honest, I didn't really care what everyone was thinking. After playing at Texas Tech, I'll take a bet on myself over anybody else. I wanted to play. Bob was everything I knew about Oklahoma football.

He looked at me and said, "Wow, you're actually here."

—Baker Mayfield

I told Baker, "I'm glad you're here, and you'll have every opportunity to be the guy."

All he said was "Thank you, Coach."

As he walked away, I couldn't help but smile. I remember thinking, *This guy has got something to him.* He had a confidence about him. You could see it in his face. I liked that. I like guys who aren't afraid of competition.

I meant what I said about Baker having an opportunity to compete for the starting job in 2015. But I'm not sure I believed he'd actually do it. We weren't in need of a new quarterback. We certainly weren't looking for one.

As winter conditioning drills began, the reports started to trickle in: "This Mayfield kid isn't backing down...this Mayfield kid is making an impression." After he was on campus for a month, we put him on scholarship.

I told my staff, "We're not going to find a high school quarterback like this."

Once spring practice began, it became obvious that Baker was going to be a factor. He was serious, and he had serious skills.

I always kept an eye on the scout team. I wanted to see how the redshirt players competed. The year before Sam became our starter, I noticed that he never threw a bad ball. It was always where it was supposed to be. I told the coaches that. Sam didn't waste plays, not even on the scout team.

Baker was the same way. Our defensive coaches told our offensive coaches that they couldn't stop him. They raved about his energy level, his throwing accuracy, his quick release. Defensive guys don't like admitting those kinds of things, but Baker's talent was difficult to ignore.

That season he was our Scout Team Offensive Player of the Year. He didn't dress for games, but he still competed on game day. He would run up and down the sidelines in street clothes, totally invested in what was happening on the field and in what his teammates were doing.

You have to remember that Baker wasn't a household football name back then. But that wouldn't last long.

Chapter Fourteen

Controversy

On July 23, 2014, I was at ESPN's headquarters in Bristol, Connecticut, doing what they call a "car wash." That's when you make the rounds to almost every ESPN TV and radio show, as well as a podcast and interviews with several of their website reporters.

I was there as part of a Big 12 contingent of head coaches. The SEC coaches had been in Bristol early in the week, and the ACC coaches would be there the following week. You ping-ponged from one interview to the next.

A day earlier, during one of his stops on the ESPN tour, Nick Saban said it had been difficult to prepare and motivate his Alabama team to play us in a "consolation game."

I can appreciate the emotional letdown that Alabama had after losing to Auburn in the Iron Bowl. It cost them a place in the national championship. But to call the Sugar Bowl and a matchup against Oklahoma a "consolation game" was an insult.

I told the ESPN reporters during the car wash, "They didn't look like it was a consolation game on that first drive when they scored a touchdown and everyone thought they were going to rout us. I've been in plenty of those [nontitle games] . . . so that means I've got a built-in excuse the next time we don't play for a national championship?"

We didn't call our Fiesta Bowl loss to Boise State a "consolation" game. Did that win mean more to Boise State than it might have meant to us? Sure. That was a huge victory for their program. The way that game ended is still talked about years later.

You can always come up with a reason that your team didn't win. We didn't get a pass—or ask for one—when a difference maker like DeMarco was unavailable for our national championship game against Florida. Injuries happen. Letdowns happen. Deal with it.

Once I was done with that situation, I flew back to Norman and soon faced one of the most debated and criticized decisions of my coaching career. It didn't happen on the field; it happened off it.

In 2014, Freedom High School's Joe Mixon of Oakley, California, was one of the most sought-after running backs in the country. He was a five-star recruit with forty-seven major college scholarship offers. We were one of them. And he chose us.

Mixon turned eighteen on July 24. In the early hours of July 25, he was involved in an incident that would have a lasting impact on his reputation—and, in a way, on mine, too.

While in a Norman deli restaurant, Mixon and OU student Amelia Molitor got into a heated argument that escalated into physical violence. Mixon and Molitor didn't know each other, but Molitor would allege that it began when Mixon began harassing her and a friend. Mixon would allege that Molitor's friend had directed a racial slur at him, and according to the accounts of the incident, Mixon had responded with a homophobic slur.

Once we had learned of the incident and understood what had actually happened, we suspended Mixon from all team activities.

When the Norman Police Department investigated, it said there was a surveillance video of the incident but that it couldn't be released publicly at the time because of its "evidentiary value."

I eventually saw the video, and it was shocking. It showed an argument between Mixon and Molitor, followed by Molitor pushing and slapping Mixon with the butt of her hand, followed by Mixon punching Molitor, which broke her cheekbone and jaw.

In mid-August, Mixon was charged with one count of misdemeanor assault. Joe Castiglione and I recommended to President Boren that Mixon be suspended from the program for the entire 2014 season. He could remain at OU as a student and be eligible for financial aid, but his return to football in 2015 was subject to review. President Boren supported the decision.

In October, Mixon reached a plea deal with the prosecutors. He received a one-year deferred sentence and agreed to undergo counseling and serve one hundred hours of community service.

Our decision to suspend Mixon rather than permanently dismiss him from the team or expel him from school remains a sensitive issue to me. It remains an issue for those who disagreed with my thinking, too.

The critics of the decision said that I was more concerned about Mixon the running back—and his ability to help our team—than I was about Molitor and violence against women. Nothing could be further from the truth.

No question, my decision was controversial—and I knew it would be, too.

No decision is made in a vacuum. As much as a coach can control such things, I controlled a young man's immediate future—and perhaps his long-term future, too. That is no small responsibility. And I didn't take it lightly.

I tried to put the entire situation in context, which, in 2014, was this: Mixon had struck a woman—a reprehensible act of violence against a person who in no way could defend herself against someone of his size and strength. In no way could I justify it, defend it, or excuse it.

Mixon hit the young woman, and he's going to have to live with that moment for the rest of his life. That is an incontrovertible fact. He had a horrific, split-second reaction. Nothing in the way he handled that situation was acceptable.

But there are other facts, and I felt it was important that I considered all of them.

Until that moment, Mixon had had no history of physical violence. And he has had none since. We had recruited him for a long time. We had gotten to know him and his family well. He was a gifted running back, to be sure, but he was a good person. Character mattered to us.

He didn't begin the night looking for trouble. It wasn't a domestic situation where he had a history of girlfriend or spousal abuse. It wasn't premeditated. These were two strangers who got into an argument, and it had escalated into a tragedy.

My first reaction upon hearing the news was shock, followed by concern for the health and well-being of the young woman. Whatever the circumstances, whatever the reasons for the confrontation, I wanted to know her condition and the progress of her recovery.

I could have cut Mixon loose in 2014. In 2019, that's the only choice that would have been acceptable. If I were faced with the same situation today, my decision would be much different from the one I made in 2014.

Back then, however, I thought the punishment was powerful and appropriate. He had never played a game for us, and critics of my decision said he never should.

If anything, the easy answer would have been to permanently dismiss him. Then OU—and I—would have been done with the incident. But I chose to take on the situation and do so in a transparent manner. We didn't kick the can down the road. We were serious about confronting the issue of violence against women, about holding Mixon—and the rest of our program—to the highest possible standard.

We removed Mixon from every part of the team for the entire season. No practices. No games. No meetings. No workouts in the weight room. Other than his access to academic services and a weekly visit with Cale Gundy and me, he had no contact with the program. In a way, he was an outcast. He had just turned eighteen, was more than sixteen hundred miles away from his family in California, and now was cut off from his new football family. He was alone.

He had been punished by the legal system. We added our own sentence.

For those who think my decision to allow him to return in 2015 somehow implicitly condoned violence against women, it simply isn't true. We took immediate action. We certainly made no guarantees that Mixon would be allowed to rejoin the team.

Mixon could have rejected our conditions and transferred to another school. I'm sure there would have been plenty of programs willing to take him. But he didn't transfer. He accepted the suspension and his responsibility in the incident.

I saw the Mixon video at the Cleveland County district attorney's office. Those are images I'll never forget. But in 2014, I thought it was punishable in a way that would teach Mixon an important, vital, life-lasting lesson, and do so in a way that gave him a chance to recover from his terrible mistake.

When law enforcement officials released the video publicly in December 2016 and the media asked me if, upon reflection, the punishment had been sufficient, I said that dismissal would be the only option. Second chances were no longer a possibility in these kinds of cases.

We had instituted a series of sensitivity training programs related to violence prevention, and five months earlier, I had invited activist Brenda Tracy, who had begun speaking publicly about her 1998 experience as a rape victim in Oregon (several of her attackers were college football players at the time), to address our team. It took courage for Brenda to share her story, but during those forty minutes, you could hear a chinstrap drop in the room. Sensitivity training is important, but Brenda's story put a face on the issue of sexual assault. I think it had a lasting impact on our players. It was powerful and meaningful. As our players left the room that day, they each stopped to hug Brenda.

There are those who will never believe me, but Mixon hadn't been a commodity to us. He wasn't just a name on a stat sheet. I didn't judge his worth by how many yards he could gain for OU, how many touchdowns he could score, how many games he could help us win. He certainly wasn't the victim in this case, but at the moment he threw that punch, he was an eighteen-year-old freshman who, in a split second, had lost his way.

Mixon wasn't the first player I'd suspended for at least a year. In 2004, I dismissed defensive tackle Dusty Dvoracek from our team after two games when I'd learned of his involvement in a series of incidents of violent behavior. He was a senior and a first-team all-conference selection the previous season, as well as a first-team academic all-conference in 2003 and 2002. He had been on numerous preseason All-America lists. His absence would hurt our team. But his presence would have hurt it more.

Dvoracek, by his own admission, had issues related to anger and alcohol. I felt I had no choice but to kick him off the team. At the time, there was no talk of him ever returning to the program. He was done.

The following summer, Dusty came to me and explained all the steps he had taken on his own to resolve his personal issues and asked if I would reconsider my decision. As with Mixon's situation, these are life-changing moments. They are never simple or clear-cut. With them, a future is at stake.

I decided that Dusty had earned a second chance and spoke on his behalf to Joe Castiglione and President Boren. I believed in Dusty as a person and was confident that he wouldn't let me — or himself — down. And he didn't.

I felt a sense of utter sadness. My everything was gone.

My senior year is when we played for the national championship. I was going to be an All-American. I had a chance to be a first-round pick. In an instant, that's gone.

When you're twenty-one years old, you think you're invincible. But I was out of control.

Little did I know that through hard work, they gave me the opportunity to come back. Man, Bob Stoops — I'll forever be grateful to him. They could have easily, easily said, "That's it; you're done here." And I would have left OU with a different legacy.

When you hit whatever your personal rock bottom is, you have to figure out how to get up. Bob Stoops helped me get up from the rock bottom. Now I have a six-year-old with me out at OU's practices. I wanted my kids to be proud of me.

I just know that Bob Stoops isn't a win-at-all-costs coach. He didn't give Joe Mixon a second chance because he was a five-star running back. He gave him a second chance the way he gave me a second chance... in Mixon's case, he gave him a chance to right a wrong.

—Dusty Dvoracek

[Mixon's] suspension was dismissed by a lot of people as a redshirt season. But anybody who saw Joe play knew he was not a redshirt candidate. Joe had a couple of stumbles along the way, but as far as I know, he's conducted himself without incident after the second chance. So far, history is bearing Bob out.

—Kenny Mossman

Every person has a right to become a better person. That situation has turned Joe around, shaped him.

He got penalized. He paid his debt. Joe handled his business. I was a team captain for two years, and I saw it. I also saw Coach Bob take a lot of flak.

The world ain't perfect. We're young men, and we make mistakes. I don't agree with a man putting his hand on a woman. Joe made a mistake.

But if we don't get that second chance, our lives might be done.

—Eric Striker, Oklahoma linebacker, 2012–2015

I saw Bob work with countless guys, and I'd think, "That light is never going to go on for that kid." But, sure enough, he'd get the light to go on.

—Matt McMillen

It won't matter to some people, but when Mixon did return, he was contrite and humbled and changed by the experience. He told me and his teammates that he had made a severe mistake and that he was grateful for the chance to prove he wasn't the same person in that video. As I understand it, Joe and Amelia eventually met, and she accepted his apology.

He wasn't perfect. I suspended Mixon for one game in 2016 after an incident involving a parking ticket.

One day, as the controversy swirled about my decision to let Mixon return after the year's suspension, there was a note waiting for me in my office. Someone on our staff had written it. It said, "If the worst thing you ever do in your life is give an eighteen-year-old a second chance, then you'll have lived a good life."

That note meant a lot to me. But for every note like that, there were ugly phone messages left at our office and hateful letters sent to both me and Castiglione. In the end, the entire incident taught me there is no perfect, elegant solution to an imperfect, terrifying moment of violence.

In 2017, after he had left Oklahoma, Mixon settled a civil case and issued an apology to Amelia for his previous actions. Despite being considered the third-best available running back prospect in the 2017 draft, Mixon wasn't allowed to attend the annual NFL Combine, and he wasn't chosen until midway through the second round. Some NFL teams refused even to put him on their draft board at all.

I wish the best for Amelia. I wish the best for Joe. I hope he makes the most of his second chance. And so far, I think he has.

That 2014 season might have been my most difficult at OU. We began it ranked number four and ended it out of the polls and with a crushing, embarrassing 40–6 bowl loss to Dabo Swinney's Clemson team to finish 8–5.

It was the kind of season where we missed game-winning chip-shot field goals and had point-after kicks blocked (Kansas State loss). It was the kind of season where we got blown out at home (Baylor) and lost in overtime at home (Oklahoma State). We were inconsistent offensively, inconsistent defensively. I knew I had some very tough decisions facing me.

> *I remember after the Clemson game, it was so obvious that we were outmatched.*
>
> *The game was in Orlando, and afterward—and it wasn't planned— Bobby said, "Let's get a car and go to the beach." So we drove to our condo near St. Augustine. It was awful: silent, tense. He was deep in his head.*
>
> —Carol Stoops

After going 11–2 and winning the Sugar Bowl in the 2013 season, it was incredibly disappointing and deflating to take a major step backwards. Once again, I seriously wondered, *Do I really want to do this anymore? Maybe I've run my course here. Maybe I need to do something else.*

I sat in Florida for a few days and just thought things through. I visited with my mentor, Coach Spurrier. I talked to Carol. I talked to Joe C, who let me vent and urged me not to make any rash decisions based on pure emotion.

It didn't take me long to go from dejected to motivated. I realized I needed to make some significant changes. If you're the face of the program, you have to take responsibility not just for what happened in 2014 but for what needed to be done in 2015.

Carol, who is such a strategic thinker, listened a lot, boosted me up, and asked me some tough, important questions that forced me to think hard about my answers. There were two options: I could leave—which meant most, if not all, of my assistants would likely be out of a job—or I could stay and try to fix things.

I was pissed at the situation. We had been good for so long. Our consistency was one of our strengths. But two 8–5 records in six years was unacceptable. We hadn't lived up to the standards we had set for the program. We weren't even close.

During this same period, there were published reports that the Cleveland Browns were interested in me. If they were, I never heard from them directly. Anyway, I wanted to repair what was wrong with my own program first.

I'm not a guy who churns through assistants, but when I returned to Norman, I informed co-offensive coordinators Josh Heupel and Jay Norvell that I was making changes in our offensive leadership.

There was no easy way of breaking that news. They weren't the reason that we had finished 8–5. While it might sound like a cliché, I thought we needed to move in a different direction.

All dismissals are difficult—you're talking about people who often have families—but with Josh, it especially killed me. He was the guy who had led OU to a national championship. He was a first-team All-American and a Heisman Trophy runner-up. Of all the players I ever coached at OU, he was the MVP—not because of his athletic skills but because of what he meant to our program. He was a great player and a legend at Oklahoma. It is his place, and I hope he looks at it that way.

Firing Josh was the worst day of my eighteen years as the head coach at OU. In the end, I just didn't feel we were operating our offensive system the way I felt it ought to be done. I thought we had drifted too far from the Hal Mumme–like system we had started with years earlier.

Josh is a great leader and a tough guy, and everything about him is positive. He did a great job for us, and I knew he'd do a great job when he was hired eventually as the head coach at Central Florida—and he has.

Why had we slipped? It was my fault. It was everybody's fault. Collectively, we had let the standard drop.

I didn't read what was being written about me and our program at the time, but I knew the vibe in the OU community. There were questions about my dedication to the job. You want to see the Youngstown in me come out? I get there really fast when someone challenges my commitment to a program I helped rebuild from the depths. Go ahead and throw whatever you want at me. I was ready to fight.

The first thing I did was look at the top offenses in 2014—specifically, the top passing offenses. Leach had the number-one passing attack at Washington State, and numbers three (East Carolina), seven (TCU), eight (Texas Tech), ten (Cal), and eleven (West Virginia) had head coaches or assistant coaches from the Leach coaching tree.

That's what I wanted. I wanted to get back to our passing roots of Leach's season at OU.

I was going to bring in two candidates: first, TCU co-offensive coordinator Sonny Cumbie and then ECU offensive coordinator Lincoln Riley. Sonny was great, and he had worked with Baker as an assistant at Texas Tech in 2013. He was familiar with Trevor Knight and his family from several years earlier. He wasn't the game-day play-caller at TCU, but he certainly had major input in the game planning each week.

Lincoln was only thirty-one years old, which might have bothered some head coaches, but I didn't care about his birth certificate. The number I cared about was this one: ECU had the fifth-best total offense in the country in 2014—and Lincoln was the guy calling its plays.

I called Dana Holgorsen. I had gotten to know him a little bit when he was on Leach's Texas Tech staff and a little more when he became the offensive coordinator at rival Oklahoma State. We really became friends when he got the head coaching job at West Virginia. Dana was very close with then-ECU head coach Ruffin McNeill and knew all about Lincoln, since they had worked together on the same Texas Tech staff.

"I've got to interview a couple of people, and I don't need you messing with me," I told Dana half jokingly. "I don't want you to be setting me up to hire the wrong guy. Don't give me bad advice."

I had gotten our O-line coach, Bill Bedenbaugh, off Dana's WVU staff in 2013. I trusted Dana's opinion. In fact, when I later hired Dennis Simmons as our receivers coach, I called Dana, too. He had worked with Dennis at Texas Tech.

"I'm giving you all your good coaches," said Dana, who highly recommended Lincoln.

It was kind of a strange deal. I'd interviewed at Kentucky with his brother [UK head coach Mark Stoops] between the end of the season and our bowl game. Ended up not being the right fit, just didn't work...I do think that perhaps Mark and Bob had a conversation about it. In this business, it's pretty good to talk to two Stoopses for a job.

I came in, had a full day in the [OU] interview, and then didn't hear for almost a week. I said, "Well, I didn't get that one."

That's the one job I interviewed for that I really was going to be crushed if I didn't get it. I knew this was perfect, the one I wanted as badly as any job I've ever interviewed for.

I was headed to the [coaches'] convention, a convention I had hoped I wouldn't have to go to. He called me at Love Field in Dallas and told me he was going to hire me.

From the outside, you knew they had all the wild success through the years but had had a tough year in 2014. Honestly, it wasn't until I got here that maybe I understood where Bob was at, where the program was at. I don't have anything to compare it to, but you could kind of feel like he was really reinvigorated.

—Lincoln Riley, Oklahoma offensive coordinator, 2015–2016;

head coach, 2017–present

Considering the way our 2014 season had ended, every starting position had to be earned again, including quarterback. It was going to be between Trevor, Cody (who had made three starts in 2014), and Baker. I always liked to quote the great John Wooden from UCLA, who said, "Competition is a coach's best friend."

It was going to be my best friend in 2015.

I did know about Baker. I'd kept up with him and some of Kliff's guys at Tech. And when I heard he was transferring, I actually had two phone conversations with him. I tried to get him to transfer to ECU. He would have been able to sit for a year and then potentially be the guy.

But I could tell his mind was already made up. I didn't know where he was going, but the second I found out it was OU, I got in contact with him and tried to talk him out of it. Told him he was crazy, that Trevor Knight

won the Sugar Bowl, and all that business. But he had his mind made up. I
tried, but I'm glad I didn't. If I had, I might not be in this office right now.

—Lincoln Riley

It was a clean slate. I didn't care about the past. I told Lincoln that whomever he thought was the best quarterback after spring and fall workouts was going to be our guy come that September.

Our first spring practice was Saturday, March 7. That night, an episode involving an Oklahoma fraternity would shake our campus and my team to the core.

I first heard the reports the following night. That's when a video surfaced showing members of the OU chapter of the Sigma Alpha Epsilon fraternity singing and chanting racist insults while on a party bus.

The video instantly became national news, and it threatened to tear our campus apart.

President Boren almost immediately shut down the 104-year-old SAE chapter. Two SAE members were later expelled from school. But the damage had been done.

The OU campus was in upheaval after the original video became public, followed by the appearance of another video that was equally disturbing. In the videos, there were song lyrics filled with racial slurs and unabashed boasting that no African American ever would become a member of the fraternity. There was also a reference to lynching.

Our roster included many African American players, some of whom didn't hide their outrage and anger. Our star linebacker Eric Striker released a profanity-laced Snapchat video of his own, and in it, he made no secret of his disdain for "phony" OU students who cheered for African American players on Saturday afternoons but then chanted about lynchings on their fraternity bus on Saturday nights.

There is no coaching handbook that covers this. Our players were angry. One of our recruits withdrew his commitment to OU. Students marched on campus—and marched to the shuttered SAE house.

The racism I've witnessed wasn't confined to that SAE party bus. I've seen it here and there throughout my career as a player and coach.

When I was growing up, there was no confusion about racism at our house. It simply wasn't allowed. My dad was a football coach, and football, he said, was the great equalizer. It didn't care if you had a vowel at the end of your name or if you were white or black, if your parents were rich or poor, or if you had an accent when you yelled out an audible. Either you could play or you couldn't. The rest was just noise.

I'm white, and watching that frat video cut through me. I'm not a guy who shows a lot of emotion, but seeing that video affected me in ways I can't fully articulate. And if it hurt me, the middle-aged white coach, I can't imagine how much it hurt the African American players on my team, the African American students on our campus, the African American folks in our town, state, and country.

You may ask yourself, how could this still be possible in the year 2015? How could something like that chant be taught and sung? How could there be not one but two videos of this hatred?

It was incomprehensible to me that this type of casual racism—racism as party-bus entertainment—existed. It's nothing that I could imagine.

But our African American players could imagine it. Some of them have lived it, been subjected to it.

In the days following those videos being posted on social media, my players chose to boycott spring football practices. And I chose to boycott it with them.

You have to understand that football coaches are creatures of habit. We live by daily schedules, and those are broken down by the hour, even by the minute. And we only get fifteen spring practices, so each one is precious from a coaching standpoint.

But as someone who had sat in the living rooms of these players and promised their mothers and fathers that I'd take care of them as if they were my own—they had a right to be angry. They had a need to vent, and I couldn't stand in their way now. They had a basic human instinct to examine the evil of that chant and see if there was a way to move forward from it.

Several of my assistant coaches wanted me to "get in the middle of the boycott." In other words, they wanted me to stop it.

They were worried we were missing too many practices. That's how coaches think sometimes. It wasn't as if they didn't recognize the severity of the situation, but they had been conditioned as football coaches to, well, think football. And that's what a few of them were doing.

I had talked to the players. I had seen the anguish on their faces. I told my assistants, "We ain't controlling this. We need to back off and give them all the time they need." And that was that.

I canceled our Monday practice and meetings. My coaches wanted me to get in the middle of it? That's exactly what I did. I was in the middle of the front row, arms locked with my players, as the entire team, all of us dressed in black, walked out of a canceled practice session at our field. I wanted the photographers (damn right I made sure they had access to that moment) to see us united against that sort of prejudice, bigotry, and hatred.

We were united against the chant, but we weren't completely united as a team. The players got together on their own and discussed how to further respond as one. They were trying to figure out what their public role was as OU football players. I was told later that those sessions were intensely emotional. There was shouting. It became so heated that several of the players almost got into fights. There was talk of boycotting games.

Some of the players didn't want to get involved. They said they were there to go to school and play football. They wanted to leave the politics to the university.

Striker, the kid who had released his own angry video, told me he had stood up in a team meeting and said the players had to confront this head-on, that they had an opportunity to bring about positive change.

That first team meeting lasted through the night. Think about that. As a coach, I constantly tried to team-build by using gimmicks or something football related. But this was life related. My players could have splintered. Instead, they came together. I was never prouder of an OU team than that one.

Because of those meetings, the players got a deeper sense of each other and of themselves. As a coach, I was impressed. But I also learned from them.

We're young black males saying, "This matters to us...hey, Coach, we think we have something that's bigger than football right now." He understood that. He said, "You're right." That was real. He loved the hell out of us.

He knows, as a white man, "Hey, I can't be affected like y'all." He got it. But he understood the history behind the moment. He understood our frustration.

Coach Bob grew, and he learned a lot about the players in that room. He couldn't feel our pain, but he understood our pain. It helped us all out. We were trying to talk out this race thing, which is still on us today.

We were nineteen, twenty, twenty-one, twenty-two years old, but we got it together, man. White men, black men.

—Eric Striker

President Boren asked me and my team captains to come to his office. He wanted those players and other members of our student body to meet with several of the SAE fraternity members who were on that bus.

I waited outside as my captains spent a long time in President Boren's office with the SAE guys. And when the door finally opened, there were my players hugging the fraternity members, showing forgiveness to them for their actions. Those two SAE members had shown complete remorse and apologized for the pain they had caused.

On their way out of the office, the fraternity members stopped and apologized to me, too. I shook their hands. If my players could find it in their hearts to forgive, then so could I.

We eventually returned to practice as a stronger, closer team. It wasn't perfect—it would take months before the divisions on campus and in our own locker room healed—but I could feel a difference in the awareness of the players. The same went for me.

As we went from spring practice to fall camp, the quarterback competition remained close. Some days, we'd get done with practice and I'd ask Lincoln, who was leading the quarterback derby, which player was our man. One day he'd say, "Probably Baker." The next, he'd say, "Probably Trevor." And Cody had his moments, too.

Everyone had an opinion, including Carol. One day during fall camp, she said, "Bobby, I haven't even watched practices, but I can tell you who your starting quarterback will be." Turns out, she was right.

In the end, Lincoln thought Baker had won the job. I agreed. Lincoln met with Trevor and delivered the news. I followed up and asked him to stay ready and, as a team captain, to keep a good attitude. I didn't really need to say that; Trevor was such a high-character individual that he'd do it on his own.

Lincoln informed Baker of the decision, and then I met with him. "Your name is on the starting lineup, but remember, you've still got to keep it," I told him.

Three quarters into our second game of the season — a tough road game at the sound chamber that is Tennessee's Neyland Stadium — there were probably lots of OU folks wondering why Lincoln was our offensive coordinator and why Baker was our starting quarterback. I wasn't one of them.

We trailed 17–0 in the second quarter, then 17–3 going into the fourth quarter. The crowd of 102,455 (almost the population of Norman) was the largest crowd an OU team had ever played in front of. A lot of teams and quarterbacks would have crumbled under those conditions.

In three quarters, we hadn't even crossed the fifty-yard line. Most head coaches would have been on the phones, saying, "What you're doing ain't working." He never said a word. Never. He believed in me and our offense. When your head coach has that much confidence in what you're doing, that same confidence comes to you, whether you're a player or assistant.

—Lincoln Riley

I never did feel I was ready to pull Baker. I trusted my coaches. I hadn't liked it when Coach Spurrier had second-guessed one of my coverage calls in the second game of my Florida career as a coordinator. I wasn't going to do the same thing to Lincoln in his second game at OU.

Thanks to our defense, we hung around, and in the fourth quarter, it all began to click on offense. We tied the game with forty seconds remaining and then won it in double overtime. During the last quarter and those two OT periods, Baker was eleven of fourteen for 103 yards and four touchdowns (one was a rushing TD). Our defense held Tennessee to 125 passing yards and only 254 total yards. Zack Sanchez's interception of a Joshua Dobbs pass clinched it for us.

Sooner Magic...

The win was our third consecutive victory against an SEC team. It also was one of the favorite wins of my career. It's always satisfying to come from behind on the road and quiet 102,000 fans.

That's the most fired up I've seen him in a long time. He was really excited after that. That was the first big win we had.

A lot of [head coaches] would have pulled me. That's the reason why I love Bob and Lincoln. They didn't crumble under the pressure. They didn't panic. At halftime, Lincoln told me, "We believe in you. Relax and go play. We're on the road and we're going to write a story today."

That's why I love that Tennessee game so much. They showed how much they trusted me. It goes a long way. What they did resides deeper in me than they'll ever realize.

— Baker Mayfield

We beat Tulsa, then Dana's West Virginia team at home. Unranked Texas beat us, and then we had a road game against K-State and Coach Snyder. One problem: we spent nearly eight hours at the airport waiting for our charter plane to arrive from another location.

Instead of complaining, we made the best of a bad situation. The coaches and administrators who had driven to the airport got in their cars and loaded up at nearby fast-food restaurants. We made it a potluck thing and had fun with it.

We didn't take off for Manhattan until 9:00 p.m. and didn't get to the hotel until after midnight. We had to be at the stadium in less than eleven hours.

"If you guys want an excuse not to play well tomorrow, you got it today," I told the team. "But we're going to get up tomorrow with no excuses. We're not going to let this bother us."

We won, 55–0, and played one of the most complete games of my eighteen years at OU.

Baker was extra motivated—maybe too motivated—for our late-October game against his old team, Texas Tech. I asked him to be careful about trying to do too much. He listened. We won that one, 63–27.

We later beat number-four Baylor in Waco. We beat number-eleven TCU at home, despite Baker getting knocked out of the game on a cheap shot and TCU having a chance to win on a late two-point conversion. I can still close my eyes and see Steven Parker knocking down TCU's final pass attempt.

We finished the regular season 11–1, and even with the loss to Texas, we won the Big 12 Championship, our first since 2012.

There was speculation that the College Football Playoff selection committee might not choose us as one of the four teams. (The playoff system had made its FBS debut a season earlier.) But I made sure to mention that OU had raised its hand when it came time to play a tough nonconference road game such as Tennessee. You should be rewarded for doing that, for taking those kind of scheduling chances.

We did get into the playoff and would face Clemson for a second consecutive year in the postseason.

As we prepared for Clemson, we were also preparing for the possibility of life without Baker. At the time, we didn't know if Baker would be allowed to play beyond 2016. Even though he was a walk-on in 2013, he had lost a year's worth of eligibility when he transferred from Texas Tech to OU. I thought it was an unfair rule—not just for Baker, but for any player in the conference who was penalized as a walk-on transfer.

In the meantime, three quarterbacks in established programs had expressed an interest in transferring to OU: Texas A&M's Kyle Allen and Kyler Murray, and Florida's Will Grier.

We had tried to recruit Murray out of high school, but it hadn't gone very far. This time, though, one of his former high school coaches reached out to us and asked if we'd consider Kyler.

Nothing against our younger guys on the roster, but we owed it to the program to look at Grier, Murray, and Allen. We called their head coaches. We went down the checklist: character, work ethic, team player, talent. Then Cale, Lincoln, and I put on the game tapes of each of the quarterbacks. They all could play.

Allen and Grier were both six foot three and looked like prototypical quarterbacks. Kyler was shorter, about five foot ten, tops.

Lincoln liked each one of them. "Every one of them can make a difference," he said. "But Kyler could win a Heisman Trophy here."

Even though it was clear from the tape that Kyler had electric skills, my eyebrows arched on that one. "Just make sure you're OK size-wise and height-wise with him," I said.

"I get it," said Lincoln. "It will be all right."

Kyler announced his decision to come to OU about a week before our playoff game.

We lost in the semifinals to Clemson. Let me tell you, there was no shame in losing to that team. We played hard and led at halftime, 17–16, but got outcoached and outplayed in the second half and lost by twenty.

Afterward, I shook Dabo's hand near midfield, and later, after my media obligations, Carol and I went back to the field and found Brent Venables and his wife, Julie, and congratulated them. Had the roles been reversed, Brent would have done the same thing. Brent's defense had played so well, and they had beat us fair and square. It was the least we could do, given our long history together dating back to when we first recruited Brent to K-State, and all the years—and shared life events—that followed.

Alabama ended up beating Clemson in the national championship, not that I paid much attention to it. I wanted to be in that game, not sitting on a sofa watching it.

Our accomplishments of 2015 weren't accidents. We were a better team because we had come together months earlier in March. It was one of the most remarkable transformations I'd ever seen as a coach. And it happened not because of anything I did, but because of the players.

I'll remember those wins from 2015, but I'll also remember something that defensive end Charles Tapper said as we prepared for the playoff game against Clemson. When Jake Trotter of ESPN.com asked him about his teammates, he said, "I want every guy on this team to be the best man at my wedding. The bond on this team...it's real."

What happened in 2015 galvanized our team. And it changed our university forever. I've had people ask me, "What makes [Stoops] so great?" After April of that year, I knew.

—Lincoln Riley

I felt good about where our program was again, however difficult the circumstances had been to get there. I wasn't completely satisfied yet, but we were pointed the right way now. We had had Baker back in 2016 and had Kyler in the quarterback pipeline for 2017.

Trevor, who couldn't have handled the 2015 season situation with any more class, requested a release from his scholarship at season's end. He transferred to Texas A&M, and we wished him our very best.

But then our quarterback situation took an unexpected twist. On June 1, the Big 12 faculty reps decided that they weren't going to change a rule that would have granted Baker an extra year of eligibility in 2017. It was a disappointing decision, but not a complete surprise.

On June 2, they changed their minds. How about that?

I was so happy for Baker. But it meant our other quarterbacks, including Kyler, would likely be stuck behind him until the 2018 season.

Chapter Fifteen

The Rivalry

Army-Navy. USC-Notre Dame. Auburn-Alabama. Michigan-Ohio State. Cal-Stanford. Harvard-Yale. They're all great, historic rivalries.

But I'll take Texas versus OU every day of the week, and twice on a game-day Saturday.

The Cotton Bowl. The grounds of the State Fair of Texas. The stadium split down the middle: OU crimson and cream one half, Texas burnt orange filling out the other half. National television. Bordering states. A rivalry that started in 1900. The smell of fried everything wafting through the air. A who's-who list of Texas-OU players that stretches from one end zone to the other. A game with usually national implications.

I wanted to win every game, but I especially wanted to win the OU-Texas game, whether it was called the Red River Shootout, Classic, Showdown, or Rivalry. Didn't matter to me. All I knew is that they gave you a big Golden Hat trophy if you won, and it sure made recruiting in Texas more fun.

When I was hired at Oklahoma in late 1998, Mack Brown had just finished his first season at Texas. He was an experienced, successful, and formidable coach.

The Longhorns had been a mess the previous couple of years. There was a lot of infighting, a lot of politics. The previous coach had sort of sucked the Texas identity out of the program. Mack put it back in. They went from 4–7 in 1997 to 9–3 during Mack's debut season in 1998.

We lost to them during my first season in 1999, but there was one footnote to that game that stayed mostly secret for nearly twenty years. I didn't know about it myself until the week after the loss.

Mike Leach is wired a little differently than the rest of us. We all know that. His outside-the-box thinking has a lot to do with his success. It's one of the reasons I hired him to be our offensive coordinator.

We were 3–1, unranked, and underdogs coming off a close loss at Notre Dame as we prepared for the Texas game. The Longhorns were ranked number twenty-three.

I basically left the offense alone; that was Leach's world. My expertise was on the defensive side and on our overall game prep. They had their usual meetings, and we had ours.

At that time, I brought something up every day. Literally every day, I'd ask, "What do you think of this?" Or, "What do you think of that?" I had all these ideas.

Mike had one sheet of paper, and that was our game-day script. That's how he did it. We were sitting around, and I said, "Let's create a fake one — all sorts of reverses and double passes, formations and shifts — and then drop it out on the field for the players and see what happens."

Mike said, "That's a good idea. Let's do it."

Was I the inspiration for it? I wasn't. It was the Tennessee game: Florida versus Tennessee, and my father versus Phil Fulmer. That's what started it.

"I'll never forget the time we did it at Tennessee. Think it was 1996. We were in the press box, and we watched the guy who picked [the fake play sheet] up walk it into the locker room.

For Texas, we had Cale Gundy's name on it. Gundy would be the guy to lose it. Then you had to kind of walk down their sideline, make sure it got picked up by the right person. That was always entertaining.

—Steve Spurrier Jr.

Leach would later mention the incident in his autobiography, and in 2018, Jake Trotter of ESPN.com did a whole story on the deception. Leach had put together a sheet of fake plays, put Gundy's name on it, had it laminated, and then had it dropped by our tight end Trent Smith near the Texas coaches during warm-ups.

According to Trotter's story, one of Texas's student assistants picked it up and gave it to defensive coordinator Carl Reese, who then met with his defensive assistants and decided it was the real thing. Once the game started, Reese changed his calls based on the fake play-call sheet.

We scored on a long touchdown pass twenty-nine seconds into the game. Then we kicked a field goal. Then we scored again on another TD pass. We were up, 17–0, in the first quarter. They looked out of sorts, and we looked unstoppable.

I thought it was kind of stupid that it came out [publicly]. We had a seventeen-point lead, but I don't think [the fake play sheet] had much to do with it.
— Steve Spurrier Jr.

Texas came back to win the game, 38–28. Turns out they finally realized they had been duped and supposedly quit calling coverages and blitzes to counter Leach's fake plays.

I still don't believe we had success just because of the script. It's not like they knew our terminology or what the exact play was. We were outplaying them a little bit at that point in the game.

I kind of chuckled when I heard about it later. I was used to dealing with Leach, so I wasn't surprised.

The first year Bob was there, he was the new, hot coach. We were down, 17–0, but we came back late, and it set the tempo for two great teams in the rivalry. Before then, it had slipped on TV, slipped on attendance. Our games [OU/Stoops vs. Texas/Brown] were always full.
— Mack Brown, Texas head coach, 1998–2013

When I first became a head coach, my mentality was that I didn't want to be friendly with anybody I was coaching against. I was respectful. I was cordial. I was professional. But I wasn't out there to be your buddy.

I actually got kind of angry at Mack before the 2000 game. I went out to shake his hand, and he put his other hand behind the back of my head and pulled me in a little bit, like you do to someone you think is your junior — at least, that's the way I took it.

My reaction was, *Wait a second…hey, I'm not ready for that.* I pulled away. I didn't like it at all.

Did I read too much into it? Maybe. But it was only my second year at OU, and I wasn't looking for any tender, friendly pregame moments with the opposing coach. And that went for everybody, not just Mack.

My assistant coaches shared that competitiveness, and they were the best. They were so determined in their prep work not to miss a thing, no matter how small. During Texas week, the intensity was palpable.

In 2000, during our midweek prep work for Texas, I started walking down the hall of the coaches' offices with a late-afternoon message: "Let's get out of here early. We're going to kick the shit out of those guys."

I wanted to project confidence, and I wanted them to project that same confidence to our team. But it wasn't fake confidence. I knew we were ready.

With 4:43 left in the second quarter, we were up, 42–0. I got on the headphones with our coaches. "You know what, boys, we're pretty good," I said.

In other words, quit worrying so much.

Final score: OU 63, Texas 14. And we called off the dogs in that game, or it could have been worse. At the time, it was the most points OU had scored against Texas in the then–ninety-five-year history of the series, and the second-largest winning margin until…we beat them by fifty-two in 2003.

We obviously had something special going in 2000. It's not often in an OU-Texas game that you feel comfortable at halftime. And I didn't feel truly comfortable until the third quarter. But that's how coaches are.

Quentin Griffin had three touchdowns in the first half and another three in the second half. Texas had minus-seven rushing yards in the game.

I gave game balls to everyone after that win, including myself. After all, it was my first victory against Texas as a head coach.

But the game every OU fan remembers (and every Texas fan tries to forget) is the 2001 meeting. If you've never seen it, YouTube it. It was the "Superman" game—when Roy Williams put on his cape and became a college football legend.

We were ranked number three, and they were number five, but they were favored. There was 2:06 left in the game. They had first-and-ten on their own three-yard line, and we were clinging to a 7–3 lead.

I've seen the replay of what happened next. But what happened before the Superman moment matters, too.

A play earlier, we had the ball and faced a fourth-and-sixteen at the Texas twenty-seven. I was talking to the coaches on the headphone and started to send in the field goal team. Even though Tim Duncan had missed his two attempts in the game and six of his last seven, a field goal would mean they'd have to score a touchdown to have a chance.

Mike had another idea. "I'd pooch it down there," he said. "Let's back them up. We *will* stop them."

Smart. We still sent out the field goal team and snapped it to Jason White, who was also our holder. He had come in the game at quarterback when Hybl got hurt.

White tossed the ball to Duncan, who punted it down the middle of the field. The ball was going into the end zone when Texas's Nathan Vasher, who was a helluva player, made a mistake and caught the ball at the three. Had it bounced into the end zone, Texas would have started at the twenty and with room to operate.

Mike decided to run a zone blitz called "Slamdogs."

There's a TV timeout before we take the field. We had the blitz on, Slamdogs, where the [middle linebacker] and strong safety go up the middle in the A and B gap. We had run it earlier in the game. We knew how they were going to pick it up. It was a great way to get Roy against the running back one-on-one and get in the quarterback's face.

—Teddy Lehman

Brett Robin, their blocking back, had cut me, hit me in the groin earlier in the game. This time, Mike said, "Don't leave your feet. Don't jump."

I said, "Don't worry, Coach." But I'm thinking, "I'm jumping," because I knew he was going to cut me again.

I was going to hit the B gap; Teddy was faking in the A gap. Rocky was showing in the A gap. too.

—Roy Williams

Cory Heinecke, our defensive end, was going to drop out underneath so they couldn't throw a hitch pattern to their Roy Williams, the Texas receiver. We told him not even to bother getting into a three-point stance. Just drop off the line into the passing lane.

They snapped the ball, and I just watched Cory. He was in the line of flight, and Texas quarterback Chris Simms couldn't throw the football in that direction. I was watching to make sure their Roy Williams couldn't get the ball.

Then I heard the whole crowd going crazy. Our guys were going crazy. I looked around and asked, "What happened?"

I came in scot-free. Robin tried to cut me, and I just jumped over him. I hit Simms, and the ball fluttered into Teddy's hands.

—Roy Williams

It just pops into my hands. I score.

—Teddy Lehman

We kicked off after the score. When I was running off the field, Mike grabbed me around the neck and said, "I told you not to f—ing jump." He was smiling.

That's my coach for you. I can laugh about it now.

—Roy Williams

Roy was quite possibly the best defensive player I've ever been around. He just controlled games. On their next series, they tried to hit a seam route, and he picked the ball off to basically end the game.

Texas is a country club. We outwork them every single day. We beat them before we even walked into the Cotton Bowl.

—Teddy Lehman

I never looked at the OU-Texas rivalry as a rivalry between coaches. It was never me against Mack Brown; it was between the players and the programs.

But I wasn't going to back down. Not to Texas or Mack, or Charlie Strong, or anybody when it came to that rivalry.

That game is important for all sorts of reasons. There's so much pride within those two programs. So much history and tradition. You wanted to be the team that got to wear that golden hat and pose on the field for the postgame team photo. Our programs were usually competing for some of the same players in recruiting, especially in the state of Texas. So that game meant a lot. For the longest time, whichever team won that game usually ended up in the Big 12 Championship.

Coach Switzer said it's like two Mack trucks running into each other for three and a half hours. They just don't like each other. It was the reason kids came to those two schools. It was the game everybody wanted to watch every year: Texas and OU.

In 1984, I was the offensive coordinator for Coach Switzer. All the Texas people wanted me to hate Oklahoma, but I couldn't do it. Or they'd say, "I guess you hate Bob Stoops." I'd say, "No, we're a lot closer than you think." I'm supposed to hate him, but I don't hate him.

When it started, we were both young, probably both a little brash, and said a few things about the two programs. We were so competitive about recruiting. You had to get players from the Dallas metroplex.

—Mack Brown

I'll be honest: I never hated Texas. At the end of the day, I never found a lot of use for that word, especially when it comes to football games. Put it this way instead: I didn't hate, but I loved to win and get a leg up on the Big 12 South and the Big 12 Championship.

There are great high school players in Oklahoma. But just from a population standpoint, we had to go into Texas and recruit. You want to talk about tradition? Oklahoma recruiting Texas has always been a tradition.

I always laughed when I heard people say that a Texas kid had to stay in-state. Huh? It's not Communist Russia. You don't need permission from the commissar to cross the border.

Here in the United States of America, we can cross between Texas and Oklahoma without a passport. I'd ask those Texas kids, "What happens if you end up getting drafted by the New England Patriots? You going to tell Bill Belichick that you can't come to Massachusetts because you'd have to leave the state of Texas? You only going to play for the Houston Texans or Dallas Cowboys?"

They never had a good answer—because there isn't one.

I'm sure it did kill Texas to see some of the best in-state high school players end up in an OU uniform. Adrian Peterson, Derrick Strait, Tommie Harris, Mark Clayton, Trent Williams, and Dede Westbrook, to name a few, were Texas kids who signed with us. Texas had its shot at Baker Mayfield, who had been born and raised in Austin. Mack took a pass. But we sort of did too, at first. When Baker decided to transfer from Texas Tech after the 2013 season and enroll at OU, we didn't make the same mistake twice.

From 2000 to 2004, we beat Texas five times in a row. During that time, we were both highly ranked when that game came around.

White had four touchdown passes in the 2003 game. That's when we first saw a Texas redshirt freshman quarterback named Vince Young. He was skinny then, and he took a pounding, just like Texas did, 65–13.

The next year, we shut out Vince and a really talented Texas team, 12–0. That was pretty special. One of the great defensive efforts.

Our streak ended in 2005. That was a tough year all around for us.

You want to bring up pain? They were way better than us. They had the best player in college football in Vince Young. We had a redshirt freshman who was still trying to figure it out.

I remember thinking, "They might not lose a game the rest of the year."

I sacked Young in the game. I hit him pretty good, but he didn't go down. I forgot how big he was.

—Dusty Dvoracek

Texas beat us, 45–12, in 2005 and went on to defeat USC in the national championship game. Didn't surprise me at all.

They beat us again in 2006. We won in 2007. They won in 2008 when we were ranked number one and they were number five. There was a lot of talent on the Cotton Bowl field that day, beginning with Sam Bradford and Colt McCoy. We still managed to reach the national championship game that year.

They won again in 2009 on their way to the national championship game, and then we won three in a row, including a 55–17 win in 2011 and 63–21 in 2012. By then, Mack was catching heat from the Texas fans, boosters, and media.

Mike Riley, the former Oregon State coach, supposedly once said that coaching in college was "a great job, but a shitty profession." I thought of that as Mack dealt with the criticism.

When Texas upset us in 2013, in what would be Mack's final season there, I was disappointed in the loss, but I was happy for Mack. I knew all the shit that he had taken from his critics. He needed a win like the one against us, and he got it.

My last game between us, Bob was so classy after the game. He shook my hand, hugged my neck, and said, "You guys just lined up and physically whipped us today. Congratulations and good luck."

I was much tougher behind the scenes than people thought, and Bob was much softer than his public perception, more giving.

—Mack Brown

As the seasons passed, I softened my stance about relationships with opposing coaches. I started to wise up. Hey, that guy is working hard, too. Maybe we even had some of the same issues with our respective teams. I realized I could win a game and not be such a hard-ass about it.

Texas is a job where the expectations exceed reality. The great jobs always are like that. Mack won 158 games there. He only lost sixteen games between 2001 and 2009. He won a national championship, and like me, maybe he could have won more. But he put his program in position to play for those titles. Given the state of Longhorns football when he took over in 1998, that was no small feat. He revived and restored that program. Since he left, Texas has hired two head coaches and two athletic directors.

We went 9–6 against Mack when I was there, and I'm proud of that record. Anytime you beat a Mack Brown–coached Texas team, that said something.

I know he wanted to get back into coaching, and I wish him the very best at North Carolina.

Chapter Sixteen

Empathy

<hr/>

Their names and faces never leave you.

Cody. Micah. Fletcher. Mackenzie. Justin. TJ. David. Robert. Dozer. Stevy. Ryan. Kennedy. Bridget. Montana. Buddy. David. Those are just a few of the hundreds of kids I've met at the Children's Hospital at OU Medicine during the last twenty years.

Their courage touches you. Their stories inspire you. Their strength humbles you.

I've always been reluctant to speak publicly about my visits with those kids. It isn't out of false modesty but more out of respect for them and their families. It's the same reason I've rarely agreed to let a TV crew tag along. Those moments weren't about me but about the children. I wanted these to be personal, authentic connections, not media events.

Not all, but many of those children that I visited every Thursday — and still do — on the tenth floor of the hospital's Jimmy Everest Center for Cancer and Blood Disorders were terminally ill. Those Thursdays have been some of the few times that I *wanted* to be Bob Stoops the OU Football Coach. If that guy could make a tiny difference in a child's morning or afternoon, sign me up.

If you think you're having a tough day, go spend time with those brave kids and their families. They keep me grounded. They put life and death in perspective. They give joy when you don't think joy is possible. Whatever small comfort I provide, they return it a hundredfold.

I write about them because their stories are important, because they need advocates, because that could be my child or your child in the hospital.

EMPATHY

A longtime volunteer at the Children's Hospital, Kay Tangner, first approached me about visiting the Everest Center shortly after we won the national championship in 2000. She said the cancer patients there wanted to throw a party for me.

For me? Shouldn't I be doing something for them?

Kay explained that if I showed up, I would be doing something for them.

I brought some of my players to the party, and we had a great time with those kids. The next week, I called Kay and said I'd like to come back on my own. One week became two. Two weeks became three. Three weeks became twenty years and counting.

We played cards. We played with dolls. We took selfies. We talked about football. We talked about anything but football. We hugged. We laughed. On occasion, we cried.

Cody Brown was seven or eight when I met him. He gave me a little gold pin for Pediatric Cancer Awareness. The next time I saw him, he asked, "Where's my pin?"

"Cody, it's in my desk," I said, "but I promise I'll start wearing it."

And I did. It had a place of honor on my game-day visor.

I brought Carol and several players, including Jason White and Mark Clayton, to see Cody at his home. It was a small gesture on our part, but again, I wanted him to know that his cause mattered, that he wasn't alone. He passed the next day.

I remember sweet Micah Walters, whose condition had slowly worsened over time. I was there near the very end. I walked into his hospital room and held Micah's hand. He rallied a little bit, opened his eyes, recognized me, and softly said, "Boomer."

"Sooner," I said softly back.

There was ten-year-old Mackenzie Asher, whose story of courage and determination was told so well by ESPN's Tom Rinaldi on *College GameDay*.

Mackenzie had been diagnosed with leukemia in June 2016 and began treatments almost immediately. I first met her and her dad, Jayson, a few months later when Kay and I stopped by Mackenzie's room.

After you left, Mackenzie asked, "Dad, are you OK?" She was fighting cancer, and she asked me if I was OK.

After the first visit, that very next Saturday, she asked, "What time does OU play?" She had never asked me that before. We watched the game together, and for the first time, she was cheering on and actually watching every play. What started out as a VIP visitor evolved into a real admiration and friendship she felt she had with you.

On the day of your visits, she always wanted to be her best. She'd even ask me, "Dad, how do I look?" She perked up and soaked up every moment with you.

— Jayson Asher, in a letter to Bob Stoops

We often invited the kids over to our practices and facilities to meet the players and become part of our team, even if only for a day. During one of our Special Spectator events at OU, Mackenzie met Baker, and they formed a fast friendship.

Mackenzie passed away in early December 2017. She was only eleven. Baker spoke at her memorial service.

We have scrapbooks full of photos from our visits. Those kids became my extended family. They honored me with their love, friendship, and trust.

They say that God works in mysterious ways. I know this to be true after spending time with these wonderful kids. How else can you explain the strength of Justin Scott?

On Friday, April 22, 2005, Justin was preparing for a procedure that would make a bone marrow transplant possible. But then his doctors learned through a blood test that Justin's leukemia had returned. The transplant was no longer an option.

On Monday, Justin and his family met with doctors at the Everest Center. Afterward, we met for lunch, and they told me the devastating news. I invited them back to my office at OU.

It was there that Justin said, "Coach, I need a favor. I need you and some of the players to be my pallbearers."

You talk about something that knocks you on your rear—a sixteen-year-old kid planning his own funeral. I asked Justin to write down the names of the players he wanted. The list: J. D. Runnels, Rufus Alexander, Jacob Gutierrez, and Jammal Brown.

Justin asked me to enforce several other requests: anyone attending his funeral had to wear OU gear. No neckties allowed.

Done deal, I told him. Then I walked him over to my personal locker and told him to take whatever he wanted.

"Would you mind if I was buried in this?" he said, pointing to a white OU polo shirt and a crimson sweater vest.

"I'd be honored," I said.

On Wednesday, J. D. went to visit Justin at his house. They played video games. At one point, Justin came out of the room and asked his dad if J. D. could borrow a shirt.

"Why does J. D. need a shirt?" asked Justin's dad.

"Because we've been crying, and J. D.'s shirt is all wet."

J. D.'s mom had died of cancer in 2003. When they talked that Wednesday, Justin reminded J. D. that he was Adrian Peterson's lead blocker. He then asked if J. D. would be his lead blocker as a pallbearer. J. D. said he would, but only if Justin would do a favor for him: when he got to heaven, he had to find J. D.'s mom and tell her how much J. D. missed and loved her.

Justin died two days later.

Through the years, so many of my players made those visits with me or separately to the Children's Hospital. Sam, AD, Gerald, Ty Darlington, Baker, Nila Kasitati, Jed Barnett, and dozens and dozens of others. Nila would bring his ukulele, and Jed would sing to the kids.

I didn't force anyone to make the trip. But I think those visits had an impact on the players. You can't meet those kids without being moved by their perseverance and strength.

We always called him a player's coach. When we walked into the Switzer Center, it was always about football: "Make sure you're throwing this route...do this, do that."

But as soon as you walked out of the facility, it was never football with him. It was, "How's your mom doing? How's school going? I'm going to the Children's Hospital, why don't you just ride up there with me?"

With him, there was more to life than football.

—Jason White

I always tried to bring a bag of OU stuff and let the kids pick what they wanted. If they wanted to attend a game, come to practice, be in the middle of our team huddle at the end of practice, go to our team banquet...whatever, I tried to make it happen. If they wanted to talk, I gave them my cell number. I looked at it this way: maybe it made their day a little bit better. I know it certainly made my day better to be with them. I gained strength from their strength.

We visited on Thanksgiving Day. On Christmas Day. There is heartbreak and struggle on the pediatric oncology floor, but I also witnessed laughter, joy, excitement, happiness, hope, and friendship.

There were little kids I would visit who had no idea I was the OU head coach. But on a later visit, perhaps after their parents had pointed me out on TV during a game, they would say, "That's my Bob Stoops!"

> *He brought encouragement and hope not only to the patients but to the doctors and nurses as well.*
>
> *If he walked into a room and the parents apologized for wearing Oklahoma State shirts, he would tell them, "Oh, don't worry about it. Everybody has to like somebody."*
>
> *I've heard many Oklahoma State and Texas fans say, "I may not be an OU fan, but I'm a Bob Stoops fan."*
>
> —Kay Tangner, Children's Hospital volunteer

> *He'll hate me for saying this, but there are mothers calling Bob their angel for helping their kids. I know he bought a handicap-accessible van for a family because they didn't have the money. He helped people across the state who had children with terminal illnesses.*
>
> *I asked him why he went to the hospital every week. He told me he did it because it balanced his perspective. It kept football from getting too big.*
>
> —Kenny Mossman

There are 314 inpatient beds at the Children's Hospital. I hope I've been able to visit every one, to offer whatever help I can. It is the only freestanding pediatric hospital in Oklahoma dedicated to the treatment of kids. There's a neonatal ICU as well as the Children's Heart Center. They do amazing work in that building.

I've spoken to state legislators about the importance of funding the efforts of all initiatives that benefit children. And through our Champions Foundation and the tireless work of Matt McMillen and Julie Watson during the last twenty years, we've donated money to those efforts and provided scholarships and support to those kids who have gone on to overcome those illnesses.

One of those survivors, TJ Hutchings, invited me to his wedding. He reminded me in a letter of how he'd celebrated his eighteenth birthday in the hospital while undergoing chemotherapy treatments. The nurses had asked him to report to the breakroom. He figured they had made him a cake.

He was half right.

When he turned the corner, there was Adrian, holding his birthday cake.

TJ has been cancer free for more than fourteen years now. I still hear from him on occasion.

There's Bridget Ford, another survivor. I first met her when she was eleven or so. She's now in her early twenties. We still meet for lunch every so often.

I have a soft spot for all children in need. Having dealt with my own daughter's medical situation, I know the helplessness you can feel as a parent about what's happening to your kids.

I'm proud of the work our foundation has done. Oklahomans have big hearts. I've seen it in the support people give to the Children's Hospital. I've seen it in other areas, such as our partnership with Toby Keith and his foundation to provide Christmas presents to kids who are battling cancer.

You should have seen the 2018 OK Kids Korral Toy Ride, which began in Toby's hometown of Moore that December 16 morning. There had to be a couple hundred motorcycles in the motorcade Toby led. We had a police escort (I was in an SUV—no chaps or riding a hog for me; Santa was in a police car) and drove from one stop to the next, delivering toys. Our convoy must have stretched at least a mile long.

What a neat experience. We delivered presents and also raised about $50,000 toward the Korral, which provides free lodging for visiting families as their kids go through treatment at the hospital. Tim Smith works on the Korral during the entire year.

Some of the biker guys were tough-looking dudes. But when we'd reach the house or apartment of a family and see the reactions of the kids when they were showered with Christmas presents, well, the tough-looking biker dudes got emotional, too.

One little girl started jumping up and down with excitement as we pulled up. When she saw Santa, she ran up and hugged him. Pretty cool.

We covered about fifty miles and about a half-dozen families.

Seeing those kids' faces... that was my Christmas present.

Chapter Seventeen

Why?

It was a Friday.

I drove home after our 7:00 a.m. practice on December 2, 2016, and found Carol sitting in front of a mirrored vanity, putting on her makeup. I usually came home after the hour-long practice, took a quick shower, changed, spent a little time with the family, and then headed back to campus.

Carol smiled and said hello and then turned her attention back to the mirror.

I knelt next to her. "I don't think I can do this anymore," I said.

I don't think Carol even looked away from the mirror. "You mean the 7:00 a.m. practices?" she asked.

"No," I said, my voice measured and even. I didn't want to scare her. "This might be it. I wanted to tell you now."

She turned and stared at me. She instantly understood. Then her eyes welled up with tears, and she was silent. "Bobby, are you sure?" she finally asked.

"I'm fine," I said. "I just feel like it's time."

I had warned everyone.

For years, I had told my family, my mom and siblings, my friends, my assistant coaches, my athletic director, my school president, and even select members of the media that I never would be one of those coaches who grew old in the job. I told anyone who would listen that my days as a head coach were numbered.

Nobody truly believed me, except maybe Carol. She had seen the cumulative effect of the job on me.

Let me be clear here: I worked for and with the best people in college athletics. I cared deeply about my players and staff. I was paid a salary far above my wildest dreams. I loved the camaraderie. I lived for the competition. Coaching football wasn't work; it was a privilege and a calling.

But I had been buttoned to football since watching game film with my dad. I had been a player, graduate assistant, volunteer coach, assistant coach, or coordinator for nineteen years and a head coach for eighteen-plus. I wasn't the man I used to be. I wasn't the husband and father that I needed to be. Whatever wall you reach in your life, I had slammed against mine—and it didn't give this time.

Was I sure? I wasn't *absolutely* sure. But as my words spilled out to Carol, I knew this time was different from any previous times I had considered walking away from the game. The words hadn't been said out of frustration, emotion, or anger. Instead, they were said out of true self-reflection. I had realized I was successful, but not content. I had probably stayed at OU too long. And in the not-so-deep recesses of my mind, I didn't want to risk dying on the side of a football field as my dad had done twenty-eight years earlier.

I chose that Friday to tell Carol because if I did walk away, I wanted her...us...to soak in the final days of our season, every bittersweet moment of it: our last home game, the players, the fans, the stadium, the roars, being with our kids, hearing "Boomer Sooner"...everything.

It was a surreal experience to discuss it. In a way, we were in a kind of shared shock. After all, our lives together had revolved around faith and family, but also football. For 365 days a year, football had set our circadian rhythm.

Carol's first reaction was to think that something was wrong, that I was ill, that I was unhappy.

Nothing was wrong. The more we talked, the more she realized that everything was positive. I had made the decision for all the right reasons. Once she understood my motives, she was 100 percent supportive.

Then we beat Oklahoma State, 38–20, in front of a crazy Gaylord Family–Oklahoma Memorial Stadium crowd to win the Big 12 Championship. There was no conference title game that year, so the winner of Bedlam won it all. It was an amazing way to end my final home game at OU—though nobody but Carol and I knew at the time that that's what it was.

WHY?

We beat Auburn in the Sugar Bowl to finish 11–2 and fifth in the final rankings.

My personal fistfight with myself began again.

Resign? Who said anything about resigning? What was I thinking?

I blew off what I had just decided. Everything was going too well for me to resign. I had a great team coming back in 2017. I had a fearless, supremely talented quarterback in Baker. I would coach another year and then reassess. That's what I told myself.

But then the thoughts returned. A whisper in my mind became a shout. A shout became something close to a final decision.

Carol and I hadn't told anyone about our December conversation. But after the Oklahoma State win and the celebration in the locker room, we pulled our three kids back onto the field for a family photo. They didn't understand why we had insisted, and we didn't tell them.

As for me, I savored the postgame celebration: the smiles on the faces of my players, the laughter, the indescribable feeling that comes with a team victory and a Big 12 title. (It was the first time one of my teams had won the championship on our own field.)

In late spring of 2017, I decided it was time to talk with Joe Castiglione. Joe was the guy who had hired me more than eighteen years earlier. Joe is the athletic department's voice of reason. He is dependable, honest, an optimist and pragmatist at the same time—a forward thinker who isn't afraid to take chances.

I owed him my honesty. I told him I was leaning hard toward resigning as head coach. He was surprised. And maybe, in my own way, I was surprised, too.

Then I met with President Boren. It isn't often that a head coach has the same athletic director and president for his entire run, especially for one that lasts eighteen and a half years. They weren't mere administrators; they were partners in our program. They were trusted friends.

I told President Boren that it was time for me to step down and that Lincoln was the perfect choice to take over the program. I wanted to make an announcement in June.

Joe called: "Bob's in my office, saying crazy things—like he might not stay for next season. You've got to talk him out of it. I've got to bring him over. You've got to talk him out of it."

Bob talked about Lincoln Riley. In many ways, Lincoln has some of the basic values and qualities and straightforwardness that Bob has. Lincoln reminds me a tremendous amount of Bob Stoops.

—David Boren

President Boren and Joe had an idea. They wanted to name Lincoln the so-called coach in waiting. I'd coach the 2017 season and then step aside for Lincoln in January 2018.

"Just think about it," Joe said.

I thought about it for a month. But something about the arrangement didn't feel right. Either I'm the boss, or I'm not. You can't *sort of* be the head coach. You can't have the players and assistant coaches wondering if they're supposed to work hard for me, or for Lincoln. It wouldn't be fair to them or to either Lincoln or me. I felt it would be more empowering for Lincoln to win and have a successful, strong team moving forward.

Plus, if I resigned in June, it would give all those recruits who had signed with us in February a chance to see that nothing had really changed. True, I wouldn't be the head coach anymore, but my handpicked successor would carry on.

Lincoln was ready to be a head coach. He knew it. I knew it. Joe knew it. The players knew it. Other schools updating their coaching wish lists knew it. I wanted to give him every chance to succeed. We had the kind of mature, strong team that could handle the transition. And I was convinced that making the announcement in June would be the least disruptive in terms of impact to the football program.

There's one other thing: usually when a new coach comes in, he brings new people with him. I didn't want to leave and see assistant coaches and support staff lose their jobs. Lincoln wasn't an outsider. He knew these people. He knew the quality of their work. I could rest easy, knowing that their positions were safe for the near future.

Not long after those meetings, Carol and I were driving back from Dallas. It takes about three and a half hours—plenty of time to talk.

When the Big 12 gave us Baker back, I thought, "Good, we've got another year." Oh, my gosh, it was going to be a fun year with Baker. I even said that to Bobby.

He said, "That's the whole point—I don't want to ride Baker out. I want Lincoln in a good spot."

I said, "Bobby, are you sure? I get it, but as someone who loves you and has watched you go through the pain of some of these years, doing the hard things like letting people go, putting together this staff, changing recruiting, getting things where they are now, you're just going to hand it over?"

He just said, "Yeah."

—Carol Stoops

There's a story about the man who falls into the river and is fighting not to drown. He yells to the heavens and says, "God, I know you'll save me. Send me a sign."

And as he's shaking his fist at the heavens and imploring God to send a sign, a log floats by. And then another. And another after that. Each time, the man is too busy to notice. Overcome by the current and high waters, the man drowns.

Moments later, he finds himself at Heaven's gate. He begins arguing with the guard there. "I kept asking God to help me, but He did nothing," says the man.

The guard answers, "We sent you three logs, but you let each one float past. You failed to see the answer because you were too busy asking the question."

I thought about that story when I was making my final decision. To everything there is a season, and my seasons were done. I didn't want to miss my moment to escape the river. Lincoln Riley was my rescue log, and I wasn't going to let it pass.

If it had been anybody but Lincoln, I might have reversed course and returned for 2017 and perhaps beyond. But I knew Lincoln was the right guy for the job.

He cares more about this program than he does about himself. He was not going to factor in the fact that we had a good team coming back, that we had a senior quarterback coming back, that we had good positioning—that was not going to be a factor in his decision, other than it being a positive for me being a first-year head coach and a positive for the transition. That's the only way he would have factored it in for himself.

That's him, man. That's what makes that guy special. I'm telling you, 99 percent of the other coaches out there would have hung on for one more year and then maybe done it after that, when the senior quarterback was gone. He's just not wired like most guys. Most guys won't retire when they're fifty-something years old and have a job like this.

But he's different. That's what separates him.

—Lincoln Riley

As June approached, I confided in my brother Mike. He was stunned. He couldn't process the idea of me giving up coaching. It was as if I'd said I was changing my first name from Bob to Bevo.

"Mike, I didn't get to this decision lightly," I said.

Carol later told me that Mike called her, asking if he should try to talk me out of my choice. He wanted to be supportive and respectful of it, but he also wanted to be sure this is what I really wanted. Carol told him I was at peace with it.

A few weeks later, I told my daughter, Mackie, and our sons, Isaac and Drake, that I was resigning. "Hey, everything is fine," I said. "It's just time."

For weeks, the decision stayed a secret. The circle of trust was very small. But inside our newly opened, $160 million football facility, it became apparent that some sort of transition was in the works. For starters, I hadn't made much of an effort to move into my eighteen-hundred-square-foot office, which Carol and designer and friend Debbie Groves had helped conceive and furnish. During the previous two seasons, we had worked out of temporary trailers, just like the old days.

The new digs were fabulous. My office, with its masonry fireplace, oversized leather chairs, floor-to-near-ceiling windows, dramatic archways, and wood floors, looked more like an upscale fishing lodge. I'd moved just enough items into it to give the impression that all was normal.

But even the media had begun to learn of some of the details. The secret was no longer a secret.

We had originally planned to make the announcement on Friday, June

9. With the leaks, we had to move up the timetable—and I needed to reach out to the people who meant the most to me.

My wife, Gina, and I went over to his house for dinner. I remember standing at the grill, thinking, "That boy has something on his mind."

We all sat down for dinner outside on the patio, and he just looked at me and said, "I'm not going to coach anymore."

I was literally stunned. I couldn't even speak at first. My mouth was open a little bit, but it was like getting hit on the head with an anvil. I was overblinking—the whole deal.

I asked, "You mean this year?"

He said, "I'm going to retire. I'm all done."

I can barely even talk as he's explaining it. Forty-five minutes. It was a roundhouse.

Chicken was served. We kind of struggled through dinner. My wife starts bawling, and she never cries. I remember going home, just sitting there. Wow. Everything changes.

I did not try to talk him out of it. I could tell he was doing it for all the right reasons. And I knew his mind was made up.

—Matt McMillen

I called my mother as well as my brothers—Mark, the head coach at Kentucky, and Ron—the day of the official announcement. I didn't want them to be worried about me or to hear the news from someone else. I tried to tell a few others, too.

I didn't see it coming. When I was told, it just went through me. There was a certain part of melancholy to it.

I think the time was right. He recognized it. He had somebody who could take over. I think it was an unselfish move.

He came in a winner. He leaves a winner.

—Dee Stoops

I was at work, and my mom called, crying. It was so shocking that nobody knew. I called him immediately. I wanted to know if something was wrong.

He picked up right away and let us know he was OK.

His words were, "It's just time."

—Reenie Stoops Farragher

It was the first week of summer conditioning. We had some guys who were late, so I ran the whole team. I was pissed, so I walked back over to the new facility so I could tell Bob that I just got done running his whole team because some guys were late.

I got over there, and the elevator opened up, and he's on the elevator. He's got some stuff in his hands. He kind of gave me a look. I'm thinking, "Why is he looking at me like this?"

"Hey, Schmidty, let's go on a ride," he said.

He waited until we got downstairs and got out to his car. The trailers were out that way.

He said, "Hey, I'm getting ready to go down there and step down as coach at Oklahoma."

As he's saying the words—I don't know how to explain it, but I thought about how we had been together since Florida: raising my kids, the ups and downs, wins and losses. He was at my daughter's graduation party.

I sort of bent over and I almost cried—I was right there with the tears. And he gave me a hug and said, "It's all good; there's nothing sad here. Hey, we started in a trailer; we ended in a trailer."

Only he would say something like that in that emotional moment.

—Jerry Schmidt

I got an email from a friend saying Bob was resigning. I laughed it off.

Common perception was that Bob was year to year. It was June, so I figured he was good for another year.

Then someone else on the staff told me. I go, "Are you kidding?"

—Scott Anderson, Oklahoma head athletic trainer, 1997–present

Someone came into my office and asked, "Did you hear?" And then they told me the news.

I said, "No way."

WHY?

I went to my knees. I went to my knees because I was scared something was wrong, because it was so unexpected.

I went to the press conference, but it was tough. He told me, "You and Carol need to quit crying."

— Sherri Coale

I was sitting on my couch. We had a team meeting scheduled for three or four o'clock. Probably about one-ish, I got a call from Lincoln. He said, "Bob and I want to meet with you. There's something Bob wants to tell you."

I told him I'd be right over. Then I started getting these messages from my buddies asking, "What's going on in Norman?" The news had already broke.

That drive over there is something I'll never forget. I walked into Lincoln's office, and Lincoln didn't say a word. Bob handled it. He told me that it was the right time for him and his family.

It might have been the hardest decision of his life, but it was the best thing for him. He could have very easily stuck it out for another year with the seniors we had, the guys who had been in the program for a while. Any normal man would have said, "Why would I not coach this out?" But he wanted to do it so it would work out best for Lincoln in his first year. That speaks volumes about him.

He's a football guy through and through. He gets it. He's not about the BS. He's going to cut to the chase.

— Baker Mayfield

It was taking him a really long time to get his stuff moved over to the new office. He was always saying, "I'll get it. I'll get it."

I should have picked up on that.

I didn't know about the rumors that morning. I was in the office; he came in and asked me to close the door. I thought, "OK, something's wrong."

He said, "Are you ready for this? I'm going to resign."

I asked, "Are you OK?"

"I'm just ready," he said. He said Lincoln was going to take over and he wouldn't have done it unless everyone was going to be taken care of.

He left my office, and it was mass chaos after that. Everything was sort of a blur. "Surreal" is probably the best word. I felt like I was floating above it and watching from a distance.

— Julie Watson, Oklahoma assistant to head coach, 2008–present

When I first got the word, I thought he was ill or there was some family matter. He just said, "I woke up, and I knew today was the day."

— Tim Headington, Oklahoma alumnus and prominent donor

Actually, I had talked to him two years earlier. Carol called me. She said, "I know you love Bob. He's talking about retiring. I'd appreciate if you'd talk him out of it."

I did.

I'll be honest with you: [this time] it did not surprise me.

— Barry Alvarez

Everything has its time. And on June 7, 2017, it was the perfect time for me to move on. It was the perfect time to hand the keys to our program to Lincoln, who at thirty-three was the youngest head coach in major college football.

I believe in faith and family. I don't wear my spirituality on my sleeve, but I felt an inner peace about my decision. What does it say in Ecclesiastes 3:1–8? "For every thing there is a season, and a time for every purpose under heaven."

I felt I had fulfilled my purpose at Oklahoma. I felt I was doing the honorable thing—the kind of thing my dad would have done. I wanted to empower Lincoln with a strong team and a great quarterback. I wanted him to have a recruiting mechanism in place that ensured success. I wanted OU and our opponents to know that the transition from me to Lincoln was going to be seamless. The name would change on the head coach's office door, but the mission would be the same.

Was my health a factor in my decision? It was. Was it *the* reason for my decision? Absolutely not.

Yes, my fifty-four-year-old dad had died on the sidelines of a high school football game after suffering a heart attack. That event had changed my life. It changed our family's life. It certainly had an impact on how long I wanted to coach.

To be clear, I have been diagnosed with a form of heart disease. It isn't major. I've never had a drastic heart episode. That's the way I want to keep it, too. But since I was twenty-something years old, my cholesterol levels have always been high. My calcium scores have never been very good, either.

From the beginning of my coaching career, I've made sure to visit a cardiologist several times a year for checkups. Cardio stress tests . . . ultrasound exams where they examine all my arteries. I have had several angiogram procedures. My diet is configured to be heart healthy, and I take certain heart-related medications. I exercise.

One night during the off-season of 2003, I felt something wrong in my chest. I sat straight up in bed and knew there was a problem. It was a quick, sharp jab of pain. Something didn't feel right with my heart.

Back then, in my early forties, I was an avid runner. But I was beginning to labor during each run. It felt as if my heart seemed to be working too hard, like a car stuck in first gear. It got to the point where I couldn't run without having to stop every so often. Something was wrong.

When I went swimming, I didn't have the same sensation in my heart. But as soon as I stood upright and jogged . . . problems.

I got an angiogram. The doctors found blockage in the small branches running from my heart but determined that I was naturally bypassing the blockage—it just wasn't complete yet. Six months later, I was able to jog again.

In October 2004, just two days after we beat Texas, I was driving to the OU football offices and suddenly felt as if I were going to pass out. I was only a block or two away from Memorial Stadium, but that area of campus has a high concentration of students making their way to and from classes. I didn't want to risk hitting anyone, so I pulled into a parking lot and called our team trainer, Scott Anderson.

They picked me up at my car, and before long, I was undergoing a brain scan and a heart scan. As a high school player and college player, I had suffered multiple concussions. Back then, in the late 1970s and early 1980s, we didn't have a full understanding of chronic traumatic encephalopathy (CTE) and the effects of concussions. Research was in its infancy.

The doctors told me my brain scan results were better than those in 90 percent of the scans they saw on a daily basis. That gave me a sense of relief, but I'd be lying if I said I haven't thought about the possibility of dealing with CTE later in my life.

In 2011, I had another angiogram. The doctor could see the areas where I had suffered blockage in the past but had bypassed it naturally. Again, everything cleared up just fine.

For the record, I've never had a heart attack, nor have I ever felt again the same sharp pain that I experienced in 2003. But I do have to monitor my heart condition.

My heart issues were 10 percent of my decision to resign at OU. When you lose your father—a man who didn't smoke or drink—it stays with you. You have an awareness that if it could happen to him, it could happen to you.

I can't remember exactly when I first considered resigning. I had always thought that age sixty was old—not in a conventional sense, but old for a college football coach. Old to be recruiting almost every day of the year. Old to be traveling so much. Old to deal with the constant demands of the job. Old to have your life dictated by a schedule that rarely lets you up for air.

I laughed when I heard fans or hot-take talk show hosts read through a just-released season schedule and say, "They should win this game, that game, this game..."

Do they know how many things have to go absolutely right for you to win even *a* game? Do they know how few things have to go wrong for you to lose one?

I've never done the math, but think about it: eighty-five scholarship players, ten coaches, twenty support staff, four medical-related personnel; another fifteen administrative, video, academic, equipment, and facilities personnel; three sports media department members; one athletic director... all of them—every single one of them—doing whatever they can to best position us to win a game. Just chicken-scratching the numbers, that's about forty-nine hundred man- and woman-hours devoted to a week of game prep. Now multiply that by twelve regular-season games—and if you reach the national championship, multiply it by three more postseason games (a conference championship game and two playoff games).

I've said many times that I don't have to be a coach. It doesn't define me. Coaching is not who I am, all I am, or who I will be. We all evolve. Stepping away from the game in 2016 was part of my evolution.

WHY?

I could have stayed at Oklahoma. The program was always built for the long run, so, barring a cataclysmic chain of events, I think we would have enjoyed annual success. And by success, I mean in OU terms: Big 12 championships, the playoffs, runs at national titles.

I could have made millions more in salary and, if everything went the way we hoped, won another thirty games or so over a three-year period. I might have added a few more banners to the wall, a few more rings on the fingers.

Money can buy stuff. It can buy comfort, but it can't buy happiness. It can't bring my dad back to life. It can't guarantee that I won't suffer a heart episode of my own. It can't replace time lost, moments forfeited, laughter and tears never seen or heard.

There's a line from a movie called *Wall Street* where Charlie Sheen asks Michael Douglas's character, Gordon Gekko, "How many yachts can you water-ski behind? How much is enough?" I don't own a yacht—and never will—but I understand the point. I made more money than I deserved, more money than anyone on our block in Youngstown would ever have thought possible.

My dad was a helluva high school defensive coordinator and could have easily coached on the college level. He topped out at low-to-mid five figures in salary at Mooney. We probably spent that much on new carpeting for the OU football locker room.

But my dad was happy. And our family was happy. It was never about the money then. It's not about the money now.

I coached just as hard as a know-nothing, no-salary graduate assistant in 1983 at Iowa as I did during my final season as OU's head coach. A paycheck wasn't going to change that. You got my best regardless of how many commas and zeroes were on the paystub.

Five, six years ago, I went out to spring practice. I was walking with Bob during this full-blown practice. You could hear guys talking and playing hard, and Bob asked, "Do you hear that?"

I said, "Well, there's a lot of action out there."

He said, "No . . . do you hear the coaching? Listen. Listen to the coaching going on."

271

When I think of legacy, I think of him as the ultimate football guy. Loved to coach as much at the beginning as he did at the end. We were lucky to have him as our coach.

—Tim Headington

The college football world was stunned when I walked away from the eighth-winningest program in the history of the game. But the key words are "walked away." I didn't run away. I wasn't fired. I wasn't encouraged to resign. I didn't have a better offer. I had simply come to a crossroads in my life.

The new question: What's next?

Chapter Eighteen

Difficulty

This is going to sound strange, but one of the hardest things I've done in my life is *not* work. The day I resigned at Oklahoma was the day my life became more difficult, not easier.

I've never second-guessed or regretted my decision. That doesn't mean it hasn't been a huge adjustment. It's been hard as hell. Harder than I thought it would be. But just because it's been challenging doesn't mean it was the wrong choice.

The fall of each year of my football life was reserved for competition, for games, for rivalries, for those on-field chess matches, for pressure. I loved every nanosecond of the competition. As a coach, there's nothing better than the intensity of game day, and you've got to make split-second decisions that can mean the difference between a win and a loss. There are eighty thousand fans stuffed into the stadium. There's a national television audience watching. Your players and assistant coaches are depending on you. And when it's done, your mind and body need to sit on a beach in Florida for two weeks.

Scott Anderson, our head trainer, would sometimes come up to me before a game to give me an update on a player's condition. I would hear him. I would digest the information. But I was somewhere else.

You don't realize the energy expended during a game until it's finished. For three and a half or four hours, you've been completely focused on trying to help your team win a game. You've competed. You've processed information at a dizzying speed. You've tried to motivate and influence your players. You've done your best to project calm and confidence, even though you want to burst with emotion.

When it's done, you're halfway destroyed. You're wiped out. If you lose, you're wiped out even more.

Coaches who did their TV highlight shows shortly after their games always amazed me. I was totally exhausted after a game. I didn't do my coach's shows until the next afternoon, when I'd had time to rest and recover.

Well...I resigned on June 7, and on June 8, I didn't know how to fill a day. I wasn't prepared for life without football. I didn't have a place to go.

I never dreamed it would be harder than some of the previous years, but it was. I mean, how could it be more difficult with all the stress and pressures removed? But we didn't know what to do or how to live. It was painful not to do what we'd always known.

It was sort of like an open wound. We were here in Norman. We were part of the program, yet not. We recruited those kids. We loved them. So you were a part of it, but not really. No one made us feel that way. That's just the way it was.

—Carol Stoops

He was a wreck at first. He'd be in my office, visiting. Then he'd get up and say, "I'll see you later."

I'd ask, 'Where you going?'

He'd say, "I don't know.

Sometimes he just drove around.

—Matt McMillen

The 2017 season opener was at home against UTEP. I literally didn't know how to watch an OU football game as a spectator. I was still too close to it all. It mattered too much to me.

Sitting in the stands wasn't going to happen. There would be a spontaneous combustion if I did that. Joe found me a private stadium box to watch the opener. It only seated six people, which was perfect. I needed a private place to deal with the unfamiliar feeling of game-day uselessness.

DIFFICULTY

This is one of my favorite stories: Carol and Bob are going to the first home game of the year—my senior year—and they're driving to the stadium, and there's a bunch of traffic.

Bob turns to Carol and says, "What's all this traffic for?"

He had no idea about the amount of craziness that came to that stadium to see him coach every Saturday. He hadn't been on the outside. He didn't know.

—Baker Mayfield

The next week against Ohio State at the famed Horseshoe (I grew up about two and a half hours from Columbus), I was on the sidelines for the pregame warm-ups (Baker sprinted over to give me a hug), then to a private box with my family, and then to the stadium tunnel for the final minutes of the game.

I hadn't been to Ohio Stadium since 1985, when I'd been a volunteer assistant for Iowa and we lost to the Buckeyes—our only regular-season defeat during a year we reached the Rose Bowl. And in my final season at OU, Ohio State beat us at home.

But this time, we—I'll always be a "we" guy when it comes to OU—beat number-two-ranked and favored Ohio State. A 3–3 halftime score became a 31–16 OU win. I couldn't help myself. The cameras caught me pumping my fist after a couple of big plays.

I didn't care. I knew there might be a TV camera aimed our way, but I was tired of sitting on my hands and looking like I was attending the opera. I just let it go.

That's the thing: when you're a coach, you're nervous, but you're working the game. You have some control over the outcome. When you're not coaching, you're more nervous, and you don't have any control over the outcome.

After the win, I stood at the tunnel's opening and watched as Baker tried to plant the OU flag on the field. I hugged and shook hands with every player and coach I could find.

It didn't get easier to watch the games, but slowly, I was coaching myself not to coach. I missed OU's fifth game of the season against Iowa State because I wanted to take Drake, a wide receiver for Norman North High

School, to Ohio University for an official football recruiting visit. Both Isaac, a defensive back/WR, and Drake were considered FBS-caliber prospects.

During the visit, Carol and Drake were sneaking looks at their phones for scoring updates. I didn't want to know what was happening. It was too stressful, especially since I couldn't have any direct impact on the game.

I later learned that after trailing for most of the game, OU, which was ranked number three at the time, tied the game late in the third quarter and tied it again in the fourth quarter...and then lost in the final few minutes. I felt like I had lost with them.

Carol was always great about writing notes to our players. If a player had a tough game, she'd write him a note of encouragement. A great game...a note. A birthday...a note. Sometimes she'd give me the notes to deliver personally.

But it was after that Iowa State game that Carol wrote a note to the opposing starting quarterback: Kyle Kempt. Kempt had played high school ball only about an hour or so from Youngstown. He had bounced from Oregon State to junior college and then to Iowa State and near the bottom of the depth chart. When he helped beat the Sooners that day, he was a fifth-year senior walk-on.

One of the many reasons I love my wife is for her empathy. She had just wanted to acknowledge Kyle's journey and offer him congratulations on the victory.

I also love her for her honesty. She reminded me that while I had never watched an OU game as a spectator, she had never *not* watched an OU game. It stressed me out to watch, and it stressed her out not to watch and know what was going on.

The following week was the Red River Showdown in the Cotton Bowl: the 112th meeting between Texas and OU. I used to love looking into the stands and seeing the stadium split down the middle like a two-color Easter egg. I loved what the game meant to our players, to their players. It is what other rivalries wanted to be when they grew up.

But there was no way I could attend that game as a fan. It would have been unbearable for me. Instead, Carol and I flew to Chicago for the weekend. That way, I wouldn't be part of the Cotton Bowl scene. The TV cameras wouldn't zero in on my reactions in a stadium box or on the sidelines. The attention would be where it belonged: on the team, not me.

I couldn't bring myself to watch the first half of the game. Instead, I turned the channel to a baseball game, hoping it would distract me from OU-Texas. It didn't.

Meanwhile, Carol told me later that she was secretly checking her phone for the play-by-play account on an app.

After a while, I couldn't take it anymore. "Come on," I said to Carol. "Let's go watch the second half someplace else."

We found two seats next to an older couple at the bar of a neighborhood restaurant. Just my luck—the guy recognized me.

But he was a football fan, and he could sense my level of anxiety and investment in the game, especially when OU fell behind midway through the fourth quarter. So he only talked to me during commercials. And his wife instructed him to leave me alone during the game broadcast, too.

They were nice people, and after OU rallied to win the game, 29–24, I did what any respectable former Sooners coach would do: I secretly bought them lunch and left without them knowing. (They later sent a very sweet thank-you note.) We celebrated the OU victory on Rush Street and toasted Lincoln and the fellas.

During the entire decision process, I wanted to do whatever I could to make the transition easier for Lincoln. But I never realized that Lincoln was determined to do the same for me.

Lincoln encouraged me to visit practice anytime I wanted, to sit in on quarterback meetings, to offer whatever advice or observations I had. A protective and insecure head coach wouldn't have done that with the previous coach. But Lincoln doesn't have a self-esteem problem. He is confident and self-assured, but in a humble way.

Lincoln knew I wasn't going to look over his shoulder or judge him, or ever use the phrase, "The way I would do it is..."

I stopped by practice a few times each week. I sat in the back of the room during the Monday and Tuesday quarterback meetings. I'd shake the hands of the players when they came off the practice fields.

No one was happier than I was to see Baker win a Heisman Trophy and later become the number-one overall NFL Draft pick. No one was happier to see Lincoln and the Sooners win the 2017 Big 12 Championship, win twelve games, advance to the College Football Playoff semifinals at the Rose Bowl, and come *this close* to reaching the championship game. (OU lost in double overtime to Georgia in the semis.)

I left Lincoln a very good team. But he and Baker and the rest of the players made it a great team. They made it a playoff team.

In 2018, they reached the playoff again before losing to Alabama in the semifinals. This time, they did it with Kyler Murray. And just as Lincoln had predicted several years earlier, Kyler won a Heisman.

After the 2018 season, Lincoln faced some of the same decisions I had faced at times during my career—mainly, did he want to stay at OU or pursue a job in the NFL?

We talked. I'm the first to acknowledge that the NFL is the elite level of football. But I've never understood why people automatically think that coaching in the NFL is a better job than coaching at an elite college program.

It might be a better job for those guys who were born and raised in the NFL world—I'll give you that. But based on what I know of NFL ownership and franchises, I would rather be the head coach at Oklahoma than be the head coach of 70 percent of those NFL teams. Coach Switzer has said it a bunch: half those guys in the NFL would rather have the Oklahoma job.

I never compared salaries, but I'm also guessing mine was higher than a lot of those of the NFL head coaches. Point being, head coaches at the top levels of college football are making just as much as, if not more than, those pro coaches. And if I did my job, we had a chance to compete for a championship every year.

Yes, there are only thirty-two NFL head coaching jobs in the world. But I looked at it this way: the president of the university is sort of like the "owner" of the University of Oklahoma. Not the owner per se, but you get my point. The president is its caretaker, and his or her decisions shape the entire university. The president is the Boss.

The athletic director is the OU sports team president of sorts. He or she oversees the financial welfare of all the OU sports, including football.

In my case, I trusted our administrators, and they trusted me. That is no small thing in the coaching business.

Because of that trust and that stability through the years, OU football enjoyed great success. We were a team.

Now then, can you say the same of every NFL franchise? Is the owner committed to winning? Is the owner committed to running a first-class program? Does the organization reflect that commitment? See what I'm getting at? Just because you own an NFL team doesn't make you a great NFL owner.

If I was going to leave OU for the NFL, I wanted to know that the owner and general manager shared my same values, work ethic, and commitment. It's like I always told recruits who were considering OU and also other programs: just be careful. Everybody has a track record. What were the other programs' track records of success? What did they do in the past? And if they didn't have track records of success, how come?

I used the same list of questions when the NFL or other college programs approached me.

I didn't have an NFL background. I never played in the NFL. I never was an assistant coach in the NFL. Do I think my coaching style and skill set would have translated to the NFL? I'd like to think so, but it is a different dynamic at the college level. At OU, I was the head coach and the de facto general manager. I decided who we were going to recruit and sign. I had control over my roster. In the NFL, that usually isn't the case, unless you're someone like Bill Belichick or Jon Gruden.

I wouldn't have been afraid to give up that sort of personnel control, but it had to be under the right circumstances. And I never had the right circumstances.

Is college football without its flaws? No, not by any stretch. It has its own issues.

Start with recruiting, which is the lifeblood of any program.

I've lost some recruits to cheating. Somebody got to them, or to the parents, or to the high school coach. They got something. It's the worst part of the game. The NCAA does what it can, but what it can do isn't enough. The conferences do their best, but they're limited by personnel and resources.

I don't know how you fix it unless you impose incredibly harsh punishments. I'm all for that. If you cheat, you deserve the worst.

Anybody who thinks the cheating goes away if we pay the players a big stipend—well, they don't know major college athletics. It drives me nuts when I hear people say that football and basketball players should receive some percentage of the CFP or NCAA Tournament financial pie. Sure, in a make-believe world, that would be great. But that isn't happening, so quit wasting time on the argument. Unless the laws are changed, specifically Title IX laws, there is nothing to discuss.

I'm all for Title IX, for all Olympic sports, for all women's sports. I'm all for diversity. That's how a university should be run: to reflect the wide range of interests of its student body. I did my best to support as many of those sports as possible.

And to think that a football program should keep its revenue and pay just its own players doesn't make sense. That's not a university.

What the general public misses, and sometimes the media, too, is that a football program such as OU's has been funneling millions of its revenue dollars to the university and its academic programs. You don't think that makes a difference to those professors and students?

Our OU players get a sum of money each week now. There's a cost-of-attendance formula used to supplement an athlete's scholarship. The NCAA is doing a better job of helping players and their families go to bowl games. We're on the right path, but there's more work to be done when it comes to helping players.

At OU, we reinvest in our players every way we can: stronger academic support, nutrition, medical, training facilities, dorms. Is some of it lavish? Compared to when I played, sure. Compared to the standards of other schools today, not really.

Player safety and welfare always has been a priority for me. In Scott Anderson, I had one of the top athletic trainers in the business. He would make me aware of studies, research, and stories related to player safety. In fact, I had read some of Scott's work on concussion research in the early 2000s.

We tested our players for sickle-cell trait. We partnered with Gatorade to do research on sweat rate and fluid consumption.

I didn't screw around with injuries. If Scott said a player was unavailable, then his word was final. I might question the specifics of the injury, but I would never question Scott's decision to hold a player out. He's the expert, not me.

When I got to Oklahoma in late 1998 and then hired Schmidty, we wanted to be the best conditioned team in the country. That was our goal. But there's a difference between a tough conditioning philosophy and one that uses conditioning as a way to humiliate and, at its extreme, endanger the well-being and health of a player. A player should never be put at risk during a workout, practice, or game. There is no scenario where a player's health shouldn't always take precedence.

In my eighteen seasons at OU, I'll bet I could count on one hand the number of times we had to get a player into an ice tub for a cooldown or to the hospital as a precaution. Every summer and at the beginning of every camp, I spoke with my strength staff and trainers about the parameters of our workouts. I made it very clear that we should never ask a player to do more in a conditioning drill than is reasonable. For example, if a player hasn't made his 440-yard dash time during the first two tries, he's surely not going to make it on the third—so don't have him try! When in doubt, err on the side of caution. I constantly reminded the strength-and-training staffs that we weren't going to win the Big 12 during winter conditioning. Same thing in the summer. It's not Bear Bryant and the Junction Boys. Drinking water at practice is not a form of weakness. At our practices, fluids and trainers were positioned at every workout station.

We also were always very aware of who had tested positive for sickle-cell trait, and we adjusted their workouts accordingly. We wouldn't let them do a complete workout. Their rest intervals were longer and more frequent.

Bob was a major supporter of our work and research. He listened to what we had to say. He came to his own conclusions.

He would make a point to coaches and strength coaches: "Train these [sickle-cell-trait] kids different. We're going to be safe."

He took some flak from some of his peers. He just laughed it off. I've never worked for a head coach this supportive in thought and in action when it came to the welfare of players as Bob has been.

—Scott Anderson

When I played at Iowa, there weren't as many protocols and procedures in place. With more research and knowledge come better protocols.

My playing career ended nearly forty years ago. Back then, there was a more casual attitude about football-related concussions. I'm not sure we even had heard of the brain condition called CTE.

I've had moms ask me why they should let their kids play football. They worry, understandably so, about player safety and health.

My twin boys played high school football. Drake is an OU player. If Carol and I didn't think the game was safe — as safe as any contact sport can be — we wouldn't let our boys play it.

I'd tell the moms that football teaches values that matter. It teaches mental toughness, work ethic, comradery, teamwork, confidence, and a developed sense of inner self. It teaches you how to deal with adversity. It is the ultimate team game because it forces you to know your teammates, to appreciate them as people, to work alongside them. The game exposes your weaknesses as an athlete and sometimes as a person, and it challenges you to turn those weaknesses into strengths. It is a game that enhances your ability to strive for something bigger than yourself. It teaches the importance of competition, of sportsmanship, of friendship, and of lifelong relationships. And these are all values that translate to our professional and personal lives.

Yeah, maybe this sounds like something off the back of a football pamphlet, but I believe every word of it. I've seen it. I've been part of it. I've lived it.

As far as the injury part of things, without question, we've taken steps to improve the safety of the game. As the information on concussions and other trauma-related injuries has evolved, so has the coaching instruction to help prevent or reduce the possibility of such injuries. We did everything we could as a staff, especially with our concussion protocol, to protect our players. At OU and other college programs — as well as the NFL — there is an increased emphasis on teaching a different and safer tackling technique. It's more of a rugby-style tackle, where the head and neck are significantly less exposed and involved.

There's no getting around it: football is a physical sport. If you've ever stood on the sidelines of a game, you know it can be violent. And because of the physicality and popularity of the game, it is a sport that gets examined, and deservedly so, more than other sports.

Our twin sons played flag football as kids. We didn't allow them to play padded football until fifth or sixth grade. They wanted to play football, and we as parents made sure they were properly coached, properly equipped, and properly educated on the game. As parents, we had to consider the risks of injury versus the benefits of the game. That's the case in every sport. How many women basketball players have torn their ACLs? How many soccer players have done the same or suffered the effects of head injuries? Any contact sport has inherent dangers.

I don't pretend that the human body was designed for football. If it were, players wouldn't need helmets and pads. And I don't pretend that CTE doesn't exist. It's real, it's a concern, and it's something I've had to consider in my own life.

But I will defend the game of football. Is it perfect? No. And nobody has a way to make it 100 percent perfect or safe. But the essence of the game outweighs its flaws. What we have to do is minimize its flaws and dangers.

Speaking of imperfect, there's the College Football Playoff system. Georgia coach Kirby Smart thought his team should have been selected for the 2018 CFP. Kirby does a great job, but with all due respect, once you lose two games and you're not the conference champion, sorry, you've got nothing to complain about.

An eight-team playoff would be ideal, but it wouldn't be fair to the players. Some of these players who are moving on to the NFL are already squeamish about playing in postseason games. Now you're going to ask them to play as many as three playoff games *and* a conference championship?

It's just too many games. It would interfere with final exams, cost the players their entire Christmas breaks in some cases, and compromise conference championship games. It also would compromise the significance and future of bowl games. That would mean fewer postseason opportunities for teams and players. That isn't a good thing for college football.

I'm not on a college sideline these days, but I still watch the game as if I were. I've always liked and respected the work that Gary Patterson has done at TCU, Mike Gundy at Oklahoma State, Chris Petersen at Boise State and Washington, Mike Leach at Texas Tech and Washington State (along with my brother Mike and Brent Venables, Leach is the all-time MVP of my assistant coaching hires), Paul Chryst at Wisconsin, Pat Fitzgerald at Northwestern, Dabo Swinney at Clemson, Nick Saban at Alabama, and Mark Dantonio at Michigan State. Before he retired, I would have included Urban Meyer at that top level.

I could keep going. To me, there are very few bad guys in coaching. (There is, however, a very bad mullet, and it belongs to Mike Gundy. I like Mike a lot, but he does some weird stuff.)

Coaches watch the game in a different way. You—Joe Fan—watch the ball. I watch the offensive and defensive schemes. I watch which coordinator is making the best adjustments in real time...which player, especially on third downs, is impacting a play. I always graded players on their production, on their ability to influence a play.

I look for leaders. Baker is a leader. At OU, he led by example. He cared. A leader understands the pulse of a team, isn't worried about being popular, isn't afraid to put someone in line if needed.

When we constructed our team, we obviously built it around the quarterback. Nobody wins without one. But the second most important position group is the secondary. When a defensive back screws up, the opposing band plays, the scoreboard lights up, the other sideline celebrates. There's no margin for error. But a talented secondary makes the difference between a good football team and a great one.

I'm a college guy, but I'll watch the NFL if one of our OU guys is playing. Baker, he's hysterical to watch. I love his body language. He walks around like every day is a great day. He energizes everybody. It isn't a put-on; that's how he really is. He has energized the Browns, and it doesn't surprise me in the least.

Patrick Mahomes, too. He didn't play for me at OU, but we played against him. During my last season at OU, he and Baker put on a show in our 66–59 win at Texas Tech. Baker had seven touchdown passes and 545 yards. Mahomes had five TDs and 734 passing yards. His NFL success isn't a shock. I knew going into our 2016 game that he was a fabulous talent. You could see all the throws: the sidearm thing, the flick of the wrist. Tough to bring down.

One of the best defensive players I ever faced at OU was Nebraska defensive tackle Ndamukong Suh. He just destroyed everything. He was better than advertised, if that's possible.

During my first year out of coaching, Carol and I traveled extensively. We weren't bound by the football calendar. I played lots of golf. I made my trips to Youngstown. I spent lots of time with my kids. I exhaled.

People said I looked better, that I was more relaxed. But I'm not sure I truly felt that way.

> *Toby Keith would tell us, "When my voice is gone, I won't be able to sing, but I'll always be able to write songs."*
>
> *But Bobby is a coach, and coaches coach. They don't kind of coach, or help, or consult. You're in or you're out.*
>
> —Carol Stoops

It wasn't until 2018 that the personal aftershocks began to subside. It still didn't feel natural not to coach, but I was more comfortable with my new life. It was getting easier.

Carol and I were empty nesters in 2018. Our kids were in college. The house was strangely quiet.

I saw Drake catch his first and second collegiate passes as an OU walk-on. I saw Mackie and Isaac find their comfort levels in school. As usual, I lived and died with the OU season.

It was a complicated season, in a way. Kyler won the Heisman. Lincoln and the team won the Big 12 and reached the playoff.

But in early October, a day after OU lost to Texas, Lincoln decided he wanted to make a change at defensive coordinator. He dismissed Mike.

In the coaching business, these things happen. It's tough.

I'm professional enough to understand that Lincoln had to make a decision based on what he thought was best for his football program. It couldn't be a decision based on emotion or on any extenuating circumstances.

Lincoln wanted to talk through the various issues with me. By then, I also had talked to Mike, who had offered to resign if Lincoln thought that would be the best for the program.

The professional side of me understood that the defense hadn't been what it needed to be, and there were arguments to be made for a change. The personal side of me felt for my brother. He had faced a lot of criticism, and I knew it had to be difficult for him.

I told Lincoln that if he thought making a change would move the team forward, then he should do it. He asked me, "If I go in that direction, do you understand?"

With a heavy heart, I said I would. Several years earlier, I had made the difficult choice to make a change with Josh Heupel. It's never easy.

On Sunday night, Mike called me and said he and Lincoln had decided it was best to part ways and move on. The thinking: OU had had an off week. The negativity toward Mike had become unmanageable. A change might do everyone good.

I'm sure it was extremely difficult for him, especially given the circumstances. I respected Mike's professionalism. He had coached at OU for almost twelve seasons and with much success.

Every fan has an opinion, but it's foolish to think that Mike suddenly forgot how to coach defense. He helped OU win a national championship in one of the best defensive games ever played. His work at OU helped him become a head coach at Arizona. And when he returned to OU, we had some very strong years defensively.

At the end of the day, it's never one guy's fault. You've got a head coach, ten assistant coaches, and one-hundred-plus players. You're in it together. Everyone needs to find ways to improve.

I would always tease our offensive coaches that when I died, I hoped the good Lord would send me back as an offensive coach. The worst thing that happens when you can't move the ball after three downs is, you punt. It's tougher on the other side of the ball. If you can't stop them, then you're on the field until the scoreboard lights up.

I'm not the first coach who has stepped away from the game, and I won't be the last. In 2018, Urban Meyer resigned from Ohio State due to health-related issues. I wasn't surprised. It had been a difficult year for him and his program. A combination of health problems and controversy had to have taken its toll.

It's difficult to win at the highest level at the biggest programs. If walking away from Ohio State was the best decision for his health and his family, then good for him. I wish him the best.

I also wish the best to Coach Snyder, who called it quits after twenty-seven seasons at K-State. I've said many times that I'll forever be grateful to him for hiring me as an assistant coach. I sent him a note thanking him for those opportunities.

I'm glad for him. He's worked long and hard, and I hope he's able to enjoy other parts of his life. But if it was hard for me to transition, just imagine what it might be like for him.

In our house in Norman is an entire wall covered with framed photos. It's sort of a photographic timeline of our lives together: Youngstown. Iowa. Kansas State. Florida. Oklahoma. Family. Friends. Players. Coaches. Weddings. Celebrations. Faraway places.

The photos are a reminder of what matters in life. And a few of the photos are almost too crazy to be true.

There's Carol and me standing with Bono as he held an OU jersey. (U2 had a tour gig at our stadium in 2009. By the way, Bono told his people to hold on to the jersey for him.)

There's me with President George H. W. Bush.

There's me with President George W. Bush.

There's me with President Bill Clinton.

When we played road games at Texas A&M, I was sometimes asked to meet with President George H. shortly before kickoff. Under normal circumstances, I would never have left my team that close to the start of the game. But when the president wants to chat, you chat. I was honored that he asked as often as he did.

President Bush's presidential library is at A&M, and he spent a lot of time in College Station. He was a frequent visitor to Aggies practices and attended more than a few games. And, of course, he's also buried on the grounds of the presidential library.

I had met him and the first lady years earlier. And I had met 43 during our visit to the White House after the 2000 national championship.

My twins were only a couple years old when 9/11 happened. We had a nightly routine before bedtime when Carol always said prayers with them.

The boys might say something like, "God bless Louie our dog. God bless Grandma. God bless Daddy."

One night, Isaac blurted out, "God bless Coach Bush."

They had seen President Bush on TV in the aftermath of 9/11. They equated such male figures with the position of leadership as coaches. They'd go to my office and see coaches. They'd see coaches on TV or at the stadium. So they looked at 43 as a coach.

I told President Bush that story during a 2002 function in Washington, DC. He burst out laughing, grabbed a program and a marker, and wrote, "Dear Isaac and Drake, Thanks for the prayers. God Bless."

And then he signed it, "President (Coach) Bush."

There will be more photos added to that wall. Life doesn't stop because I'm not on the OU sideline.

I learned a lesson from my parents long ago: that the sum value of your life is determined by much more than a national championship ring on your finger or a career win-loss record. Am I a worthy husband, father, brother, son, friend? Am I dedicating myself to making the lives of others better? Can I find another kind of personal challenge? Those are what matter most to me.

I'm still a work in progress, and at times, I can still feel the gravitational pull of the game. I haven't completely relaxed my grip on the laces of a football. And maybe I never will.

But Carol says I'm in a better place than I was. She says the time away from the game has allowed me to piece myself back together, that I'm once again the man she married in 1988, that I'm healed.

You know what? I like being *this* Bob Stoops.

Epilogue

Thursday, February 7, 2019

I'm standing on a small stage at Globe Life Park in Arlington, Texas, my wife, Carol, sitting in the audience as XFL commissioner Oliver Luck introduces me as the new head coach and general manager of the league's Dallas franchise.

I'm fifty-eight years old, and unlike at the beginning of this book, I'm now 100 percent sure I will coach football again.

What changed? I changed. Circumstances changed.

In June of 2017, when I resigned at Oklahoma, and in April of 2018, when my statue (still a strange concept) first was unveiled at the Bennett Event Center, and during the many months that followed, I had had no intention of returning to coaching. I'd thought I was done—and I felt good about that decision. It was the right decision at the right time.

But this is a different time, and I'm a different person from the guy who walked away from the game back then.

After being out of coaching for two seasons, I realized I've got too much of my own time. There is only so much golf you can play.

Dick Vermeil told me one time, "Don't ever say you'll never go back. I stayed out fourteen years and then went back and won a Super Bowl."

Coaches coach. Somebody's going to call you, then you get excited, and then you'll have lied about not wanting to coach. So leave room.

I was lucky to transition to TV, but there, you still don't have a win or loss on Saturday. Coaches are used to that…I once had a schedule every day, but now, what do you do? I told my wife, Sally, "I woke up and had nothing to do for the rest of our lives."

I miss planning those seasons. I miss those comebacks in the fourth quarter and trying to rally the troops.

I'm out four years now. And every year you're out, it gets a little bit better. I've been to movies and grocery stores, done things that I've never done before. I'm that guy—"Which mayonnaise do I buy?"—because I've never been to a grocery store.

—Mack Brown, August 9, 2018, four months before
being named North Carolina's new head coach

It's been twenty years and three months since I was introduced as OU's head coach. I held on to that podium at Evans Hall that day for dear life. I white-knuckled it.

But today, as I'm introduced to the small crowd and reporters, I'm not nervous at all. I can't wait to coach again.

Who knows how long it will last? But right now, it fits my world. In fact, it reminds me of what it was like when I started at OU. There's a sense of excitement and the unknown.

Mack and Carol are right: coaches coach, and eventually, I missed it again. But if these two seasons away from the sidelines have taught me anything, it's this: I'm a coach's son who loves the game.

Two years ago, I got to write my own ending. I needed that time to decompress and recharge. I didn't mind having to figure out which mayonnaise to buy.

Now I get to do something even better.

I get to write my own beginning.

Acknowledgments

Writing a book has never been on my bucket list. I never had the time when I was coaching, and I wasn't sure I had the interest when I wasn't coaching.

But time has a way of altering your views. The longer I coached, the more often aspiring young coaches—at both the high school and college level—would write to me or approach me asking for advice on their coaching careers. They were interested in the journey I had taken and the paths—some by chance, some the result of careful planning—that I had followed during my life.

I never had an answer for those young coaches, and I'd always respond that there is no magical formula. So maybe this book helps to clarify what I meant by that. Maybe my journey from working-class Youngstown to working-class Norman helps explain the joys, challenges, pain, sacrifices, and rewards involved in coaching. Maybe it connects the dots between hard work, family, and team.

Writing this book took me out of my comfort zone. But my entire life has been a series of events that tested me and made me choose between the safe and comfortable or the challenging and risky. As I look back, challenging and risky turned out to be my go-to choices in most cases. I hope people will feel what I felt, that it's OK to take a chance, that you can't succeed or fail *without* taking that chance.

So I wanted people to see, for better or worse, my life's road map. I also wanted to give my view of how things happened over the years. It isn't about setting the record straight, but more a matter of providing my perspective and context.

Acknowledgments

My map begins in Youngstown, Ohio, with my mom and dad, Dee and Ron Sr.; with my brothers and sisters, Ron Jr., Mike, Mark, Kathy, and Maureen; and with all those neighborhood friends, coaches, teammates and teachers who helped shape me. If we are a product of our upbringing and environment, then I am proudly a product of *that* city and *those* people.

I think I was born to coach. It is part of the Stoops DNA. But I couldn't have done it without the support and the sacrifices made by my own family: my wife, Carol, and our children, Mackie, Isaac, and Drake.

The life of a coach isn't normal. The schedule, the pressure to succeed, the travel, the responsibilities, the public scrutiny...they can all be difficult for a coach's family to endure. Carol and the kids have been very understanding of the demands of the job. In their own ways, they have contributed to any success I've had as a coach. Carol isn't just my wife and my friend; she's a trusted voice whose instincts and leadership skills have helped me become a better coach, husband, and father.

I would tell any aspiring head coach that it's almost impossible to have long-term success without the support and stability of your school's administration. From the day I took the OU job to the day I stepped away eighteen years later, I had the steady, dependable leadership and support of athletics director Joe Castiglione.

The university administration, Joe, and myself considered ourselves a team. We worked toward a common purpose. To do what OU did at that time—rebuild the football program, create a standard and culture, and maintain that standard and culture over decades—is a testament to the administration's commitment.

Without question, our success was the direct result of hundreds and hundreds of players who wore the interlocking OU during my tenure. I cherish more than anything the opportunity I had to develop relationships with those young men, and it's been my honor to watch so many of them grow into mature and successful adults. The credit also belongs to the assistant coaches and staff members who, through their commitment and dedication, created fun, excitement, and victories over the years. None of this happens without those players, those coaches, and those staff members.

Special mention goes to my longtime right-hand man and close friend,

Acknowledgments

Matt McMillen, as well as Julie Watson, who was my personal assistant at OU. I thank them for their patience and many years of hard work.

I'd also like to thank Neil Cornrich, who has been a great adviser and friend since long before I became a head coach.

I've had many valuable mentors, friends, and colleagues in the coaching profession. But it was the influences of Steve Spurrier and his wife, Jerri, that helped refine me and polish me as a head coaching prospect. My three years at Florida under the Head Ball Coach were invaluable to me. The time spent on his staff prepared me and convinced me I was really ready to run my own program. That support continued during my career at OU. I'm fortunate to call him a close friend.

One of the most rewarding aspects of my time at Oklahoma has been my affiliation with the Children's Hospital at OU Medicine. For that, I have Kay Tangner to thank. Her dedication to that hospital, to those kids and families, and to that cause is inspirational. It certainly has been to me during the past twenty years.

I'd like this book to be a connection to that cause, which is why I'm donating a percentage of all profits from this project to the OU Children's Hospital. I've been honored to meet those children, those families, those doctors and nurses who fight the good fight every single day.

And finally, I'd like to thank the OU fans who make that university and that football program so special. I was proud to be part of it. And always will be.

Bob Stoops

May 2019

An acknowledgment of gratitude to Bob and Carol Stoops, whose enthusiasm and commitment to this book made these pages possible. Their partnership, friendship, and openness are genuine and never-ending. Years pass, but the Youngstown and Iowa in them remain—as does the Oklahoma. And those are all good things.

Much appreciation also to the many Stoops family members, relatives, and friends who made themselves available for multiple interviews. Their help, insights, and generosity with their time were invaluable.

The same holds true of those connected to Bob's football life, including coaches, players, administrators, staff members, teammates—even opposing

Acknowledgments

coaches, past and present—all of whom were quick to offer interview time on behalf of this project. In all, more than fifty people spoke about Bob for the book.

A special mention to Oklahoma's Mike Houck and Kenny Mossman, Iowa's Steve Roe, Florida's Steve McClain, Kansas State's Kenny Lannou, and Washington State's Bill Stevens. OU athletics director Joe Castiglione, OU head coach Lincoln Riley, OU administrative assistant Julie Watson, former OU assistant athletics director for football operations Matt McMillen, and Texas A&M's director of athletic performance Jerry Schmidt were especially helpful.

Thanks, too, to David Black and Phil Marino for their tireless efforts from start to finish, as well as to Elizabeth Gassman for her assistance in tying up the daily loose ends.

And, as always, a special thank-you to T. L. Mann for his desk-side inspiration. And if, according to the late, great Audrey Hepburn, "the best thing to hold on to in life is each other," then I count my blessings with my wife, Cheryl, whose considerable love, patience, and support got me through another one.

Gene Wojciechowski
May 2019

Notes

Unless otherwise noted, all italicized quotes from head coaches, assistant coaches, teammates, players, family members, family friends, administrators, staff members, bowl representatives, athletic directors, and sports information directors are the result of interviews, sometimes multiple in nature, with the coauthor.

In addition, some material in this book was gathered during the coauthor's coverage of past games, events, and press conferences. In several instances, interviews conducted by the coauthor during that past coverage also were used.

Facts, figures, and assorted statistics were found in the NCAA database, school media guides, record books, and school websites, as well as NFL-specific websites such as Spotrac.com and Overthecap.com.

When Bob Stoops spoke in a group setting at press conferences or media days, those comments are not attributed to a specific publication but rather as a "told reporters" designation. Material used from a specific, stand-alone interview is attributed in the text.

Supplementary background material was used from *ESPN.com, ESPN, Oklahoma Today, Los Angeles Times, Associated Press, United Press International, Des Moines Register, Daily Oklahoman, Norman Transcript, Tulsa World, The Athletic, Oklahoma Daily, Cedar Rapids Gazette, Dallas Morning News, Omaha World-Herald, Gainesville Sun, Orlando Sentinel, Austin American-Statesman, Boston Globe, Kansas City Star, Houston Chronicle, Forbes.com, Miami Herald, Sports Illustrated, USA Today, Wichita Eagle, Chicago Tribune, South Bend Tribune, Columbus Dispatch, Cleveland Plain Dealer, St. Louis Post-Dispatch,* and *Youngstown Vindicator.*

Index

Index

Index

Snyder, Bill: coaching approach of, 84–87, 106–107; effect of Stoops and, 8; at Iowa, 65; at Kansas State University, 80–84, 87–90, 92–93, 95, 120; Minnesota rumors and, 110; national championship and, 167; retirement of, 287; Stoops's move to Florida and, 97, 100; Texas A&M upset and, 114–115

Southwest Louisiana University, 104

Speronis, Jamie, 100, 102–103, 117–118

Spurrier, Steve: at American Football Coaches Association convention, 96; as coach, 101–103, 106–107, 120; effect on Stoops of, 8, 11, 120–121; at Florida, 95; hiring of Stoops and, 97–100; offense of, 101–102; resignation of from Florida, 177; on Stoops's head coach interviews, 116; on Stoops's Minnesota offer, 109–110; Texas rumors involving Stoops and, 112

Spurrier, Steve, Jr., 143, 244

Stanford, 212–213

Stead Family Children's Hospital (University of Iowa), 174–175

steel industry, 21, 29–30

Stewart, Bill, 202

Stolz, Denny, 31–32

Stoops, Bob: adjustment to postcoaching life and, 273–277, 285; Arkansas offer, 112–113; "Big-Game Bob" nickname, 193; boycott over Sigma Alpha Epsilon video, 234–237; Cardinal Mooney High School Hall of Fame induction, 79, 99; childhood of, 16–20, 22–23, 25–27; Children's Hospital visits and, 252–258; Cleveland Browns and, 170–171; college prospects of, 30–33; courtship with Carol and, 60–61, 64–65, 67–69; death of father and, 72–79, 269–270; doubts after 2012 and 2014 seasons,

217, 230–231; effect of national championship on, 167–169; at Florida, 101–108, 110–112, 114; Florida head coach offer, 178–179; as graduate assistant at Iowa, 65–67; on having fun, 153–155; heart disease and, 269–270; injuries of, 44–45, 46, 54, 56–58; interview with Oklahoma, 116–119, 122–125; Iowa rumors and, 113–114; at Kansas State University, 80, 83, 87, 90; at Kent State, 72; loneliness at OU and, 137; Minnesota offer and, 108–110; Notre Dame and, 92–93, 179; Ohio State and, 169–170; public appearance for OU and, 6; resignation of, 3–5, 11–12, 259–266, 268–271; on SEC vs. Big 12, 217–218; Spurrier and, 97–99; statue of, 7–8, 10; strategy at OU, 130–131, 133, 139, 141, 147–149, 152, 231; team standards and, 161–162; Texas rumors and, 112; values of, 91; wedding of, 70–71; XFL and, 289–290

Stoops, Carol: on autographs, 211–212; on Bob's life postcoaching, 274; Bob's resignation and, 7–8, 10, 259–263; courtship with Bob and, 60–61, 64–65, 67–69; death of Ron Stoops Sr. and, 75; in Florida, 102–103; Mackenzie's surgery and, 172–176; move to Florida and, 98–99; pregnancy with twins and, 138; on Ron Stoops Sr., 77, 166; Texas rumors and, 112; wedding of, 70–71

Stoops, Drake, 150, 275–276, 282, 287–288

Stoops, Evelyn "Dee": Bob's resignation and, 265; Bob's time in Iowa and, 38–39; death of husband and, 73–75, 78; money and, 20–21; 1981 season and, 53–54; trip to Iowa with, 34–35; work of, 14

Index

Index

About the Authors

Bob Stoops was the head football coach at the Universtiy of Oklahoma from 1999 until his retirement in 2017. During his career he led the Sooners to an Orange Bowl victory and a national championship and coached three Heisman Trophy winners. He continues to live in Oklahoma with his wife and children.

Gene Wojciechowski is a reporter for ESPN. He has authored or coauthored multiple bestsellers, including *The Last Great Game: Duke vs. Kentucky,* as well as autobiographies with Jerome Bettis and Paul Finebaum. He lives in Wheaton, Illinois.